JUNE '36

CLASS STRUGGLE AND THE POPULAR FRONT IN FRANCE

by Jacques Danos and
Marcel Gibelin

translated by Peter Fysh
and Christine Bourry

Edited by Peter Fysh and Peter Marsden, with an
introduction for English-speaking readers by
Peter Fysh

Bookmarks
London and Chicago

JUNE '36:   100079277X
CLASS STRUGGLE AND THE POPULAR FRONT IN FRANCE
by Jacques Danos and Marcel Gibelin
translated by Peter Fysh and Christine Bourry

Published May 1986
by **Bookmarks**,
265 Seven Sisters Road, Finsbury Park, London N4 2DE, England
and PO Box 16085, Chicago, IL 60616, USA.

ISBN 0 906224 23 3

First published in French as **Juin '36** by *François Maspero*, Paris 1952. This
edition published by arrangement with Marcel Gibelin and *Editions la
Découverte*, Paris.

Printed in Great Britain by A. Wheaton & Co. Ltd, Exeter
Typeset by Kate Macpherson, Clevedon.
Cover design by Peter Court.

EDITORS' NOTE
To our great regret we learned only when preparations for this English edition
of **Juin '36** were well advanced that Marcel Gibelin had prepared a revised text
for publication in France by *Editions la Découverte* in 1986. This translation is
therefore that of the 1972 edition published by *François Maspero*.

BOOKMARKS is linked to an international grouping of socialist organisations:

AUSTRALIA: **International Socialists**, GPO Box 1473N, Melbourne 3001.
BRITAIN: **Socialist Workers Party**, PO Box 82, London E3.
CANADA: **International Socialists**, PO Box 339, Station E, Toronto, Ontario.
DENMARK: **Internationale Socialister**, Morten Borupsgade 18, kld, 8000
    Arhus C.
FRANCE: **Socialisme International** (correspondence to Yves Coleman, BP
    407, Paris Cedex 05).
IRELAND: **Socialist Workers Movement**, PO Box 1648, Dublin 8.
NORWAY: **Internasjonale Sosialister**, Postboks 2510 Majorstua, 0302 Oslo 3.
UNITED STATES: **International Socialist Organization**, PO Box 16085,
    Chicago, Illinois 60616.
WEST GERMANY: **Sozialistische Arbeiter Gruppe**, Wolfgangstrasse 81,
    D–6000 Frankfurt 1.

CONTENTS

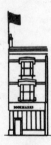

This book is published with the aid of the **Bookmarks Publishing Co-operative**. Many socialists have a few savings put aside, probably in a bank or savings bank. While it's there, this money is being re-loaned by the bank to some business or other to further the aims of capitalism. We believe it is better loaned to a socialist venture to further the struggle for socialism. That's how the co-operative works: in return for a loan, repayable at a month's notice, members receive free copies of books published by Bookmarks, plus other advantages. The co-operative has about 130 members at the time this book is published, from as far apart as East London and Australia, Canada and Norway.

Like to know more? Write to the **Bookmarks Publishing Co-operative**, 265 Seven Sisters Road, London N4 2DE, England.

Dunkirk
Calais
Boulogne   CALAIS   Lille
Lens   NORD
SEINE-INFERIEURE   SOMME   Amiens
le Havre   Rouen   OISE   AISNE
Rheims   MOSELLE
SEINE-ET-OISE   SEINE-ET-MARNE   Strasbourg
Paris   Bar-le-Duc   Nancy
SEINE
Troyes   HAUT-RHIN   Colmar
FINISTERE   Orleans   Belfort   Mulhouse
Vesoul
Saint-Nazaire   Dijon   DOUBS
Nantes
VIENNE
La Rochelle   Riom   RHONE
HAUTE-VIENNE   LOIRE   Lyons
Clermont-Ferrand   ISERE
Saint-Etienne   Grenoble
Périgeux
Bordeaux
GIRONDE   ARDECHE
ALPES-MARITIMES
Nîmes   Avignon   Nice
BOUCHES-DU-RHONE   Cannes
Toulouse
Tarbes   Marseilles
Toulon

Towns: Lyons
DEPARTEMENTS: NORD

CHRONOLOGY

1934

6 February	Fascist-inspired demonstration outside Chamber of Deputies in Paris. Government resigns.
9 February	Communist anti-fascist protest demonstration.
12 February	General strike and Socialist anti-fascist demonstration, with Communist participation.
5 March	Formation of Vigilance Committee of Anti-fascist Intellectuals, including both Socialists and Communists.
March	Austrian Social-Democrats crushed by Dolfuss regime.
31 May	**L'Humanité** reprints article from Russian **Pravda** which hints that *'front unique'* may be offered to Socialist Party leadership. USSR joins the League of Nations.
30 June	'Night of the Long Knives' in Germany, as Nazism eliminates its populist wing.
2 July	Socialist Party *Fédération de la Seine* holds joint meeting with local Communist Party federation.
27 July	Joint Socialist-Communist pact signed.
29 July	Joint demonstration of Socialists and Communists in Paris to commemorate anniversary of the death of Jean Jaures.
9 October	Nantes: Communist Party leader Maurice Thorez proposes extension of Socialist-Communist pact to include the Radicals.

1935

18 February	Joint propaganda meeting, chaired by member of the League for the Rights of Man, includes Communist, Socialist, Radical, CGT and CGT-U leaders.
2 May	Stalin-Laval Pact between USSR and France.
12 May	Paul Rivet, of the intellectuals' anti-fascist committee, runs as the only left candidate in Paris municipal by-election and is elected.
14 July	First joint demonstration, half a million strong, of Radicals, Socialists and Communists in Paris. As a result a committee begins the elaboration of a joint programme for the 1936 elections.
August	Comintern Congress in Moscow officially adopts the 'Popular Front' line.
September	Congress of Toulouse: fusion of CGT and CGT-U union confederations. Throughout the year there is a rising level of strikes.
October	Italian forces invade Abyssinia.

1936

January	Popular Front programme agreed and published.
13 February	Street attack on Socialist Party leader Léon Blum.

7 March	Hitler denounces Treaty of Locarno and remilitarises the Rhineland.
26 April	First round of voting in French general election.
3 May	Second round of voting: victory for Popular Front. A rising wave of mass strikes and factory occupations spreads through France.
4 June	The Popular Front government takes office, with Léon Blum as premier. He at once sets out to defuse the strike movement.
7 June	First Matignon Agreement between government, employers and unions.
10 June	Second Matignon Agreement. Strikers persuaded back to work by Popular Front and union leaders.
18 July	Franco leads rebellion against elected Popular Front government in Spain.
23 August	Non-intervention committee formed in London in which France, Britain, Germany, Italy and the USR agree to aid neither side in the Spanish Civil War. Germany and Italy at once break the agreement in order to supply Franco with arms.
August	Hitler extends military service in Germany.
28 September	French franc devalued.
15 November	Suicide of Popular Front Minister for the Interior, Roger Salengro.
4 December	Communists abstain from supporting Blum government in parliamentary vote of confidence.

1937

16 March	Anti-fascist demonstrators shot and wounded by police at Clichy, suburb of Paris.
22 June	First Popular Front government resigns.

1938

January	Second Popular Front government, under Chautemps, resigns. Succeeded by Radicals-only 'caretaker' government, also headed by Chautemps.
13 March	Blum sets up Third Popular Front government, after failing to set up a 'national' government.
10 April	Resignation of Third Popular Front government.
21 April	Right-wing government headed by Daladier voted into office by parliamentary vote of 575 to 5.
21 August	Government attacks one of the principal gains of June '36, the 40-hour week. Frossard and Ramadier resign from government.
30 September	France signs the Munich Agreement along with Britain and Nazi Germany, allowing the dismemberment of Czechoslovakia.
10 November	Radical Party officially withdraws from government.
30 November	Failure of call for general strike against the imposition of general austerity measures of workers by the Daladier/Reynaud government.

THE AUTHORS

JACQUES DANOS was born in 1921. His first political affiliation was to the youth section of the Socialist Party (SFIO). Later he joined the Trotskyist *Parti Ouvrier Internationaliste*, which fused with another such group to become the *Parti Communiste Internationaliste* (PCI). After writing this book, he left the PCI in 1955 to join the *Parti Socialiste Unifié*. He was principally active in campaigns against France's colonial wars in Indochina and Algeria. He died in 1969.

MARCEL GIBELIN was born in 1920, joined the youth section of the Communist Party in 1934, then in 1935 joined the more left-wing youth section of the Socialist Party. From 1938 to 1953 he was in the *Parti Ouvrier Internationaliste* and *Parti Communiste Internationaliste*, where he met Danos in 1940. He was a member of the POI's wartime clandestine leadership. After leaving the Trotskyists, Gibelin devoted himself to trade union activities, as a leader of the Paris organisation *Force Ouvrière* confederation, and took a leading role in a workers' co-operative. He is now retired and lives near Paris.

INTRODUCTION

by Peter Fysh

THE EVENTS described in this book took place in France between 1934 and 1939, years of acute social conflict, inevitably coloured by the shadow of the approaching war.

The year 1934 saw British hunger marchers in Hyde Park and Downing Street. In Austria clerical conservatives tore up the republican constitution and turned their guns on the workers' movement, literally destroying their strongholds in the Viennese residential districts. In October the Spanish mining district of Asturias saw a strike, occupation and local insurrection crushed by troops.

In Germany, Hitler had been in power for one year. All political parties but the Nazis were dissolved, all trade union organisations had been forcibly amalgamated into the state-run German Labour Front, and all Communist and Socialist leaders were either dead, in exile, or behind bars.

In Italy, fascist since 1922, more than a decade of pitiless exploitation, aggravated by the world economic crisis which began in 1929, had not solved chronic problems of uneven development, which left a large pool of rural unemployed and semi-employed. Mussolini chose October 1935 to launch armed aggression against Abyssinia, a campaign designed to revive his popularity at home and his prestige abroad.

In May of the same year one of Mussolini's French admirers, Pierre Laval, went to Moscow to sign a pact with Stalin in which the Russian dictator 'recognised and approved' France's need to maintain strong armed forces for the sake of her national security. Using the Stalin-Laval pact as an excuse, on 7 March 1936 Hitler denounced the treaty of Locarno, and sent German troops to occupy the Rhineland, from which they had been barred since the end of the first world war.

Then, in the middle of 1936, international attention suddenly switched to dramatic events in France and Spain. The French 'Popular

Front' government, a coalition of Radicals and Socialists supported in parliament by the Communists, took office on 4 June 1936, in the midst of the biggest mass strike till then seen in French history, just three months after Hitler's threatening gesture on the Rhine, and six weeks before the Spanish fascists' rebellion would begin on 18 July.

For Socialists today there is an obvious interest in studying events which have remained surprisingly little-known in Britain. Imperfect knowledge of the facts have led to a variety of interpretations of the events of 1936, from mere hiccup in the long-term degeneration of the Third Republic, to successful anti-fascist defence, to revolution betrayed. In particular, the Popular Front has been claimed as vindication of their views by advocates of divergent 'roads to socialism'. For some, a broad parliamentary coalition including elements of the middle class is a necessary condition for the growth of workers' self-confidence and political awareness. For others, the mass strike is the essential source of revolutionary energy and inventiveness, on which parliamentary combinations act essentially as a brake. This book sets the record straight.

* * *

Though inevitably intertwined with events in other countries, the development of the Popular Front in France cannot be fully understood without some knowledge of French traditions and institutions. What follows is the briefest of guides.

The parliamentary arena

The French third republic, which lasted from 1871 to 1940, had a two-chamber National Assembly, of which the lower house was called the Chamber of Deputies, or simply the Chamber, and the upper house, with a smaller membership, was the Senate. The two houses had essentially similar powers, in that the government had to win a vote of confidence in both, and all legislation had to pass through both. Of the two, the Senate was considerably more conservative, the stronghold of petty-bourgeois provincial and rural interests, since its members had to be at least 40 years old and were elected by a restricted franchise, that is by the local councillors in the areas which they represented. The Chamber was elected by universal male suffrage. The Chamber and the Senate together elected the president of the Republic, a post with mainly representative functions.

In the British system of government, the strength and discipline of parties results in one-party cabinets which usually control enough votes to push their programme through parliament. The executive dominates the legislature. In France in the 1930s the relationship was the other way round.

A newly-elected deputy would come to Paris weighed down by the promises he had made to various individuals or groups of constituents in respect of obtaining funds for municipal development, a permit for private business development, the granting of a war pension, and so on. The deputies formed groups among themselves for the promotion of certain interests, such as those of cereal farmers, wine-growers, or simply the inhabitants of a particular region.

In this situation, the formation of cabinets had only the most tenuous connection with election results, advertised programmes, or a politician's formal position in a party hierarchy. Much more important was the horse-trading between the various pressure-groups. Between 1875 and 1940 there were 107 cabinets, whose average life was nine months before 1920, and six months after 1920. Against this background we can imagine the shock produced in ruling circles by the arrival in 1936 of a government for the first time headed by a Socialist prime minister, who announced his party's intention of governing according to the Popular Front programme on which they had campaigned along with the Communists and Radicals, and for which they had a majority which ought to last them a full four years.

The new government lasted one year, a fact which allows us to measure by how far it had really burst the existing pattern.

The Right and Centre

The political right and centre in France between the wars were in a state of flux and political redefinition.

The traditional right had by the 1930s been reduced to the status of a fringe which refused to accept the republic as the institutional form for the French nation, hoped for the restoration of the monarchy, and defended the privileges of church and army. Divided amongst themselves over the constitutional arrangements for any new regime, uncertain whether to participate in the democratic arrangements of the republic, hampered by the anti-democratic aura of their aristocratic supporters, the representatives of the right in parliament never matched the strength of Catholic feeling in the countryside. This was important in that, apart from a motley group of independent Catholic deputies, the activities and energies of militant Catholics focussed *outside* parliament, where they inevitably in time coalesced with those of the fascist leagues which were operating as street protest organisations.

Politicians whom we would recognise as unequivocally conservative variously described themselves as either of the right or of the

Centre. The Centre groups were technically divided from the right by their attachment to the tradition of republicanism, and by their support for the separation of the church and state. Party labels and composition changed frequently throughout the 1930s. From the left, the Centre was of course distinguished by its conservatism on social questions. As the economic crisis worsened, nearly all the Centre politicians espoused the same policy of deflation and cutting civil servants' pay which was followed in Britain.

The Radicals

In the continually renewed struggle between liberal-agnostic republicans and Catholic monarchists in French history, the 'radical' wing of the republican movement defined itself by its espousal of the most democratic institutional forms (abolition of the presidency, single-chamber parliament, election of judges), social reform (income tax, social insurance) and, above all, an all-out attack on the privileges of the Church, particularly its role in education.

The Radicals' traditional constituency was the mass of small-holding peasants created by the land redistribution of the great revolution of 1789, and their activists were the small-town doctors, lawyers and school-teachers who serviced the small rural communities. In the 30-odd years since its foundation in 1901 the party had given itself a programme put together by piecemeal additions at various congresses. The shopping list included defence of private property (preferably small), law and order, the nationalisation of private monopolies such as rail, electricity and insurance, and profit-sharing, which was expected to lead to the abolition of classes.

By the 1930s, with their reformist zeal long since exhausted and facing an electorate more concerned with the impact of the great depression than with set-peice confrontations between church and state, the Radicals found themselves more and more often needing the Socialists' help in getting elected. In 1932, in 50 per cent of Radical-held constituencies the Socialist Party had more than 10 per cent of the votes, while in 20 per cent of these they received more than 20 per cent. In a general election decided by two rounds of voting, a Radical who faced a Centrist opponent in a second ballot run-off was careful to stress the anti-capitalist elements of his or her programme, so as to pick up the votes of the eliminated Socialist candidate. Once in parliament the new deputy nonetheless felt no compunction in voting for a motley string of cabinets composed of Radicals and Centrists committed to deflation and wage cuts as a remedy for the depression.

The Left

Socialism was represented in France between the wars, as in the rest of Europe, by two parties which were the product of the split provoked in the old pre-war socialist movement by the shock of radicalisation during the war and by the Bolshevik revolution: the SFIO, normally referred to here as the Socialist Party, and the PCF, the Communist Party.

One should not however underestimate the extent to which the SFIO (*Section Française de l'Internationale Ouvrière* — French Section of the Workers' International) which was founded in 1905, was marked by essentially French experience. In France there was no mass trade union movement of the sort which had contributed powerfully to forming the openly reformist character of Labour and Social Democracy in Britain and Germany.

The French socialists' political paralysis on the outbreak of war in 1914 therefore need not be attributed to creeping bureaucratisation, nor to a long experience of controlling and channelling workers' restiveness into economic demands, (though there was a current of municipal reformism in the party). What the several varieties of rhetoric which flourished in the SFIO had in common (from the mechanical Marxism of the Guesdists through to the 'humanism' of Jean Jaurès) was precisely a *failure* to involve themselves in the day-to-day struggles of France's growing army of workers — the mechanical separation of politics and trade unionism.

After the war and the split from the Communists in 1920, the SFIO appeared as a curious anachronism. Neither a party of government nor a revolutionary force (though it continued to describe itself as a 'Marxist' organisation right up to the 1960s), its congresses continued to ape the doctrinal debates, precisely-worded mandates and card votes of the pre-war International. While the party officially expected eventually to win a majority in parliament and be able to bring about socialism from above, it resolutely refused to 'join' a bourgeois government. (Participation in the wartime coalition was regarded as an exception). The left-dogmatist current was strong enough to ensure that any deputy who accepted a ministerial portfolio between 1917 and 1936 was immediately expelled — a procedure which led to the slow accretion of a group of Independents in parliament, known as the *néo-socialistes*, or *néos*, and positioned somewhere between the SFIO and the Radicals.

In reality of course, there were tensions between those who feared contamination by any sort of collaboration with the Radicals, and those, like Popular Front leader Léon Blum, who were more attracted by the possibilities of power but feared that to reach for it too openly would risk splitting the ranks. As each general election approached, debate focussed on what attitude to take to the Radicals. There was a long tradition arising from the two-ballot electoral system that candidates eliminated in the first round would recommend their supporters to vote for the best-placed 'left' candidate in the second round, a procedure known as 'republican discipline'. In the 1928 and 1932 elections the two parties elevated this to a semi-formal agreement whereby in certain agreed parts of the country one would withdraw its candidate from the second ballot in order to give the other a clear run. This arrangement was known as the *cartel des gauches*, or simply the *cartel*, and its logical extension was that in time the *cartel* would win enough seats in parliament to form a solid governmental majority. The Popular Front majority elected in 1936 was thus in one sense simply an extended version of the *cartel*, this time with an agreed programme published before the election.

But, as many authors have pointed out, the 1936 election did not register a large swing to the left compared to 1932. The total left vote was barely above the 1932 level. What made the crucial difference was the intervention of the Communists. In all previous elections, shunned by and shunning the other parties, the Communist votes had usually been wasted on the second ballot, or indeed had split the left electorate. Now they threw in their lot with the other left parties and the result was a landslide for the Popular Front.

The Communists

For the Communists, the 1920s had been a decade of declining fortunes.

The wave of class struggle and enthusiasm for the Bolshevik revolution which split the SFIO at its Tours congress in December 1920 certainly drew into the new Communist Party some of the most militant elements of the working class, including the best of the pre-war revolutionary syndicalists. But at first the party contained a large majority of those who had been represented at Tours, and many of these converts were inevitably only skin-deep. As a result, between 1921 and 1923 the leadership of the Communist International repeatedly intervened against reformist and opportunist tendencies in the party.

Soon the balance of strength between Communists and Socialists swung rapidly in the wake of international events. The defeat of the German revolution dimmed prospects for the hoped-for Europe-wide upheaval; the consequent isolation of the Soviet Union, Lenin's death, Trotsky's disgrace and exile — all served to ensure a difficult childhood for the infant party. After 1924, when the Comintern came under the control of Zinoviev and then Stalin, the party was slowly but surely transformed into a loyal agent of Moscow, a process which involved the expulsion of genuine revolutionaries such as the veteran trade-unionists Rosmer and Monatte. In France a serious split in the trade union movement coincided with the ebbing of the post-war wave of class struggle, and a new phase of capitalist expansion based on reconstruction of war-damaged heavy industry and Poincaré's successful stabilisation of the currency in 1928. Communist Party membership dropped from 121,000 in 1921 to 52,000 in 1928.

In 1930, the French Communist Party was given a new general secretary, the 30-year-old miner's son Maurice Thorez. Carefully chosen by Stalin and trained in Moscow, he would remain in office until 1964. Danos' and Gibelin's narrative opens at the moment when Thorez is searching for ways to break the isolation imposed on the Communists by their espousal of the Comintern's sectarian 'third period' line, in force roughly from 1928–34, when reformist socialist parties and trade unions had been denounced as 'social fascists', and 'the main enemy of the working class'.

French trade unionism

A short way into this book, the authors speak of 'trade-union re-unification' as giving a crucial impetus to the formation of the Popular Front. We need to examine briefly therefore what the union movement consisted of, and how a split originally came about.

We have seen already that the SFIO tended to neglect mass work on day-to-day issues; the obvious separation between politics and trade unionism had scandalised Krupskaya who noted during a stay in Paris with Lenin in 1909–10 that the party had stood aside from an important strike by post-office workers which 'agitated the whole town'.

But this attitude was largely reciprocated by trade unionists. On one level this was the reflection of an attachment to anarchist ideas which saw the unions more as self-help societies than class-combat organisations; on another it reflected the views of those who embraced the class struggle but subordinated systematic propaganda to the exemplary actions of a core of self-selected leaders. These two logically contradictory strands co-existed in the *Confédération Générale du Travail* (General Confederation of Labour) which from about 1903 successfully claimed to represent the bulk of existing craft, industrial and geographically-based unions which had grown up piecemeal in the 1880s and 1890s.

The two tendencies accepted the CGT's classic self-definition in a Charter drawn up by its Amiens congress in 1905, which stated that the CGT 'is preparing that complete emancipation which can only be accomplished when the capitalist is expropriated; it commends the general strike as a means of action, and it believes that the unions, which are now the nucleus of resistance, will in future become the nucleus for production and distribution, the foundations of social reorganisation . . . Affiliated organisations must not . . . pay heed to the parties and sects which, outside and by their side, are completely free to pursue their aim of social transformation.'

This syndicalist *credo* was in due course used to justify the limitation of workers' activity to strictly industrial and economic issues. The unions did indeed participate in production and distribution — as they were drawn into joint administration of the war economy during 1914–18.

But this burgeoning collaboration was first challenged and then shattered by a wave of class struggle, beginning with an engineers' strike in 1917, which coincided with widespread mutinies at the front and demonstrations for peace. The government hastily voted the five-day week and a pay-rise. CGT membership rose from 970,000 in 1910 to 1,200,000 in 1919, to 2,400,000 in 1920.

In April 1919 the government voted the eight-hour day without loss of pay after strikes by Lorraine miners and Paris bank and rag-trade workers. The workers' response was a 24-hour general strike and a half-million strong victory demonstration in Paris. Throughout the summer and autumn, following the lead of 150,000 Paris engineers, workers in industry after industry and district after district struck to enforce the employers' acceptance of the essential gains of the post-war period — the eight-hour day, collective agreements and wage rises.

Towards schism

But the crucial year was 1920. Beginning in February, the railwaymen's federation, the biggest and most important in France, with 250,000 members, was drawn into an all-out strike in defence of its organisation and for a wage rise. The titanic dimension of the struggle was such that the CGT was inevitably drawn in. The reformist leaders agreed to help the railmen on condition that control of the dispute was handed over to the CGT.

In a remarkable parallel with the 1926 General Strike in Britain, the movement's 'general staff' called out during May successive waves of workers in other industries. When the government and employers showed no signs of retreating, and mobilised troops to do the strikers' work, the CGT's National Confederal Committee gave in and called off the strike.

A hundred and ninety thousand railmen continued the struggle. But with the revolutionary leadership in jail, a reformist clique headed by Bidegaray took control of the federation and managed to end the strike on 29 May. Twenty thousand strikers were sacked. In June, Bidegaray organised a Federal Congress to legalise his usurpation of power. Unexpectedly acquitted at their trials, the revolutionaries were released from prison, made their way to the congress and defeated him in the vote. Bidegaray then left the hall to organise a new federation, which was promptly recognised by the CGT.

The first schism in an industrial federation affiliated to the CGT had thus occurred as a result of differences over tactics in an industrial dispute, some months before the founding of the Communist Party, which took place only the following December.

The struggles of the post-war years had long since forced a polarisation between an activist minority and the reformist leadership in other industries apart from the railways. In many areas, the minority had organised themselves openly into *Comités Syndicaux Révolutionnaires*, Revolutionary Union Committees, to which they tried to persuade their federations and *Unions Locales* (the equivalent of trades councils) to affiliate.

After the debacle of the railway strike, the right moved sharply against the 'minority'. In the agriculture, textile, building and white-collar federations, where the reformists had a controlling majority, they proceeded to expel individual militants, and organisations controlled by the minority. In 1921, the schism was driven to a conclusion. Depending on their relative strength in the various federations and *unions locales*, the majority either expelled the opposition, or withdrew in order to set up new and competing organisations which were immediately officially recognised by the CGT.

The revolutionaries held an open congress in December 1921, during which, as a conciliatory gesture, they decided to dis-affiliate their unions from the revolutionary committees, and called for a special CGT congress to be held in January 1922. The appeal fell on deaf ears, with the result that a second national confederation, the CGT-U, *Confédération Générale du Travail Unitaire*, or Unified CGT, was founded at St Etienne in June 1922. The new organisation began life with 360,000 members, and was politically dominated by the Communist Party and revolutionary syndicalists. In January 1922 the membership of the old CGT had been 920,000. One year later, the figure was down to 373,400. For the next dozen years, the French workers' movement was ruinously split.

The difficult years

In the years that followed, the tempo of the struggle inevitably turned down. While the CGT continued to affirm its non-involvement in politics, the Communist Party systematically built a fraction organisation in the CGT-U. To organisational schism was added political rivalry. The employers profited from this situation to impose wage cuts and unpaid overtime, and refuse the renewal of collective agreements. There was no such thing as union recognition or collective bargaining, and workers were frequently sacked for union membership.

From 1924–27 there were no more than 1,000 strikes per year. The maximum number of strikers was 300,000 in a year and the strikes were almost always provoked by wage cuts. But 1929–30 saw a slight upturn. In 1929 there were nearly 1,200 strikes, involving 430,000 strikers, while the figures for 1930, nearly 1,700 strikes and 850,000 strikers, included 300,000 miners on a 24-hour general strike. Gradually the strikes assumed a more offensive character, including demands for wage increases and reduction in hours and the tempo of work.

12 February 1934 saw a million strikers in Paris, an event described by Danos and Gibelin in their first chapter, accompanied by meetings and demonstrations in 346 other places. The authors concentrate on the political and national repercussions of 12 February, but they could have added that the incidence of strikes grew rapidly in 1934 and 1935, and included tram and textile workers in the North, anthracite miners, Marseilles dockers, rubber-workers at Clermont-Ferrand, Berliet vehicles workers at Lyons. These struggles provided the essential context of the authors' oft-repeated assertion that the workers 'forced' their leaders to bring about trade union unity.

The CGT's Public Service federation, at its September 1934 Congress, was the first to call for immediate contacts between the leading bodies of the two union confederations 'with a view to fusion'. During December 1934, various of the railwaymen's local organisations, forcibly split in 1920–21, decided to fuse. Workers in building, public services, lighting and transport formed *comités d'entente* (joint committees) across the confederal divide.

In June 1936, horrified observers spoke of a 'social explosion' which had burst, as it were, from a blue sky. As these briefest of details show, however, the French working class was already sketching the plot of what would be the finest chapter in its history.

* * *

Fifty years after June '36

June '36 was first published in 1952. Its republication today is the first full-length record in English of the French mass strike of June–July 1936, and the attempts by the Socialist, Communist and the trade-union leaderships to head it off. Though the book has stood the test of time remarkably well, the perspective of 1986 allows us to deal with one or two omissions and questions of interpretation.

For example Danos and Gibelin mention that Léon Blum included women in his Cabinet, but they do not mention the agreement by all the Popular Front parties that female suffrage should not be raised as an issue because they feared that women would vote for the right.

Secondly, while Danos and Gibelin follow Trotsky in arguing that the petty-bourgeois class of small businessmen, peasants, civil servants, and so on, could, in a situation of economic crisis, be won either for fascism or for the workers' movement, they also state that in 1934 fascism lacked the decisive support of the 'capitalist bourgeoisie', or *big* business. They do not offer an explanation of why this might have been the case, nor do they return to the question of big business support for fascism as the struggle progressed through 1936 to 1938.

It would be a mistake to believe that what was at stake in France throughout the 1930s was a direct contest between socialism and fascism, which had to end in the victory of the one or the other. All available evidence shows that the riot of February 1934 was *not* part of an organised attempt to seize power. In the critical years of 1937 and 1938 the employers worked through their own control of the factories and through Radical governments headed by the former Popular Frontists Chautemps and Daladier to begin to roll back some of the workers' gains of June '36. In this they were aided by the socialist and trade-union leaders' acquiescence in the use of mechanisms such as compulsory arbitration in industrial disputes. While it is undoubtedly true that a fraction of capitalist big business had long personally been admirers of fascist Italy (just as they had in Britain) and some welcomed the German invasion and the collapse of France in 1940, it is not certain that these were the sentiments of the whole capitalist class.

In accounting for the variety of aims and organisations among fascist and business circles in France between the wars, one should remember that not only social structures but also *business* structure was quite different in France from that in Germany. French big business had a much smaller proportion of national production and employed a smaller proportion of the workforce than its German counterpart. As Danos and Gibelin show, employers' organisations in

France were divided, backward, and open to domination by small business mentality. In these conditions *big* business could not play the decisive role in France which its German colleagues had played in helping fascism to power.

This is not to say that the Vichy regime established after the collapse of the republic in 1940 was not a species of fascism, of which the Italian, the German and the Spanish were other variants. It was. But like the Spanish version, French fascism could probably not have come to power without assistance from outside forces.

On another point, Danos and Gibelin's book is perhaps marked by the need to combat a certain mythologising of the events of the Popular Front. The post-war official Communist version of 1934–6 paints a picture of party and people marching forward together in their finest hour, successfully fighting off the fascist menace. In this context, Danos' and Gibelin's stress on the role of the PCF and the unions in holding back the spread of the strikes and channelling all the energy into economic demands was a necessary correction.

But in emphasising the failures and weaknesses of the existing organisations, the authors at times seem to fall into an opposite error — the neglect of *any* need for political organisation, so that the strike movement is seen as something elemental or instinctive. The fact is, however, that in every strike and occupation a role is played by individual militants who have at least *some* political ideas, though these may be composed of bits and pieces of whatever is current in society. In 1936, those militants who did want to press the mass strike to a decisive contest with the capitalists lacked an organisation which could link them up and *systematically* combat the ideas coming from the Socialists and Communists — that is, they lacked a revolutionary party.

The text also tends to skip over the close connection between the development of the Popular Front and the course of the Spanish Civil War. Franco's rebellion against the elected Popular Front government in Spain began on 18 July 1936, when the French Popular Front and mass strike had been under way for six weeks. On 20 July, Blum received an urgent request from the Spanish government for the delivery of planes and other war material. Blum, and the Socialist ministers whom he consulted, at first made it clear that they intended to comply with the request, which would have been no more than fulfilling the terms of a commercial treaty concluded in 1935.

Opposition was immediately expressed by the British government, with whom Blum had some contact on 23 July, and by the French right, who launched a press campaign denouncing Blum as a Jewish war-monger. But ultimately more fatal to a policy of fraternal aid to the Spanish republic was hostility from inside the Popular Front itself. Right-wing Radicals, who had never supported their party's alliance with the Communists and Socialists, seized their chance to play on all the arguments of the right, especially the danger of a European war in which France would be pitted against Germany and Italy. On this issue they threatened to bring down the government. Their domination of the Senate ensured that they would be well able to carry out this threat.

Though there is evidence that Blum considered fighting the issue, being defeated in parliament, and returning to opposition, he essentially succumbed to these pressures. By 2 August he had produced his plan for a Non-Intervention Pact which Hitler and Mussolini found no difficulty in signing before the end of the month while continuing more or less openly to supply arms and men to the Spanish fascists. Originally a signatory, the Soviet Union denounced the violations of the pact towards the end of September and began sending arms to Spain through French territory.

Thus by the beginning of August, barely two months after the government's formation and when the strike wave had only just receded, the Spanish question broke the unity of the Popular Front, a point perhaps not adequately brought out by Danos and Gibelin.

The Radicals as a party remained true to their principle of looking both ways at once. (Within the government, Pierre Cot and Jean Zay remained firm supporters of sending aid.) Inside the Socialist Party, the classic battle was fought out between those, led by Blum, who put their faith in multilateral international agreements between governments, and the activist militants who campaigned passionately through meetings and demonstrations for arms for Spain, a call which was clearly and unequivocally echoed by the Communist Party.

But the Communists and the Socialist militants abstained from urging (and organising) the workers in the aircraft factories, in engineering and on the railways to ignore the niceties of parliamentary control and themselves ensure the delivery of the needed supplies. This would have meant an immediate break with the Radicals, and indeed pushing the Popular Front 'experiment' well beyond the confines of parliamentarism and down the road to revolution. Many Socialists would no doubt have been prepared to consider this. But not the Communists. Their policy, concerted in Moscow with the Comintern leadership and taking account of Russia's need for allies in the events of a possible war with Germany, refused to go outside the framework of the Popular Front alliance which included the Radicals.

The result was that Blum's government sent only a few undercover arms deliveries to Spain through Mexico. Blum said at the time that if his government had sided openly with the Spanish republic the result would have been civil war in France. We cannot be certain about this, nor about the possible outcome of such a struggle. But what we can say with certainty is that the all-class alliance, which dictated a policy of standing aside, contributed to demoralising and demobilising the French Popular Front's own supporters just as surely as it eased Franco's path to power.

Later, as Danos and Gibelin show, the Radicals chose their own moment to denounce the pact and side with the employers in systematic attacks on the gains of June.

Finally, it might be thought that there is a small contradiction between Danos and Gibelin's assertions that the gains of June–July 1936 were irreversible, and their account of the employers' largely successful attempts to eat into the wage-rises, reinstate piece-rates and unpaid overtime, and even claw back some of the traditional bank holidays. To this were added in due course the Nazi occupation and the Vichy regime, which together reduced the workers' movement to the same status of semi-slavery which obtained elsewhere in Nazi-occupied Europe.

But after the war, when a new Republic was established, many of the 'social laws' were reinstated on the statute book. Thus French workers again enjoyed the legal right to paid holidays, legal recognition of their right to belong to a trade union and to elect workplace delegates, while the employers were legally obliged to abide by the collective agreements concluded in their industry. These did indeed amount to a fundamental improvement in the workers' condition which can be indirectly traced to 1936.

This provokes an obvious comparison with 1968. The strikes in 1968 involved an even larger number of workers than in 1936 and likewise at first escaped the unions' attempt to control them. For a moment, as de Gaulle flew to Germany to consult with French army generals, it seemed as if the regime itself was in danger.

As a chapter in the history of the French working class, however — and indeed in the history of the movement generally — 1936 was incomparably more important than 1968. We cannot ignore the fact, for instance, that in 1936 the movement occurred in the context of and inevitably against a government which included Socialists and was supported by the Communists, whereas in 1968 the right was in power. But more crucially, in 1936 the factories were occupied and remained occupied *en masse*. In 1968 in many areas a relatively small number of Communists and CGT officials succeeded in taking over the occupations and sending the workers home. In 1968, for a young worker-militant moving towards revolutionary ideas, the focus of debate and action was not his factory but the local college or university, a state of affairs which aided the rapid dissolution of the collective experience gained once the movement was over.

Finally, in 1936 the workers won a wide-ranging set of new rights which enhanced their sense of dignity as well as their institutional role in society. In 1968, apart from the inevitably temporary wage rise, the only institutional change was a minor concession on the organisation of union factory-branches.

PETER FYSH

1
THE MASSES TAKE
TO THE STREETS

ON 6 FEBRUARY 1934 fascist leagues and right-wing political organisations launched a physical attack on the *Palais Bourbon*, the symbol of French parliamentary institutions. Thousands of Parisians, gathering in response to the appeals of *Action Française*, the *Croix de Feu*, the *Jeunesses Patriotes* and *Solidarité Française*,[1] alongside thousands of military veterans responding to the call of the National Union of Former Combattants, launched their assaults to cries of 'Down with the Thieves',[2] and 'Vive Chiappe!'[3] Battle raged the whole evening on the *Place de la Concorde*, leaving a hundred wounded and twenty dead. In the end the police emerged victorious. **Le Quotidien** of 7 February was able to headline its front page 'The Republic Goes On'. Nevertheless, the Daladier government resigned, and Gaston Doumergue formed a 'Government of National Unity' to the applause of the previous day's rioters.

The fascist leagues had driven from power a government headed by a Radical, to find it replaced by the worst reactionary politicians.

So what had happened? Who were these people launched by the leagues into an attack on the Republic, only to be obliged the next day, when they were ready to renew the struggle, to become the supporters of the worst and most reactionary politicians? Were the conditions which had allowed the rise to power of Italian fascism and German Nazism not present in the France of 1934?

Since 1931 France had been paralysed by an economic crisis of unprecedented magnitude, which was as deep as similar crises in the other capitalist countries and would last longer. Unemployment, bankruptcies, a fall in real wages, the collapse of agricultural prices — the crisis obsessed everyone, be they workers, peasants or middle classes. The latter especially were the main victims of the crisis, and the parties to which they traditionally gave their votes proved incapable of providing a solution to their problems. They were losing faith in the Radical Party, discredited by its years of power, as well as in parliamentary institutions seemingly impotent and tainted by financial scandals.

In Italy and Germany the petty bourgeoisie[4], exasperated by economic chaos, had turned to the new fascist or Nazi parties, which were financed by big capital and worked in its interest, but made use of middle-class anger to smash the divided workers' organizations and conquer state power.[5] In France, while the workers' movement was rent with divisions, the economic crisis gave rise to the birth or development 'of a whole number of interest groups of uncertain ideology, operating in a social milieu where capitalism and anti-capitalism are inextricably linked in most people's minds.'[6] At the same time the fascist leagues were growing in strength and bidding for the leadership of the discontented masses by trying to turn them against the parliamentary regime and against the workers' organisations.

The *Croix de Feu* rapidly made itself the biggest and the most dangerous of the leagues. It had all the characteristics of a fascist movement; a nationalist and anti-democratic mystique in place of a programme, the cult of personality, a very well-developed military organisation, and the support of quite wide circles of capitalists. While its leader, a certain Colonel de la Roque, engaged in behind-the-scenes dealings with right-wing politicians and even — as it later became known — was able to draw on secret funds, spectacular mass demonstrations prepared the shock-troops for the decisive assault.

In February 1934, the middle classes' exasperation was at its height. Financial disorder, economic chaos which held down personal incomes while prices remained as high as they had been in more prosperous times, the Stavisky scandal which uncovered corruption in Centre and Radical parliamentary circles, all these factors helped to explain the events of 6 February.

However, the riot failed in its objective. It failed because of disarray amongst the leagues, whose leaders were rivals more than allies and who shared only their mediocrity; French fascism was lacking in leaders of common origin, capable of moving the masses. If the riot did not overthrow the Republic, and seemed to be leading nowhere, the main reasons were that fascism in France lacked both the total support of the petty-bourgeosie, at least a part of which remained undecided, and the unqualified backing of the capitalist bourgeoisie — big business.

The truth was that the latter did not see fascism as an immediate necessity.[7] The political and economic crisis appeared serious, but not insoluble; the capitalists had managed to maintain their profit-levels, while the workers' movement was not yet a pressing danger. So the bourgeoisie held back from throwing the decisive weight of its own power into the scales on the side of the fascists. They preferred to continue making use of the leagues in the role of anti-worker militias and as political counter-weights to the unions and workers' parties.

But the fate of fascism was not decided solely by the unfavourable outcome of the events of 6 February. In Germany too fascism had lost its battles. Its fate depended ultimately on the position taken by the petty-bourgeoisie. In a period of crisis the bourgeois centre parties suffer an inevitable process of attrition. So a decisive choice is imposed on the middle classes; to side with fascism, which is to line up alongside big capital against the working class and its organisations, or to fight alongside the working class against the capitalist order. Which of the two great classes in French society would succeed in winning the confidence of the petty-bourgeoisie, and in responding to its imperative need for a change in the system?

In the end it was the working class which responded to this challenge. By their energy and enthusiasm the workers obliged their leaders to accept unity in their ranks. The establishment of this united front strengthened the political weight of the working class and in so doing created the conditions necessary for a vast popular movement against poverty and the threat of dictatorship.

The workers' response to 6 February

In the period leading up to the fascist riot, the workers' organisations, both political and trade-union, were divided and seemingly impotent. The Socialist Party (SFIO), though rejecting participation in the Radical government, belonged to the parliamentary majority elected in 1932. Its opposition to the government was sporadic and inconsistent; the party played the delicate game of trying not to alienate its electoral support while at the same time maintaining certain governments in office. In October and November 1933 it brought about the fall of Radical governments which were seeking to cut public employees' wages.

But as far as the hard-pressed and rebellious petty-bourgeois masses were concerned these occasional shows of opposition were indistinguishable from what they condemned as the usual sterile parliamentary games. The accusation of demagogy levelled against the Socialist Party was not without justification — the left phrases of their Sunday-afternoon speeches about the 'future socialist society' were no substitute for a programme of action, or indeed for action itself.

The French Communist Party (PCF) followed the political line laid down by the Communist International, a sectarian policy, not the least error of which was to lump together as agents of capitalism both the fascists and the Socialist leaders. It was this slogan which had brought Communist war-veterans on to the *Place de la Concorde* alongside the fascists on 6 February.[8] The Communist Party reserved its main attacks for the Socialist Party; calls for a united front were conceived entirely with a view to separating the Socialist Party's base from its leaders. The 1932 election results proved the futility of this tactic, for the Communist vote fell by nearly 300,000.[9]

Within the trade union movement the conflicts between the reformist CGT union confederation and the CGT-U, which was led by the Communist Party, were equally violent. The main consequence of this was the small number of union members; the two confederations together numbered less than a million members, among whom the blue-collar sections were the weakest.

Despite its weaknesses and divisions, and at first taken unawares by the apparent attempt at a coup, the French working class roused itself against the fascists in the days following the riot. On 6 February the Socialist leadership called for a 'Party Mobilisation'. The members were told to 'prepare to defend your organisations', but there was no accompanying call for any practical action. It was thought to be enough to rely on the 'firmness and cool heads of the local leadership'. However, the same day, the local Socialist Party organisations in the *départements*[10] of *Seine* and *Seine-et-Oise* where the feeling for united action was particularly strong, asked the Communist Party for a meeting, 'in order to establish the basis for a genuine agreement, and to bring about workers' unity in action'. 'Please reply as soon as possible,' they added, 'we will wait in our office until midnight.' Failing to get any reply, a delegation of socialists went to the offices of the Communist Party paper **L'Humanité** shortly after midnight. This second attempt to provoke a response had no more effect than the first.

L'Humanité of 8 February reported the Socialist proposals, but its reply was a violent attack on the Socialist Party leaders. 'We are ready,' wrote **L'Humanité**,

> to fight alongside all who really want to defeat the fascists. But how can we have unity of action with people who vote for governments who cut wages? With people who break strikes? With people who abandon the class struggle to collaborate in the defence of the capitalist system, and who, in France as in Germany, prepare the ground for fascism?

The paper appealed for Socialist workers to join the demonstration which the Communist Party was organising on the 9th. This sectarian tactic, with its attempt to separate supposedly sincere social-ist workers from their allegedly traitorous leaders, was inevitably doomed to failure. It was absurd to try to mobilise the socialist workers against the fascist gangs by setting them against their own party just at the moment when its leaders had proclaimed their readiness to fight.

All commentators are agreed that the CGT trade union leaders had paid scant regard to the fascist threat. After 6 February things changed. On the morning of the 7th the CGT's *commission administra-tive*[11] decided in principle to call a 24-hour general strike for Monday 12 February.

On the evening of the 7th there was a meeting between repre-sentatives of the CGT, the Socialist Party and various other left-wing bodies. A co-ordinating committee was set up which included 'The League for the Rights of Man', the CGT, the Socialist Party, parties formed by expelled or former Socialist Party members, the so-called 'neo-socialists' (French Socialist Party, Socialist Party of France, Republican Socialist Party) as well as the *Union Anarchiste*, the *Parti de l'Unité Prolétarienne* (PUP), the 'Workers' and Peasants' Federation' and the *chambre consultative* of the workers' producer associations. On being told of the CGT's decision to call for a general strike, the Socialist Party decided to begin preparations for a big demonstration on 12 February.

In the provinces, the workers' organisations were put on alert. In certain areas preparations were made for a march on Paris when and if fascist agitation began again.

On the evening of the 9th the Communist Party's demonstration took place. The main slogans were:

> Immediate arrest of Chiappe and the leaders of the fascist gangs! Down with the butchers Daladier and Frot![12] Disband the fascist gangs! Defence of wages and salaries! Down with the reactionary and fascist National Government prepared by the Radical and Socialist Parties! Long live the workers' and peasants' government.

An entire district of Paris around the *Place de la République*, where the demonstration was to take place, was put under a state of siege. From seven in the evening until midnight eastern Paris was the scene of violent battles between police and Communist milit-ants, particularly in front of the police stations and at the workers' barricades. 'The demonstrators,' the Socialist Party daily paper *le Populaire* was to report the following day, 'showed admirable courage and energy throughout the night'. Workers' blood flowed; six dead were counted when the battle subsided.

12 February was marked by the general strike called by the

CGT 'against the fascist threat and in defence of civil liberties'. The CGT-U joined the strike, and its success exceeded the most optimistic expectations. Police figures were obliged to record that 30,000 out of 31,000 post-office workers stopped work. The Paris papers failed to appear, and theatres failed to open in the evening. In the morning few trams and buses were in circulation, and the *Métro* operated a reduced service. By the afternoon there was an almost complete lack of all forms of transport. The government workshops were all out, as was a large part of the Customs service. Response to the strike call was significant in the tax collection service; in gas and water — nearly all-out strike; 3,000 on strike in the slaughterhouses; building sites deserted nearly everywhere. In engineering it was uneven; at Citroën in the morning there was 85 per cent absenteeism at the Javel plant, 75 per cent at Gutenberg, 80 per cent at Levallois. By afternoon the strike was almost total. On the other hand, at Renault barely a quarter of the workforce struck. The CGT estimated the number of workers in the Paris region who had responded to their call as about one million.

In the provinces the movement was on the same scale. In almost all the big cities there were significant strikes. Powerful demonstrations took over the streets. One hundred thousand people demonstrated at Marseilles; big crowds appeared in Toulon, Perigueux, Toulouse, Montluçon, Saint-Etienne, Rouen, Bordeaux. In Algiers a large number of indigenous workers took part in the 20,000-strong procession. An overall estimate put the figure at 4½ million strikers, with one million taking part in demonstrations.

That afternoon the Socialist Party demonstration took place in Paris. The previous day the Communist Party had decided to take part. In one unforgettable moment the two columns joined together to cries of 'Unity! Unity!', and then proceeded in tightly-packed rows along the whole width of the *Cours de Vincennes*. For the first time for years Socialist and Communist workers were marching side by side.

'An unforgettable occasion,' l'**Humanité** reported the following day,

> which has not been seen by the old *Place du Trône* for thirty-four years, and which far outshone the previous occasion, that of the triumph of the Republic, both by the number of workers taking part and by their revolutionary spirit.

Even the reactionary press reported the scale and the 'truly impressive calmness of the procession. There were very few incidents. On the other hand, at Boulogne-Billancourt, an industrial suburb of Paris, violent confrontations had gone on between police and workers since midday. There were several wounded, and one more dead on the workers' side.

But the martyrs' blood helped reinforce the unity in the workers' ranks. On 17 February the Socialist Party federations of Seine and Seine-et-Oise took part in the funeral procession of the Communist workers who had been killed on the 9th and the days that followed.

Socialist and Communist Unity in Action

After 6 February, the fascist menace lingered. The leagues continued their agitation, and their violence against workers, of whom a mounting number fell victim to the paramilitaries. The *Croix de Feu* held a continual series of motorcades, and their leader took every opportunity to announce that the 'Day of Reckoning' was at hand. At the same time the deflationary policies pursued by various right-wing governments strangled the economy and ruined public employees, while the factory owners reduced their workers to misery. The workers could put up only a feeble resistance; any attempts at strikes were paralysed by the existence of large numbers of unemployed. But the workers' greatest weakness in the fight against fascism and the bosses was more and more clearly the division in their own ranks.

The example of what had happened in Germany was close at hand. 'It seems that, divided, the workers' forces are condemned to impotence and defeat; united, they would command irresistible power and enthusiasm.'[13] But not all the leaders saw it this way. The Communist Party insisted on its desire for unity in action 'at the base' in a central committee resolution of 15 March 1934. The leaders of the Socialist Party, and of the CGT, on the other hand, were obviously afraid that the dynamism and militancy of Communist Party members would give the party a tremendous advantage in any united front. For the Communist Party's central committee, unity in action had to take effect in the course of 'revolutionary struggle', that is, on the party's own terms. For the Socialist Party national committee (11 March 1934) 'the fight against fascism can only be carried out in the overall context of socialist action and with the aid of socialist ideas.'

But pressure from the working class was to prove irresistible. It would sweep away all hesitations, and force the two leaderships to accept unity in action. Socialist Party leader Léon Blum showed that he had recognised this when he wrote in 1935:

To have turned our backs on this first unification of the workers' movement just at the moment when popular feeling and interest were crying out for it . . . would have led only to misunderstanding and alienation.[14]

From June 1934 onwards the Communist Party executed a

political turn involving both a reappraisal of the tactic of the united front, and a more moderate tone in polemics with the Socialist leaders. What were the causes of this new course?

First of all, serious internal problems. An increasing number of members and sympathisers were not happy with their party's sectarianism, and could have been tempted to regroup around Jacques Doriot, a parliamentary deputy and mayor of St Denis. Already one of the most popular figures in the party, Doriot chose at this moment to come out into open opposition to the leadership, which he particularly criticised for its narrow sectarianism towards the Socialist Party. He stressed that the united demonstration of 12 February took place not in opposition to the socialist leaders, but with their participation, saying that 'to pretend otherwise is dangerously to underestimate reformism, both its grip on the masses, and its capacity to manoeuvre in the present period.' Despite the efforts of the Communist International to smooth over the crisis, the conflict between Doriot and the leadership grew sharper, and eventually led to his expulsion from the party.

But this expulsion took place at precisely the moment when the party itself was preparing to adopt the two main points of the programme that Doriot had been defending since February. The party's turn was executed under the direct influence of the Communist International. The Russian Communist Party paper **Pravda** set the tone in an important article reproduced by l'**Humanité** on 31 May:

> The Communist International considers that the call for a united front against the fascist threat . . . is necessary under certain conditions . . . Such a call is possible in a country like France where social-democracy has not yet been in power, where . . . the socialist workers think that their party will not follow the path of [German] social-democracy.

This text was one result of the new attitude which the USSR was obliged to adopt in the light of the developing international situation and Hitler's rise to power in Germany. The USSR was in need of allies who could balance the power of the Nazi Third Reich, whose overtures towards Poland justifiably unsettled the Soviet leaders. As a result they began to extoll the virtues of 'collective security' and even joined the same League of Nations which had been condemned by Lenin as a 'Den of Thieves'. So for the Comintern one of the objectives of the new turn was to break the isolation of the western Communist Parties, especially the French.

The French Communist Party's conference, assembling on 23 June 1934 to study 'The organisation of a united front of anti-fascist struggle', authorised the party's *politbureau* to propose to the Socialist Party a pact of unity in action in the struggle against fascism and war.

By the 25th the Socialist Party's *commission administrative* (administrative committee) had received the Communist proposals. It made a show of hesitation. On the other hand the party's left wing gave a warm welcome to the Communist offer.

On 2 July, the Socialist federations of *Seine* and *Seine-et-Oise* and the Communist Party's Paris region organised a big joint meeting. The tremendous desire for unity among Communist and Socialist workers was amply demonstrated. In fact the *salle Bullier*, where the meeting was held, was not big enough to hold the whole audience, and a second meeting had to be rapidly improvised at the Huyghens gymnasium. Enthusiastic applause punctuated the speeches; Jacques Duclos, Cachin, Maurice Lampe (secretary of the Paris region) for the Communists; Zyromski, Claude Just, Farinet (secretary of the Seine federation) for the Socialist Party. 'I have waited fifteen years for this evening,' declared Claude Just, 'and now I hope it has not been in vain.' Maurice Lampe echoed him: 'What we have achieved today at regional level will be achieved tomorrow at national level.'

The Socialist Party's left wing campaigned for the acceptance of the Communist proposals, and on the eve of the party's national council meeting, their spokesman Marceau Pivert wrote: 'We hope that the national council will say with maximum clarity: Communist Party comrades, for joint action at national level, here is our signature, here is our fraternal handshake.' On 16 July 1934, the national council voted by a huge majority to accept the proposal for a pact of unity in action, which was signed by representatives of the two parties on 27 July.[15] The first joint demonstration brought together Communists and Socialists for the anniversary of the death of Jean Jaurès, the founder of the Socialist Party, in August.

The Popular Front

The first initiative towards bringing together all anti-fascist activity had come from a group of intellectuals centred around Paul Rivet, Langevin, the philosopher Alain, and Pierre Gérôme. The manifesto launched at the end of March 1934 by the *Comité de vigilance* of anti-fascist intellectuals was immediately signed by thousands of scientists, teachers, artists and writers.

But the political conditions for an alliance between anti-fascist organisations and parties were only realised some months later. The first step came from Maurice Thorez, the secretary-general of the Communist Party. 'For us,' he wrote later in his book **Fils du Peuple**, 'the pact was less an end than a beginning. We had laid the foundations for working-class unity; we had to widen the alliance, extend it to the middle classes, in order to ensure the defeat of fascism.' But for

Thorez and his party, 'to extend the alliance to the middle classes' came to mean 'widen it to include the Radical leaders'. And if some of these sat in governments alongside the likes of Doumergue, Flandin or Laval, a subtle distinction had to be made between the 'good' and the 'bad' Radicals. At this time Daladier personified the former, and Edouard Herriot the latter.

On 9 October 1934, during a meeting at the *salle Bullier*, Thorez launched the call for the setting up of a 'Popular Front for work, peace and freedom'. On the same day the Communist representatives at the co-ordinating committee proposed to the Socialist delegates that they jointly prepare a programme which would form the basis for setting up such a 'front'. Despite Socialist hesitations, a working party was established.

On 24 October, Thorez addressed the Radicals directly in Nantes, the day before their party conference was to be held there. 'We Communists are fighting for Soviet power . . . But we are determined to neglect nothing in supporting the demands of manual and intellectual workers, and in the defence and extension of democratic rights.' That was why the Communist Party addressed itself 'to all the workers' and peasants' organisations, to radical groupings which are opposed to reaction, and generally to all the workers of town and country.' He proposed a programme of action which included the defence of the constitution against all attempts at reform which tended to restrict the rights of the people, the disarming and disbanding of the fascist leagues, general international disarmament, special progressive taxes on the rich, defence of wages and salaries, and measures to assist small peasants and small shopkeepers.

This speech did not have much of an effect on the Radicals' deliberations. These were brought to a close by the adoption of the type of composite resolution for which Herriot had a particular flair; various middle-class longings and grievances were enumerated, but Radical participation in the Doumergue government was not to be disturbed.

This in no way prevented Maurice Thorez from declaring to his party's central committee on 1 November that he was in agreement with the Radical Party programme. 'Of course, all that is not the Communist programme; but we can be sure that the demands and aspirations which form the Radical Party programme are there because they correspond generally to the French people's desires.'

The Socialists' reticence did not diminish. 'From the beginning the Socialist Party has been hostile to our idea of the Popular Front,' Thorez would tell the Comintern congress which took place in July–August 1935.

They have a tendency to consider every problem from a parliamentary point of view, and display a certain fear of the masses. But they are trying to give themselves a more left face. They consider our programme too moderate . . . But of course we Communists are not presenting the Socialists with our complete programme. We are asking them to come to an agreement with us on what it is possible to do here and now.

For several months the disagreements continued. It was not until June 1935 that the Socialist Party's Mulhouse congress produced a definite decision to join the Front.

But meanwhile there were new developments elsewhere — and the Radical Party had succumbed to the siren voices of the Stalinists.

First came a domestic event which was inevitably of the greatest import to the Radical leaders; the changing allegiance of the electors. The local government elections of October 1934 and May 1935 revealed a distinct move to the left. In October the Communist Party's vote increased by 100,000 and the number of its elected councillors rose from 11 to 26. In the *département* of *Seine* in May the party's vote rose from 75,000 to 139,000, and the number of seats from four to 25 (out of 50 contested). In contrast, the Radical Party was in serious trouble, discredited by its participation in various reactionary governments. With parliamentary elections approaching, it was time for them to try to revive their fortunes.

A different event, this time of international scope, lent plausibility to the Communists' new tactic in Radical eyes: the Stalin-Laval pact.

Laval, who was in Moscow for the signature of the Franco-Soviet mutual assistance pact, had various political conversations with Stalin from 13 to 15 May. The official communiqué that followed declared that both countries had the duty 'to see that their national defensive capability was in no way weakened', and added: 'In this respect, Mr Stalin understands and fully approves the French national defence policy which requires a level of armed force sufficient to meet the needs of her security.' Faced with this unexpected declaration, which stupefied a number of Communist Party members, the party immediately issued a poster bearing the motto 'Stalin is right'.

With the Socialist hesitations and Radical opposition both overcome, the Popular Front could become a reality.

In June 1935 the International Committee against war and fascism,[16] of which the co-chairmen were the writers Romain Rolland and Henri Barbusse, came up with the idea of a massive popular demonstration on 14 July, Bastille Day. Taken up by the *Comité de vigilance* and the 'League for the Rights of Man', this proposal rapidly found wide support and soon Victor Bash was chairing a committee representing some 100 organisations which proclaimed 14 July as 'people's republic day' and called for a gathering of all citizens in defence of democratic rights, the workers' bread, and peace.

14 July 1935: the afternoon began with a meeting at the Buffalo Stadium where all present took a solemn oath to 'stand together in defence of the democratic rights won by the French people, to secure bread for the workers, work for the young, and the peace of mankind for the world.' Afterwards Paris witnessed the enormous demonstration which remains an unforgettable memory for all those who took part. Hour after hour seemingly a whole population, maybe 500,000 people, filed through the *faubourg St Antoine*. Their songs and slogans gave voice to their hopes and their confidence in the triumph of social justice and their faith in the eventual emancipation of the workers. Manual workers, clerks, intellectuals, petty bourgeois, shoulder to shoulder in a procession the like of which working-class Paris had probably never seen before, all felt part of an immense force which nothing could stand against. Throughout the rest of France the same fervour welled up at countless meetings and demonstrations.

Carried away by the general enthusiasm after this great success, the organising committee for 14 July decided to continue its work. Taking the title of *Comité National de Rassemblement Populaire*, they gave themselves the task of drafting an electoral programme to be applied after the 1936 elections — which they were already beginning to believe would be won by the parties of the left.

The job turned out to be long and arduous. Once again resistance came from the Socialist leaders who were loth to accept the omission of certain so-called 'structural' reforms from the common programme — by which they meant nationalisations. Their attitude contrasted with the conciliatory mood of the Communist representatives, Duclos and Gitton, who often formed a 'bloc' with the Radical delegates, Auband, Kayser, Lange and Perney. At length, agreement was reached. 'Was it easy?' asks R Millet in his book **Bilan du Communisme**.

> No; the Communists had to call on all their subtlety. In contrast to what is commonly thought, throughout the whole affair they showed themselves to be less revolutionary than most of the Socialists and many of the Radicals.[17]

The programme of the *Rassemblement Populaire* was not published until January 1936. As Millet pointed out, it was limited to a few chapter-headings, to demands which were more moderate than the Front's left wing would have preferred:

We have to be quite clear that the left wing was not the Communist Party, for the Communist Party had wanted a very moderate programme and it was at their express wish that the nationalisation of banks and industries was not included.

The first part of the programme was devoted to the defence of civil liberties, and included specifically an amnesty for political offenders, the disbandment of the fascist leagues, reforms affecting the financing of the press and radio broadcasting, as well as defending the cause of secular education and union rights in the workplace. Since no agreement with the Radicals had been possible on measures to improve the position of France's colonial subjects, the text could do no more than envisage 'a parliamentary commission of inquiry into the political, economic and moral condition of the overseas territories.'

The second part of the programme, dealing with the struggle for peace, had only one concrete proposal; nationalisation of the arms industry. The other points were only general formulae along the lines of 'appeal for the collaboration of the labouring masses in supporting the struggle for peace', or 'unceasing efforts to be made to ease the transition from armed peace to peace-through-disarmament', or 'renunciation of secret diplomacy'.

The third part, dealing with economic demands, was the most concrete. It was a charter of economic and financial policies which Léon Blum's first government later began to put into practice. The aim was to restore the masses' purchasing power and give a boost to the economy. The main points were a reduction in the length of the working week without loss of pay, provision of old-age pensions and unemployment benefit, the setting up of a programme of public works and the abolition of the decrees which had cut civil servants' pay. As far as agriculture was concerned, changes in the price structure were to be accompanied by action against speculators whose activities harmed the interests of both producers and consumers; a national cereals bureau was to be set up as part of this project. Alterations to the statutes of the *Banque de France*, 'today a private bank which will become the *Banque de la France*',[18] were aimed at bringing about a reform of the credit system. Other points in the financial part of the programme were a 'democratic reform of the tax structure', action against fraud — with the introduction of a tax identity card — and controls on the export of gold and capital.

Le Temps saw in the programme 'the deep influence of Marxism and statism'. This judgement was decidedly exaggerated. The programme seemed on the contrary to give ample ground for confidence that the normal functioning of the capitalist system would not be impaired. Without striking the slightest blow against property rights, it pretended that a simple change of policy — abandoning deflation, increasing purchasing power, the easing of credit — would be enough to bring about a return to prosperity.

All available evidence indicated that the mass of ordinary people were well to the 'left' of this electoral programme. Drawn up with the aim of bringing the middle classes into an anti-fascist front, was it really any different from, did it really go any further than the old Radical Party programme? One had only to scratch the newly-applied coat of paint to lay bare all the old slogans of classical Radicalism, which managed to appear new only to the extent that the Radicals, in their rightward evolution, had put them away on the shelf for safe-keeping.

Trade Union Unity

Since the split of 1921 every effort to bring about a reunification of French trade unionism had met with failure. Until 1934 the reformist CGT[19] and the Communist-led CGT-U[20] did little but attack each other continually, and though they took it in turns to propose fusion, this was generally only a tactical manoeuvre to show the other in a bad light. The two confederations had serious differences, concerning possible methods of re-organisation: the CGT favoured organic unity, while the CGT-U proposed the formation of unified federations with a single leadership grouping under itself local or plant sections which would preserve their existing separate organisations.[21] They had also different notions of trade union independence; the CGT wanted to force the Communists into giving up political fractions[22] within the unions.

However all these difficulties were overcome. It took a long time, but the events of 1934 and the strong desire for unity to which they gave rise forced the two leaderships into a serious attempt at unification. This occurred in three stages. In October 1934 the CGT-U submitted to the CGT proposals for fusion of unions at the base, and for the convocation of a unity congress which would decide the statutes, orientation and leading bodies of the single confederation. The CGT's reply was encouraging, and raised hopes of a possible agreement along these lines, but the problem of union independence from political parties led to a breakdown in talks. This turned out to be a temporary setback, for in June 1935 first the Communist Party and then the CGT-U agreed to give up political fractions.[23] Negotiations began again, and once a definition of union independence had been agreed in July, the two confederal conferences, which both took place in September, voted for the reunification.

This was consummated at the congress of Toulouse in March 1936. More than a thousand delegates took part. The early debates on the statutes produced a considerable majority for the ex-CGT wing. The votes relating to the federal structure, to the prohibition of the joint holding of political and union posts by one person, and to the question of international affiliation gave an average of 5,500 to the former CGT tendency and 2,500 to the former CGT-U tendency.

The debate on the new confederation's programme and future action ended with a compromise resolution; the two reformisms, the old and the new, managed to come to terms with each other. The Communists defended the Popular Front programme, while the old reformists, criticising this for its timidity on economic questions, put forward instead the 'CGT plan', which was a reflection of the current vogue for 'plans'. This plan for 'economic and social renewal' included the specific measure of the Popular Front programme but demanded in addition partial nationalisation of credit and extensive nationalisation of industry, to be carried out by a 'higher economic council' composed of workers' and employers' delegates. The final resolution, unanimously agreed, included both the Popular Front programme and the CGT plan:

> This conference reaffirms the adherence given by the trade union movement's representatives to the programme drawn up by the *Comité de Rassemblement Populaire* with the aim of mobilising the French people to improve their lot and to bring the triumph of peace and freedom . . . This conference reaffirms the need to break the enormous power of big business which blocks the people's aspirations, cheats workers, consumers and people with modest savings alike and everywhere flouts the public interest . . . The CGT plan helps in this task by calling for profound changes in the economic structure, such as the nationalisation of credit and key industries where all the power of the financial and industrial oligarchy is concentrated.

[handwritten marginalia: not for the few but for all MT]

The conference also unanimously approved the participation of the new confederation in national and international governmental bodies, taking care to add, however, that this participation 'should not be considered as a form of integration into the state or collaboration with the employers.'

The Toulouse congress finished its work by organising the new leading bodies of the confederation. The *comité confédéral national* elected 33 ex-CGT and ten ex-CGT-U men to the *Commission Administrative*; the provisional *bureau confédéral* had its mandate confirmed; Jouhaux became general-secretary, and Dupont (ex-CGT) treasurer, while the secretaries were Belin, Betherau, Bouyer, Buisson on the one hand, and Frachon and Racamond on the other.

The new-found union unity was quick to bear fruit. From March to May 1936 250,000 workers joined the unified CGT; workers' struggles became more numerous, more often offensive in character, and ended more frequently in victory. May Day 1936 was a great success. Despite threats from the bosses, 120,000 engineering workers in the Paris region struck for the day, including Renault, which had to close its doors for the first time in 20 years as 25,000 stopped work.

On the eve of the strike movement — victory at the polls

The pact of unity in action, trade union re-unification, the pact of the Popular Front, all of them owing their origin to working-class pressure, reflecting the workers' readiness to fight fascism and poverty, wrought a profound change in the political atmosphere of the country. People began to hope that a new life was really possible. Little by little this wave of confidence overtook the middle classes, who were inspired by the workers' militancy, by the desire for a complete break with the past which animated the Popular Front's battalions. They began to put their faith in the new men who had upstaged the old Radical leaders.

A feverish atmosphere surrounded the 1936 elections. Political tension mounted. No one doubted that the Popular Front would perform impressively in the two rounds of voting on 26 April and 3 May. Political 'commentators' all looked forward to important gains for the Communist Party and the Socialist Party, and were already wondering which Radical leader would soon form the Popular Front government with Socialist participation.

The first round gave the workers' parties more than three and a half million votes, and, as a result of each withdrawing in the other's favour in the second round, the Socialist Party won 146 seats, and the Communist Party won 72.[24] The Socialists now became the largest single group in the Chamber, where the Popular Front as a whole had a majority of more than 100 seats. It was a triumph for the Socialists and Communists whose united action had beaten back fascism, and who now seemed to represent the best hope for all who really wanted to fight for bread, peace and freedom.

2
BEGINNINGS OF
THE STRIKE MOVEMENT

THE RESULTS of the second round of voting showed that on the whole the Popular Front candidates had stuck to the electoral deal agreed between their parties. Examples of discipline having broken down, eagerly played up between the two rounds by the right-wing press, were extremely rare, and where they did exist, could largely be explained by local circumstances; in the majority of cases a Socialist-Communist bloc had opposed the Radical candidate, who was then supported by the right. Of the 38 cases of broken discipline discovered by **le Temps**,[1] 29 involved a context between Socialists and Radicals, and only four the opposition of Socialists to Communists. This fact is easy to explain. On the one hand it was because the Radical Party did not possess an apparatus similar to those of the two workers' parties; discipline was looser, and the selection of candidates controlled more by the local committees than by the centre. On the other hand the great public enthusiasm for unity, which we have repeatedly stressed, effectively curtailed too numerous or too flagrant breaches of the pact of unity in action.

So the picture was of almost total discipline among parties and candidates.

But it is perhaps more interesting to consider the discipline of the voters, who followed closely the advice given by the local Popular Front committees. Before the second round the left papers' political commentators had been able to forecast to within one or two seats the composition of the expected parliamentary majority. The reactionary press, for their part, made a big fuss about the defeat of Jean Piot, the Radical candidate in the Paris 14th *arrondissement* or district, but they were able to do so since it was in fact one of the few upsets in the second round.

As the results came in on the evening of Sunday 3 May, spontaneous demonstrations took place. There were victory processions in the suburbs and workers' districts of Paris, and ecstatic gatherings in front of the town halls and in the squares, where the results were thoroughly discussed by everyone. Shopkeepers and workers, clerks and housewives all equally convinced that now at last 'things will change'. Groups of youngsters launched into '*Au-devant de la vie*' and everyone took up the chorus of the Internationale which was heard late into the night. In Paris the fascists went to ground. In Bordeaux, Marseille and Menton their attempts at counter-demonstrations were rapidly broken up, after short battles in which the police already began to see which side it was better to be on.

On Monday 4 May **le Populaire** published a special edition containing an important article by party leader Léon Blum, headed 'The Socialist Party is ready':

> The Socialist Party has become the biggest group not only in the majority, but in the whole chamber. So we are anxious to declare without a moment's delay that we are ready and willing to fill our allotted role, namely to organise and lead the Popular Front movement.

Nobody, it seemed, was ready to dispute this leadership. **Le Temps** noted that it was 'the rules of the democratic game', and the editorial added: 'Political morality, and even just morality plain and simple . . . dictates that the Socialists will now have to put their money where their mouths are. Mr Léon Blum will be responsible for the inviolability of the frontiers,[2] for the prosperity of France, the soundness of the currency and the national bank balance, for a recovery in the economy, the reduction of unemployment, and for much else besides.'[3]

Political negotiations began straight away, and were to last for one month, until 4 June, a month during which the Sarraut government[4] remained in office, and a month which would see the burgeoning and growth to maturity of the greatest strike-wave ever mounted by the French working class.

Following Léon Blum in his early negotiations gives us the opportunity for a rapid survey of the political landscape. The leader of the Socialist Party had claimed the premiership in a Popular Front government; he therefore logically invited the participation of all the parties which had joined the pact and approved its programme.

Before the elections the Communist Party had already stated its position on the question of participation in the government. On 7 May the party leaders Maurice Thorez and Jacques Duclos held a press conference, of which the themes were: unconditional support of a government applying the Popular Front programme, undeviating loyalty, but no ministerial responsibility.[5]

The Communist Party justified its refusal to participate, despite earnest appeals from the Socialist Party,[6] by arguing that it would not help the cause at this moment. 'We are convinced,' wrote the Communist Party politbureau to the Socialists on 14 May, 'that the Communists would better serve the people's interest by loyally supporting the Socialist-led government without reserve than by participation in the cabinet, which might offer the class enemy a pretext for panicking and scaremongering.'

Those prudent remarks were of a piece with various repeated declarations from the Communist leaders throughout the period, the aim of which was to reassure anyone who might be dismayed by their presence in the new parliamentary majority. Examples were Duclos' declaration to the press that the Communist Party would respect private property,[7] a politbureau communique which came out in favour of safeguarding the franc and defending the gold standard.[8] There was also the letter to the Socialist Party in which the Communist Party denied that it proposed the formation of peoples' committees with revolutionary aims, but favoured rather, 'improving what exists, the liaison committees of the Popular Front, which played such an important part in our victory,'[9] and finally Waldeck-Rochet's speech at Villeurbanne,[10] in which, after remonstrating with the Socialists for supporting some of their own candidates against Radicals 'at the risk of throwing them into the arms of the right', he again insisted: 'The people's verdict was not in favour of immediate revolution; we are neither putschists nor extremists. We shall shoulder our responsibilities by working to improve the lot of the working classes within society as it now is.'

Léon Blum should have had few illusions concerning the French Communists' reply to his offer of a share in power. He also knew, even before the decision of the CGT national confederal committee was made public, that the confederation's response would be similar, for he was aware that on the morning of 10 May its general secretary Léon Jouhaux had called to a semi-official meeting the important non-Communist leaders of the confederation. In the absence of any spokesman for the former CGT-U, the leaders of the majority tendency took the position which was unanimously accepted by the national confederal committee on 19 May: the CGT would agree to collaborate with the government, but intended to preserve its independence; none of its members would accept a ministerial post. On the other hand, the confederation demanded a place on the social and economic planning and research bodies which the government was pressed to set up or resuscitate. The CGT also demanded executive and administrative powers which were needed for the implementation of immediately realisable reforms, as called for in its 'plan'.

Léon Blum, making the best of this two-fold refusal, which, as he noted,[11] 'is accompanied by a double encouragement that will not find us wanting,' turned to his future partners in government and began the usual horse-trading with the neo-socialists and Radicals which was the time-honoured method of distributing the ministerial portfolios.

The Radicals had been the great election losers. They had lost 400,000 votes, and that this meant a loss of only 51 seats was due to the support they obtained from workers' votes through the application of Popular Front discipline. Whatever **le Temps**[12] had to say on the subject, the Radical leaders were well aware that the bulk of their remaining 116 seats were owed to the Popular Front; and they preferred to be second officers rather than not be officers at all. On 14 May the party's Valois executive committee approved participation in the forthcoming coalition, a stand which was unanimously endorsed by the assembly of presidents of Radical federations.[13] Nevertheless the press remarked on the reticence of Edouard Herriot, who was known to have refused the foreign secretaryship, offered by Blum at Communist insistence, and to have said he would not be a candidate for president (or speaker) of the Popular Front *Chambre de Députés*.

For several weeks Léon Blum's apartment at the Quai Bourbon was the future government's headquarters. Senior politicians, representatives of parliamentary groups, defeated deputies, Socialist militants and union delegations all followed each other in and out. It was also possible to meet there, 'the same hangers-on . . . whose faces could be recognised four years later in the mirrored halls of Vichy.'[14]

The parliamentary right-wing and centre opposition for the moment caused the future prime minister little anxiety. They seemed shattered by the recent election defeat; not so much by the defeat itself, which they had begun to get used to, but by the prospect of a new kind of parliamentary struggle. It seemed as if the elctorate had put an end to the routine. What had happened, after all, in 1924 and 1932? Then the Radicals had allied with the Socialists for the election itself, their coalition had triumphed . . . and then the Radicals had proceeded to govern along with the right. But 'this was a trick which could not be repeated indefinitely', as **le Temps** commented.[15]

Despite grandiose declarations about 'the tasks of the national opposition', the right was divided and uncertain. In the country, the bourgeoisie was full of confusion, alternately scared by its defeat, and by the size of the workers' demonstrations, then reassured by the honeyed words of the Popular Front leaders and by the usual slow pace of the inter-party negotiations. Their nervousness was accurately mirrored by the fluctuations in the stock exchange, which they were obliged to check daily. A speech by Jouhaux of the CGT would cause shares to collapse, only for them to shoot back up again the next day after some declaration from Léon Blum. It was a speculator's paradise. The big financiers, however, preferred more dependable measures; every week the Bank of France's balance sheet revealed the flight of gold and the export of capital. The example of Spain, where elections had seen the triumph of a Popular Front government a few months earlier, was not conducive to peace of mind among 'savers'; strikes, violent demonstrations, workers' control in certain factories followed each other in quick succession for several months, and the government seemed quite overwhelmed by the scale of public unrest.

The fascist gangs for the moment halted their attacks on the workers. *Croix de Feu* leader Colonel de la Roque continued his speeches, and the one had made at Neuilly on 19 May, a classic of the genre, indicated the degree of disarray among the fascist leaders: 'Already our ideas are taking power; those who are trying to apply them are not worthy of the task. It was Moscow gold which paid for their election. But we are on the eve of a great victory, and those who are our brothers will soon come to our side . . . Our decisions will depend on those taken by our enemies. To make them known now would be premature. We never say in advance what we are going to, but what we have decided to do will be done.'

The leagues still managed a big demonstration in front of the statue of Joan of Arc on 17 May. But in the continuous guerrilla warfare between sellers of the workers' and fascist press, the latter rarely commanded the field. They were usually isolated, while the worker militants received the support of the local people.

The working class had never flocked with such enthusiasm to all the meetings and demonstrations to which they were called. A big crowd swarmed along the *Avenue de Wagram* when the Socialist Party organised their victory meeting on 15 May, no longer the usual bunch of party members and close sympathisers. Now a whole population was on the march, listening to Léon Blum from the street if they couldn't gain entry to the hall, and ready to applaud him when he declared: 'Let us give the country the *impression*[16] of the change which it wants.' The same flood of people was to be found at Communist meetings; everywhere the 'men of the party' were in the majority. There was complete unity of action between members of the two workers' parties, who took part in demonstrations organised by the Popular Front, especially in the provinces.

The Front's national committee devoted several meetings[17] to plans for a massive victory demonstration. The Radicals were against the demonstration taking place at the *Mur des Fédérés*[18] on 24 May, and the date finally agreed was 14 June. Processions were to take place throughout France to celebrate the electoral victory, and to proclaim the people's desire to see their favoured programme put into effect.

We shall see that the 'people's desire' was to be expressed in a somewhat different way, and the national committee would be obliged to cancel the Paris demonstration.

Léon Blum, observing that he 'would not be flustered by the masses' impatience',[19] carried on his negotiations and made one speech after another. Reaction kept silent. The masses, disciplined and confident, were ready to go on to the attack. When they did, Léon Blum was the first to feel it as a slap in the face.[20]

Strikes at Le Havre and Toulouse

The first strikes directly connected with the movement we are studying date from 11 May, when they broke out almost simultaneously at Le Havre and Toulouse. Both strikes were characterised by occupation of the workplace.

The strike of 10 April 1936, which saw the occupation of the Boutillerie factory at Amiens, has sometimes been treated as part of the events surrounding the Popular Front.[21] But this episode had certain characteristics which were too specific to allow it to be linked with the class struggles of May 1936. The occupation was in fact carried out with the boss's agreement, in an attempt to prevent the plant's seizure by the tax authorities. In the end, the owners abandoned the factory to the workers, who set up a co-operative.

It was a different story with the strike at Le Bréguet aircraft factory which broke out at Le Havre on 11 May. The day after the May Day celebrations the management had sacked two workers who were known union members, for having taken the day off as tradition demanded. Various workers' delegations approached management to try to get the two men reinstated. This peaceful initiative, several times repeated, had no effect. Then the engineers' union called a strike for 11 May, and the workers responded 100 per cent. That evening the 600-strong workforce remained in the plant, and spent the night there. On the 12th the local Mayor, Léon Mayer, made an offer of arbitration which was accepted by both sides. His verdict found on behalf of the workers: he ordered the two strikers' reinstatement; he recognised the workers' right to absent themselves on May Day, and even ordered the management to pay wages for the strike days of 11 and 12 May.

On the 13th, at the Latécoère factory in Toulouse there was an identical train of events. Its point of departure was likewise the sacking of three workers who had struck on May Day, and who the management refused to take back despite approaches from the local full-time union officials. The workers downed tools and remained in their shops. Arbitration by the Mayor of Toulouse found in favour of the workers, who won recognition of their delegates at the same time.

These events remained purely local. The Parisian workers' papers did not mention them. **Le Temps** dealt with the Toulouse strike in a few lines without even mentioning the occupation. The local press, in conciliatory mood, congratulated everyone on the rapid solution of the conflicts, and heaped praise on the municipal authorities whose tactful intervention had calmed heated tempers and smoothed away bitterness.

Nevertheless, for the time at which they took place, these strikes had some very unusual features. They had included the whole of the workforce, who remained in control of the workshops in order to limit the risks implied by a work stoppage at a time of unemployment. They had the benefit of moral and physical support from the local people. Finally they resulted in rapid and complete victory. But these struggles were still strictly defensive; for no new demands were raised. Beginning with the same characteristics, the strike at the Bloch aircraft plant at Courbevoie was soon to raise a new set of problems.

The strike at the Bloch plant began on 14 May, after management had refused to consider a set of workers' demands of which the main points were a pay increase and changes in working hours. After the first day on strike the workers, who were still in the factory, decided to spend the night in the workshops. The Popular Front municipality promised to provide them with food and bedding. The next day management agreed to talks, and finally met all the demands. A collective agreement was signed which formalised a modest pay rise, payment for the days on strike, and recognition of the right to paid holidays.

What was especially remarkable about this victory, as well as about the partial struggles which began at Vénissieux, a suburb of Lyons, and at the Longwy steelworks in Lorraine on 18 May, was the consistent silence of the press. The first comments of the Communist Party paper l'Humanité on the Le Havre strike did not appear until 20 May, and we had to wait until 24 May before the paper, in an article by Pierre Delon, examined the three strikes together and drew activists' attention to the nature of the victories and the methods of struggle which had achieved them.

The Demonstration at the *Mur des Fédérés*

24 May was not without significance. It was the day that the ad hoc Socialist-Communist committee and the CGT had chosen to call the people of Paris to the traditional demonstration in memory of the martyrs of the Commune. The vast turn-out was without precedent; more than 600,000 people marched until midnight past the *Mur des*

Fédérés, where Blum and Thorez stood side by side, surrounded by the Socialist and Communist leaders. The throngs of workers were gradually, slowly waking up to their numbers and their power.

The Communist leaders were also alive to their growing impatience, and the next day the party's central committee, meeting at Ivry, passed a resolution including the following: 'The central committee understands and sympathises with the people's evident desire, given that nothing has been achieved in the three weeks since the Popular Front victory, to see put into practice with the greatest urgency the measures agreed in the joint programme,'[22] measures which **le Temps** itself emphasised were of a moderate nature.[23]

On 26 May the strike movement began to turn into a wave in the Paris region. Doubtless, wrote **le Temps**, 'it would be wrong to be too pessimistic about this latest development,'[24] which, according to **le Populaire**, was 'only a movement for higher wages which will soon turn into a series of victories.'[25]

[handwritten note: sit-ins reaction to built-up hopes from victory & joint programme promises.]

3
THE MOVEMENT UP TO 4 JUNE

FOLLOWING the example at Bloch, the union representatives at the Nieuport engineering factory at Issy-les-Moulineaux lodged with their management on 21 May a list of demands which included the following main points: a guaranteed minimum daily rate, the recognition of delegates elected by the blue-collar workers alone, no overtime and the 40-hour week. On Tuesday the 26th the union reps asked for a meeting with management, who refused to see them. An immediate strike was decided on, and the delegates announced that the workers would not leave the workshops until all the demands were met. At midday the strikers' meal was brought in by their neighbours and the local councillors. At four o'clock the management granted a meeting which achieved nothing. The workers got ready to spend the night in the factory after Piginnier, the Communist deputy and mayor, had come to promise them his support.

Meanwhile at Lavalette, in Saint-Ouen, a strike began in the afternoon in response to an attempted wage-cut. Here the union reps immediately went on to the offensive: they not only demanded withdrawal of the new piece-rates, but also put forward a list of demands which adhered closely to the Popular Front programme. At six o'clock the reps sent the women home, and 300 workers began the organisation of their occupation-strike. In the evening a delegation which included Berlioz, the communist deputy for Saint-Ouen, and Colin, the engineering full-time official, sought out the management. The bosses suggested that all the demands in question should be discussed the next day, promised that the doors would remain open, and asked the workers to go home. This was rejected by a mass-meeting, which immediately set about organising pickets at all the entrances.

At Hotchkiss, in the suburb of Levallois, attempted sackings provoked the same response: strike, occupation, and lodging a list of demands; but in this case talks began immediately and produced an agreement which the workers ratified. At 9 o'clock in the evening the workers quit the factory to the strains of the Internationale.

The Hotchkiss workers' victory was important in that the management gave in on all points; reinstatement of sacked workers, recognition of workers' representatives — whom the management undertook to see once a fortnight, a guaranteed minimum hourly rate of from 5.50 francs for labourers to 7.80F for tradesmen, and early consideration to be given to the question of paid holidays and the abolition of overtime. Finally, there were to be no victimisations and the hours lost through striking would be paid.

One wonders whether the Hotchkiss workers, who we will come across again later in the forefront of the struggle, fully realised the extent of the agreement which they enthusiastically ratified, which prefigured the later Matignon deals and the eventual collective agreement in the engineering industry as a whole. From this moment on, during negotiations aimed at tidying up outstanding details, they made full use of the fear their militancy inspired in the bosses.

By this time the struggle had become generalised to take in the whole of Parisian engineering. There were victorious, if slightly less far-reaching strikes the same day at Lioré-Olivier of Villacoublay, at Sautter-Harlé, in shop 221 of the Renault combine, at Corbeil, at the big Creté printworks, and among quarrymen. Finally, there was growing agitation among miners at Marles and among agricultural workes at Mesnil-Amelot.

27 May was a day of marking time. The Farman factory at Billancourt stopped work. A communiqué issued by the strikers at Nieuport announced that they 'seemed on the point of an agreement which would allow a rapid resolution of the conflict'. But at Lavalette the strikers rejected management proposals which sought to postpone discussion of wages, paid holidays and a collective agreement, while conceding on a few points such as the distribution of milk to sanders and polishers, the extension of meal breaks, the formation of a committee of workers' delegates, and abolition of overtime.

There was a growing awareness that the movement could not remain limited to these few factories. Either they would go back, and the old routine would begin again, or some chance event, as yet unguessed, would bring the entire Parisian engineering industry into the battle. In every conversation the same question cropped up again and again; what will Renault do?

The bourgeoisie were already shedding crocodile tears for Léon Blum and the difficulties which faced him. 'What a prospect for Léon Blum, who has to try out his ideas and prove himself, knowing beforehand that he must embellish his every step, every action, every thought with the clenched-fist salute,' wrote **le Temps**.[1]

Revolutionary outbreak or economistic strikes?

The events of 28 May were decisive. At 9.30 in the morning 35,000 Renault workers downed tools. There was some uncertainty caused by the mechanics of organising an occupation; at midday some workers left the plant, but the majority remained behind.

The Renault strike dragged behind it a few score of other factories in the Paris region, and at midday on the 29th the list of occupied workplaces included Farman, JJ Carnaud, Fiat, Citroën, Rosengart, Gnôme-et-Rhône, Caudron, Chausson, Salmson . . . to which were added in the afternoon Brandt, Talbot and le Matériel Téléphonique. Then, in the first important extension of the move-ment to a new industry, several building sites involved in preparations for the International Exhibition stopped work.

The occupation of the factories had already begun to follow something of a pattern. The workers' papers emphasised the perfect order reigning in the plants, where the strike committees controlled a network of services such as health and safety, supply, maintenance and security. But there was widespread debate about the nature of the totally unexpected strike-wave, and about the significance of this new phenomenon, this 'sensational initiative'[2] which was the occupation tactic.

For the bourgeoisie these were revolutionary actions striking at the freedom of labour and private property. 'The maintenance of order inside the factories has no bearing on the matter; in fact it only emphasises even more the lack of spontaneity and the concerted nature of this violation of the law,' said **le Temps**.[3] The workers' demands also had a revolutionary aspect to them, since 'they affect the general relationship between employed and employer,'[4] and 'the strikes are a kind of epidemic which at bottom has political causes.'[5]

For the other side, the working-class parties and the unions denied any political, let alone revolutionary, meaning to the strike movement. All that was required, wrote Doury in **l'Humanité**, 'was a better understanding of what was happening in the factories, and the problems could have been resolved without a withdrawal of labour.'[6] And Croizat, writing on the same day, underlined the point: 'The wave of strikes in the Paris engineering industry can be brought to a close very rapidly if there is a real willingness on the employers' side to meet the workers' legitimate and reasonable demands. At the moment, close on 100,000 engineers have stopped work and remain day and night in their factories to ensure that no damage or sabotage takes place. They are maintaining perfect order, and desire not the slightest disturbance. They are asking their employers for certain improvements in their wages and conditions.'

These very moderate attitudes, together with repeated attempts to limit the significance of the strikes, encouraged the government to attempt conciliation.

The conciliation attempt

There was one immediately pressing question facing Sarraut's 'provisional' government. Should the factories be forcibly cleared? Should the police and army be enlisted to remove workers who were violating the sacrosanct principles of the *Code Civil* relating to property rights? Sarraut reported to the Senate that he and Frossard, the minister of labour,

> had meetings . . . at all hours of the day, some of them quite dramatic. Should we use force? . . . At this moment I consulted the employers . . . I got Mr Frossard to ask them: 'Would you like us to try forcible evacuation?' The employers straightaway replied: 'No, definitely not that . . . don't involve the police . . . there would be a risk of bloody confrontation . . . the shedding of workers' blood would be laid at our door, and we might be prevented from regaining control of our factories.'[7]

It must be assumed that the former prime minister used such terms to describe his conversations with the employers in order to boost the impact of his speech to the Senate, upper house of the French parliament; otherwise it is rather disconcerting to find the guardian of public order, personifying all the authority of the state, going thus cap in hand for advice to the representative of . . . private interests. Whatever may have been the form of the dialogue, its essential point was the conclusion reached; the forces of law and order would not intervene to put a stop to the factory occupations.

Instead the government tried its hand at conciliation between the parties, and Frossard tried to bring together the *Syndicat Ouvrier des Métaux* and the *Groupe des Industries Métallurgiques*, the workers' and employers' organisations of the engineering industry for the Paris Region.

The engineering employers' first move was to try to set a formal condition on any discussion of a collective agreement involving ministerial arbitration, namely an immediate return to work. On the other hand the intentions of the workers' leaders did not seem all that threatening, and their desire to reach a rapid agreement was shown clearly in the statements made the same day by both Communist Party politbureau member Jacques Duclos and the union full-timers. Duclos, coming out of a meeting which he had just had with Albert Sarraut, explained the unions' intentions: 'We are guided by a dual preoccupation; first of all, avoidance of any disorder; secondly, to ensure that talks begin as soon as possible with a view to a rapid settlement of the conflict.'

After a conversation with the minister of labour, the employers' leaders stuck to their intransigent position. Frossard informed the workers' delegation of this and proposed another meeting, composed of equal numbers from both sides, for Friday 29 May at four o'clock in the afternoon. The representatives of the CGT-affiliated union 'declared that this proposal seemed to them to offer hope for the settlement of the conflict,' and called a meeting of delegates from the strike-bound factories for the next day, which was the 29th, at nine o'clock in the morning.

So a hundred and fifty strikers' delegates gathered on Friday morning at the *Bourse du Travail*[8] and unanimously passed a resolution noting

> with satisfaction that the movement is continuing to spread today; [the engineers] declare that they are determined to obtain satisfaction on the question of a collective agreement; they record their pleasure that conversations are to begin on this subject this afternoon. They therefore decide to call a mass meeting in each factory in order to discuss the details of a return to work. This return will be on the basis of the new collective agreement, which will apply retrospectively.

The meeting of delegates from the occupied plants had thus fallen in with the bosses' demand for a return to work prior to the talks. But they refused simply to rubber-stamp Frossard's proposals, and in their turn put forward a preliminary condition of their own; that there should be an agreement between each strike committee and the management of their factory on the 'conditions of the return to work', and there must be a formal written undertaking that there would be total adherence to the future collective agreement.

The bosses were not satisfied with the workers' position. By late morning Richemond had demanded a meeting with the minister of labour, at which he gave the latter a note which stated: 'The conditions stipulated yesterday not having been fulfilled, the planned talks will not now take place.' The note was brief and to the point. Thus Croizat in vain returned to the fray with new assurances that the unions were in basic agreement with the main points of the bosses' conditions:

> The conditions put forward [by the employers] will be observed by the workers as soon as the factory agreements are concluded . . . . The return to work would take place as planned, without delay. *Afterwards*[9] the main thing will be to discuss and sign the regional contract which will settle once and for all wages and conditions in the Paris engineering industry.

The strike delegates' resolution was indeed somewhat ambiguous, and the union negotiators took the chance to put their own interpretation on the vague formula 'to discuss the details of the return to work' in each factory. They accepted at face value the assurances that there would be no victimisations for going on strike, and that the strike days would be paid, at least in part.

On this basis negotiations got under way in various places and in the afternoon came the announcement of an agreement at Gnôme-et-Rhône, where the occupation was about to end. But the most important piece of news was made known at about 7 o'clock in the evening by Frossard. As he left a meeting with Richemond, he informed the press that the evacuation of Renault had begun at 6.30 pm.

A false lull

Agreement between the workers' delegates and management of the most important engineering factory in the Paris region had indeed been reached towards the end of the afternoon. This agreement included seven points which are worth recording in full:

1. There would be urgent consideration of a wage rise for those on the lowest rates (less than 4F per hour).
2. No overtime to be worked while negotiations for the collective agreement were still in progress.
3. No victimisation for striking.
4. The half-day of 28 May and the afternoon of the 29th to be paid.
5. The work in progress on the installation of lockers and toilets to be pushed forward rapidly.
6. Two sacked workers to be reinstated.
7. The factory occupation to end as soon as this agreement was signed, with the return to work on Tuesday 2 June.

At 8.30 pm the gates closed behind the last occupiers leaving for home.

The usual psychological chain-reaction was widely expected: when Renault stopped work, all the other big factories would follow suit — with the Renault occupation ended, agreements would be signed by one, and there would be a general return to work. That is certainly what the government thought; it must also have been in the minds of those workers' leaders who had signed such a shoddy compromise which went nowhere near meeting the workers' wage demands. And it was emphasised the same evening by an employers' communiqué. 'In contrast to what has been stated elsewhere, the Renault management has not been obliged to deal with any points coming under the collective agreement, particularly the general wage rate, which remains to be discussed between employers' and workers' representatives when total evacuation of all factories has taken place.'

The employers were conscious of having won a victory, and Richemond declared during the night: 'We are ready to resume negotiations as soon as the factories have been evacuated, *or* there is a return to work.' Was this alternative the sign of a slight concession? Were the employers ready to accept that the simple ending of the occupations would be enough for negotiations to begin again?

In fact it was simply a question of practical necessity; it was Friday; most workers had Saturday and Monday off. Renault would start back only on Tuesday. So talks were bound to begin before the return to work. Keeping the workers away from their factories for several days could also be seen as a clever tactic, a manoeuvre which came very close to success.

Despite the beginning of a strike by lorry-drivers employed by the firm Bernard, 30 May was notable mainly for the resolution of several conflicts. Factories which had followed Renault out on strike also followed their example in putting an end to their occupations. Workers at Nieuport, Caudron, Farman, Brandt, Talbot, then Citroën, Panhard, JJ Carnaud, Chausson, Rosengart all evacuated their plants. A variety of agreements were signed but few gained substantial immediate advantages for the workers like the one signed at Gnôme-et-Rhône a few hours before the Renault deal.[10] Most of the deals were based on the Renault model, which went a long way to meet the employers' organisation's wishes since it had advised its members not to commit themselves before the talks took place at regional level.

Le Temps announced:

> On the whole, the movement is on the decline. Our overriding impression is that the workers' delegates, perhaps deferring to suggestions or instructions, are trying, in their negotiations with management, to win satisfaction on a number of local issues which will enable them to present the eventual outcome as a victory.[11]

The employers indicated their pleasure in a new communiqué on Sunday 31 May:

> A relaxation of tension . . . is even more marked this morning. It seems likely that those workers who are still on strike will abandon the struggle in the course of the afternoon. If this were to be the case, the Parisian Association of Engineering, Mechanical and Allied Industries is ready to begin discussion on general issues. The first meeting of the two sides will be at four o'clock at the Ministry of Labour.

As soon as the negotiating committee began its work, they insisted that the actual negotiations took second place to the question of ending the remaining occupations.

At that moment no one doubted that it was only a matter of time.

From 70,000 the number of strikers had shrunk to 10,000. It is true that this number did not diminish further during Monday 1 June. But no one seemed to pay this any attention. The new National Assembly held its first session and listened to the Father of the House making the usual boring speech. The engineering negotiating committee discussed definitions involved in the question of the right to join a union, and nominated four specialist sub-committees. Everyone hoped that a deal would be signed on Thursday 4 June, especially Frossard, for whom it would be the last day of power.

Fifteen plants are still occupied, said the engineering employers. If the managements would only be more conciliatory, everything could be sorted out, replied the union, who at the same time called on the delegates in question to 'get in touch with management by tomorrow morning in order to come to an understanding on the points still at issue, and thus permit a complete return to work.'

The next morning Renault and Citroën went back, but at midday 66 engineering factories were on strike, and by evening 150 were under occupation.

Rapid spread of the strikes

Tuesday 2 June saw a swift escalation of the strike movement, which now became general and affected a range of different industries. We have already seen that the building labourers on the Exhibition sites had struck, but they had returned at the same time as the engineers went back to their workshops. In the past few days there had been small strikes in a Paris restaurant, in a chemical factory, and in laundries — short strikes quickly ended by an agreement of some kind. But on 2–3 June plants including chemicals, food, textiles, industrial design, furniture, transport, and oil were paralysed by strikes and then occupied.

Engineering, however, remained the industry most affected, and here it was soon possible to count 200 occupied factories, of which several, let it be remembered, were on strike for the second time. At Fives-Lille 2,500 engineers occupied their factory and raised the red flag while the strike spread with extreme rapidity; a similar incident occurred at Lyon. Various partial agreements were signed, usually involving an increase in pay. Some strikes lasted only a few hours, while others carried on even after an agreement had been signed. The movement now affected all kinds of workers, and it was tending to spread to the whole country.

The masters' voice still came out of the mouths of the engineering employers, who organised general assemblies and issued communiqués in ever-increasing numbers. On the 2nd and 3rd there were

turbulent meetings at which each boss recounted his own mis-
fortunes. The total was impressive,[12] but there were some absentees,
and not all had been able to send their excuses . . . they were stuck in
their offices; the workers had bolted their doors and cut off the
telephone. But the employers' communiqués stuck to their moderate
tone. The assembly noted the extension of the strikes, and acquainted
itself with progress in the continuing negotiations, 'nevertheless our
impression is that the employees do not seem to see the solution of the
conflicts in the same light as when negotiations were begun.'

The government called in the CGT, who appealed to the workers
on 2 June to desist from incidents involving the bosses personally,
who 'should remain free to come and go from the plants.' The
engineers' union stuck to their tactic and still recommended a return
to work after the signing of individual plant agreements. 'Certainly
other industries are affected,' noted the Paris regional *Union des
Syndicats Ouvriers* the same day, 'but these are cases where exploitation of the workers in the past few years had been particularly intense.'
There was no truth in the rumours of a general strike, 'no decision of
this kind having been taken or envisaged.' The *Union* called on the
workers' to preserve the movement's 'calm, discipline, order,
prudence and dignity,' since it should remain 'peaceful, controlled
and correct,' avoiding all 'exaggeration, bouts of demagogy, and
dangerous disorder.'

The next day, 3 June, the various unions published more communiqués. The engineers' union 'invites delegates from all workplaces
still on strike to redouble their efforts to conclude plant-by-plant
agreements and to show the same spirit of conciliation which has
never ceased to animate them.' The CGT *bureau confédéral* and the
Paris *Union des Syndicats* issued a joint communiqué to the press:

> Since we are determined to retain the same discipline, peaceful charac-
> ter which the movement has had since the beginning, we are ready to
> call a halt wherever and whenever the workers' demands are satisfied.

4 June: Léon Blum in power

But on 4 June the strikes spread even further, affecting lorry-
drivers, newspaper distribution (only **l'Humanité**, **le Populaire** and
the Radicals' **l'Oeuvre** were distributed normally), restaurants, hotels,
printing, locksmiths, goldsmiths, petrol distribution, pharmaceutical
laboratories, tailoring, building, gas, agriculture, in Lille, Vierzon,
Rouen, Brive, Nice, Toulouse, Marseilles. These industries and towns
are chosen more or less at random from the seemingly endless list of
trades and regions afflicted by the epidemic. But some qualifications
must be made — engineering was still the only industry suffering a

general strike, while Paris was still the only region where several trades were on strike and where a large number of workers had occupied their workplaces.

But everywhere where strikes broke out there were also occupations. Everywhere the strikes involved 100 per cent or all but 100 per cent of the workforce, and everywhere they received the immediate and active sympathy of the local population, together with help from the local Popular Front supporters organised in local committees or the municipal councils. And everywhere was the vague feeling that the seeming chaos of sectional actions could be transformed into a crushing demonstration of workers' power, into a unified movement with scarcely calculable consequences.

4 June was also the day on which the Popular Front government was formed. Sarraut and Frossard hastily handed over their powers to Léon Blum, the new prime minister, and his new minister of labour, Lebas. President Lebrun begged Blum to 'do something'. The employers advised him to 'shoulder his responsibilities'.[13]

Léon Blum, carried to power by the workers, formed a government 'sympathetic to the workers' whose aim was to 'bring forward measures in their interests'.[14] It had the support of a Communist Party which gave assurances of its confidence and its closest collaboration.[15] It expected also the support of the CGT, which had endorsed the governmental programme. Everything pointed to the reasonable conclusion that the workers would follow Léon Blum when he asked them the next day to 'submit to the law of the land'.[16]

4
THE POPULAR FRONT TAKES OFFICE

LÉON BLUM defined the limits of his intended 'experiment' before the Socialist Party congress which met from 30 May until 1 June. The common threads of all the speeches he made between the elections and 4 June — threads which were drawn together in the congress's final resolution — can be summarised under four headings.

First, the electorate had voted Popular Front, and not Socialist. They had not given power to a Socialist Party endowed with a mission to bring about socialism, but to a coalition of the left-wing parties. The coalition had a definite programme and it was this programme which the Socialist-led Popular Front government would now set about implementing.

Secondly, there was not and there could not be any 'holiday from the law'. The Popular Front was to be a legal government, taking over the management of public affairs in conformity with the 1875 constitution and observing the usual parliamentary procedures.

If we recall the position taken by the Socialist delegates at the first meetings of the committee responsible for working out the Popular Front programme, it will be seen that Blum's first two principles were designed to bring the Socialists more closely into line with the position adopted by the Communist Party, which the latter indeed still defended.[1]

Thirdly, if the Popular Front experiment, taking place as it did within the framework of capitalist society and a parliamentary system, should happen to be abortive, this would in no way call into question the validity of the socialist cause. It would simply prove that 'there was nothing else to be expected from this society and that it cannot be reformed from within.'[2]

And fourthly, fidelity to the party and the working class. 'I tell you this: as far as I am able, I am prepared to confront every type of adversity except one thing — discord with the party, or discord with the working class as a whole.' Blum believed that the test of power would not corrupt the men placed in government, they would remain faithful servants of the party.[3]

As well as giving unanimous endorsement to the principles which Léon Blum spelled out, the conference produced an address to the striking engineers, which expressed the Socialist Party's 'complete solidarity with this struggle backed by the reunited trade union movement. Its eventual victory will prepare the ground for the application of the more urgent measures in the Popular Front programme relating to employment law.'[4]

Léon Blum forms his government

When President Lebrun, following constitutional procedure, formally invited the Socialist Party leader to form a government, Léon Blum had his list ready and was able to present his colleagues to the head of state that same evening. The governmental structure had a new look to it; a team of senior members presiding over six groups of ministries. This was in conformity with ideas elaborated earlier by Blum in **Governmental Reform**, a little pamphlet which had appeared anonymously in 1918.[5] Without giving a complete list of the members of the government, we can mention some of the more important personalities. In the leading group, alongside Blum, were three Ministers of State, Chautemps, Violette, and Paul Faure, supplemented by Blumel, director of Blum's private office, and Jules Moch, the Cabinet Secretary. The six groups of ministries were Defence (with Daladier, and Pierre Cot), General Administration (with Salengro at the Ministry of the Interior, and Jean Zay Minister of Education), Foreign Affairs and overseas French territory (Delbos and Moutet), Finance (Vincent Auriol), Economic Affairs (C Spinasse and Georges Monnet) and 'la Solidarité Sociale' (Lebas as Minister of Labour, and Léo Lagrange). In total, 35 people, of whom three were women.[6]

'What we expected,' Delmas would write later,

> was a sort of 'Committee of Public Safety', a small group of men, each with a long list of responsibilities . . . what we got was an unwieldy cabinet of 35 people, in theory arranged hierarchically . . . And when we tried to work out why such and such a person had been chosen, it became sadly apparent that concern to balance the respective influence of various groups, sub-groups, and grouplets had weighed more heavily with Blum than the vital need to bring together men capable of identifying problems and acting quickly without regard to out-dated theories and meaningless traditions.[7]

Parliamentary tradition had been scrupulously observed.

The government takes office

This tradition had, however, been somewhat dented in the matter of presentation to the head of state. This took place at 9 o'clock in the evening of 4 June. As soon as it was over, President Lebrun addressed Léon Blum and his colleagues.

> I have a request to transmit to you from Mr Sarraut, Prime Minister and Minister of the Interior, and Mr Frossard, Minister of Labour. In their view, the situation is so serious that they request that you do not wait until tomorrow morning for the handing over of power. In the present circumstances they do not wish to prolong their interim governmental responsibilities.[8]

Lebas and Salengro immediately left to take up their posts. President Lebrun then took Blum on one side and begged him to broadcast a radio appeal to the strikers.

> Tell them that parliament is about to meet, that as soon as the session begins you are going to ask for immediate passage of the [social] laws without further delay . . . They will believe you . . . and then perhaps the movement will come to a halt.[9]

Despite his juridical misgivings, Léon Blum agreed, and the new head of government's first act was an appeal for the confidence of the striking workers.

Despite an ambiguous statement by Salengro to a caucus of left-wing parties in the National Assembly,[10] which provoked a bitter-sweet reply from Ramette, and despite the Radicals' anxiety, the new cabinet absolutely discounted the use of force against the workers' movement. In its first hours of existence, the government was convinced that emergency passage of the 'social laws' would be enough to calm the agitation. This idea was the theme of Blum's speech on the radio at midday on 5 June. It underlay the government's statement of aims, and informed all their interventions in parliamentary debates.

The ministers issued communiqués and declarations in rapid succession with the aim of convincing the workers that 'the situation has changed completely', since 'the government's programme is designed to meet all the demands put forward by the working class and backed up by the strike movement.'[11] The very large vote of confidence which the government received in parliament meant that 'it was as if the Chamber was showing its willingness to vote for the measures which will enable us to look forward to the end of the strike wave.'[12]

At the same time the government tried to take on the role of conciliator and get talks going again, particularly in engineering. In a series of urgent telegrams they encouraged the prefects to assume the same role of intermediary. In parliament they asked for emergency procedures so that discussion on the new laws could go ahead without delay.

Finally, where the struggle was at its sharpest they tried to make use of their prestige and popularity to lessen the effects of certain strikes. Thus when Blum, Salengro and Lebas received a delegation from the CGT's *commission administrative* on the evening of 5 June, the new government was worried about the effects of an all-out strike in oil-storage depots on the bakeries' continued ability to function. They decided to try to convince the workers of their case. Henri Raymond, a Communist and a union secretary in the Paris region, went with Blum's aide Jules Moch to the depots at Ivry, to ask the occupiers if they would let the necessary fuel out.[13] On their return they had to admit that the workers had refused to open the doors to them. This incident was indicative of the relationships between strikers and workers' leaders. The workers continued their strikes, which spread, and came closer than ever to engulfing every industry.

The development of the strikes, 4–7 June

The expected détente did not take place. From all over France came a flood of reports produced 'en bloc' by the newspapers, with no semblance of order, not even grouped according to regions or industries affected by the strikes. It is possible nevertheless to extract the general tendencies that characterised these days, and to summarise them under a few headings.

ONE: The last effects of the 'false lull' which we have dealt with already were disappearing. The great majority of Paris engineering factories which had gone back to work on 1 or 2 June now stopped work again and the occupation-strike took over once more.

It will be remembered that Renault had reopened its doors on Tuesday the 2nd, as the result of an agreement which contained little more than vague promises. As work restarted, the atmosphere in the plant was still electric. The workers were at their stations, but there were frequent arguments, and passionate debate during the breaks and after work. Many had abandoned the strike unwillingly, not understanding why the delegates had given up the struggle when nothing concrete had been won. Various delegations went to the management, who refused further discussions on wages, maintaining that this question fell within the ambit of the regional commission. On Thursday the 4th partial stoppages took place in various departments, and, after a delegates' meeting towards the end of the afternoon, Costes, one of the Communist leaders of the Engineering Union, announced that the management were 'going back on their promises', and that the union was calling for immediate and total stoppage of work. That same evening the occupation was once more in full swing.

The next day, Friday 5 June, delegates from the Citroën plant delivered an ultimatum to its owner, Mr Michelin: if substantial progress on meeting the workers' demands had not been made by the end of the day, a strike would be declared that evening, and the factory occupied. Thus it came to pass that for the second time in a few days the entire workforce of the Citroen plants were occupying the premises.

The same phenomenon occurred at more than 15 Paris engineering works on the same day, and in the following days the strike spread to the small and medium-sized workshops, even those employing fewer than ten workers. Meanwhile, those who had been among the first to enter the struggle held fast. 6 June was the twelfth day on strike for Lavalette, where the workers' militancy was still as high as on the first day.

TWO: What was the situation in other industries in the Paris region? Let us read more or less at random a page from a newspaper dated 7 June, in its 'new strikes' column. We find: total strike among the night train workers; all-out strike in private firms contracting for the railway network; 350 have stopped work at the Singer company plant at Bonnières; 60 workers (50 of them women) of the *Société Nantaise* at Boulogne are occupying the factory. Also on strike: the Pillot shoe factory at Paray-Vieille-Poste, 500 workers at the *Compagnie des Emeris*, boulevard Serrurier, 350 flag-stone layers and asphalt workers, the Say sugar refineries, Sommier-Lebaudy and Lefrançois, 400 workers at Dunlop, *les Grands Moulins de Paris*, the Villejuif building site, 700 workers at le Caiffa, the staff of Géo. Choisy-le-Roi accounted for ten factories on strike, in the 19th *arrondissement* more than 70 firms were shut down, including the *Société Maggi*, the Lang printworks, fuel depots, the Gaumont studios, and the Antoine ink company.

In some industries, such as locksmiths, carpets and bedding, and the cinema, the strike was more or less general. Printing and the building industry were also particularly affected.

THREE: The provinces had joined the movement 'en masse'. Here too whole industries joined the battle. In the department of Nord, in engineering at Valenciennes, in textiles at Roubaix-Tourcoing, in the mines at Anzin, Denain and Lens, the strike spread rapidly to thousands of workers. Reports from all sides named Rouen, le Havre and Nantes as places where they had lost count of the number of occupied factories, while southern workers in Bordeaux, Toulouse and Marseilles were also moving into action.

FOUR: No longer were the strikers only industrial blue-collar workers. These were joined by those who are sometimes called 'layers close to the proletariat', or 'white-collar workers'. On the 5th, the big Paris stores, the *Galeries Lafayette, le Printemps, les Trois Quartiers* all stopped work and occupied; newspaper-sellers and kiosk holders stopped selling and demanded improvement in their working conditions from their employer, the *Messageries Hachette*. Next it was the turn of the white- and blue-collar workers in the music-halls; then lorry-drivers at *les Halles*, the Paris central markets, followed by the market-dealers' clerks, and finally the office and sales staffs of the big food shops.

The agitation spread to the public services: the railways, Paris transport, certain postal services, water, gas and electricity workers all threatened to stop work. The government was extremely alarmed by this and the unions intervened vigorously to prevent such a stoppage.

FIVE: As long as the strikes had simply silenced the machines and walled up the engineers in their factories, the mass of the population was relatively unaware of their implications. Now it was different. The strikes penetrated every district, every moment of the workers' daily lives. The small firms were all shut down; the housewives found that the Potin branch where they usually bought their fresh food was closing its doors; the corner shop still received its supplies, but only after some delay; the baker's wife continually repeated that they would run out of fuel the next day and would be unable to heat the oven; the grocer dropped his voice to advise stocking up on tinned food, and of course the district's well-to-do women — their husbands well-placed to be in the know — were to be seen struggling along with heavy shopping bags filled with dried vegetables and tins of sardines which the shopkeeper had already marked up (no one knew when they could get supplies again . . . and at what price?).

Professional panic-spreaders, nervous alarmists and politically-motivated rumour-mongers went about their work, aided by the lack of newspapers.[14] Of course street-vendors were selling the workers' papers, which were eagerly seized from their hands. But even those petty-bourgeois who had voted for the Popular Front felt lost without their **Parisien** or their **Journal**.

Many people were worried by the disturbances wrought to their daily lives and by the problems which seemed to surround Léon Blum. But when they passed by the strike-bound factory near their home they would see a handful of workers peacefully sitting on chairs in front of a gate adorned with a red flag and a tricolour; through the gates they could see groups of men playing cards in the sun while others, hanging out of the windows, refereed hotly contested games of *boules*; in a corner of the yard more workers surrounded groups of young people singing to the accompaniment of a harmonica. And before going on, the passers-by would turn and drop 20 centimes into the box rigged up on the gate by the strike committee treasurer, for they knew in their hearts that the workers' demands were just.

The tactics of the CGT

The unions were alive to the dangers of a possible split between the petty-bourgeoisie and the workers in struggle, and played upon it as best they could. In his radio broadcast on the evening of the 5th, Jouhaux of the CGT insisted on the strictly sectional and economic aspects of the movement, and advised the workers to avoid cutting themselves off from the people, in particular by safeguarding food supplies. The brave tone of his speech was unconvincing, however, and everyone felt vaguely that the union leaders had been overtaken by their own troops and were no longer in control of the strikes.[15]

The tactics of the various union federations differed from industry to industry. In the press and the food industry, where talks had not been broken off, the unions took an active part in the negotiations, and, for reasons which Jouhaux had indicated, moved rapidly to the conclusion of an interim agreement on wages which allowed a return to work.[16] In other industries the bosses had broken off talks. We have seen that the engineering employers had broken off negotiations for a collective agreement. The managements of the big stores refused to talk as long as the occupations lasted. In textiles the position was the same, as was confirmed by a letter from Duchemin, president of the national employers' organisation, the *Confédération Générale de la Production Française* (CGPF), and by a message from Mr Donon, president of the *Union Textile*.[17]

But the bosses' sense of confidence was mainly verbal, and they were soon overcome by panic. Their much-vaunted concerted action of the first days gave way to a policy of individual self-defence. Self-defence required concessions — or such was implied by the returns to work announced by interior minister Salengro on 6 June, as well as the victories reported in big headlines by **l'Humanité**, **le Populaire** and **le Peuple**.[18]

In effect the unions' tactics were to go for plant-by-plant bargaining. Thus on the evening of the 4th, the engineers' union had asked their delegates to 'present the collective agreement to their managements and demand that it be signed.'[19] A few bosses conceded. But the discussion of a collective agreement covering a number of firms is a long and difficult business, slow to produce results. Accordingly, on 7 June the engineers' union changed its position, and had a resolution adopted by strikers' delegates which read as follows: 'Taking into account that the 40-hour week, paid holidays, and collective agreements will be the subject of future legislation, [the delegates] resolve in the face of this new situation, to carry on negotiations in an attempt to get a return to work *on the basis of wage claims presented* in each factory.'[20]

But certain large unions had already gone a step further. Learning from the experience in engineering, they evolved a different tactic. The strikes had broken out in no particular order, in every region of the country, with varying degrees of participation, different objectives, tactics and methods of struggle. In many respects they were already beyond the unions' control. Some had broken out in workplaces where there were no union members. To regain the leadership of the movement the unions would have to place themselves at its head. The re-establishment of discipline required unity, and for the movement to run its course it had to be generalised. The example of engineering showed the ineffectiveness of plant-by-plant deals, for in many cases the signing of an agreement was not followed by a return to work, or was negated the next day by a new strike if the workers learned that a nearby factory had won better terms.

On the evening of 6 June, the Miners Federation of the Pas-de-Calais and Nord issued a call for a general strike on 8 June. The terms of the strike instruction itself gave a good indication of the intended purpose. After listing the demands, it went on: '*To maintain order and calm, and make the government's task easier*, the regional miners' committee has mandated the day-shift technical committee members to direct the strike movement in their areas.'[21]

Two points need to be stressed. Firstly, the strike was already solid in a large number of pits involving several thousand workers. As **l'Humanité** reported on 7 June:

> At the Anzin mines, the strike is 100 per cent — a total of 6,300 miners are on strike and occupying the pits. The situation at Douchy is the same. The stoppage is also 100 per cent at Thivencelles. At the number four pit at Ostricourt 1,200 miners have stopped work.

Secondly, the general strike instruction related only to the departments of Nord and Pas-de-Calais. These were in fact the only areas where the miners were already on strike. So the call for a general strike made sense only as a tactic designed to regain control of the spontaneous walk-outs.

The same story was repeated in construction and public works. The relevant CGT federation called for a general strike on Monday 8 June. The sectors involved were those requiring the use of steel in construction, lock-making (already on all-out strike), cement workers (several thousand were already on strike and the unions leadership's intervention was to 'co-ordinate efforts'), excavating, and carpentry. Each union organised meetings of strikers' delegates in an attempt to maintain contact with the sites which were on strike.

Finally, in engineering itself, the union federation issued a communiqué stating that it 'remained in permanent contact with all the factories', while the national committee, meeting on 7 June, voted the following resolution:

> In view of the widening of the struggle, the national committee of the Engineering Workers Federation resolves to *shoulder its responsibilities* and to co-ordinate the strikes in order to give them maximum effectiveness and discipline.[22]

But there was already discipline — the discipline established in each factory by the workers themselves. And for every problem which arose, they found a solution. A group of bosses tried to forestall occupation of their premises by declaring a lock-out? The workers broke in and installed themselves in the workshops. The bosses refused to negotiate? The delegates from the aviation industry decided to look for new means of bringing pressure to bear, and they approached government minister Pierre Cot to tell him they were ready to run the machines under the supervision of the ministry of aviation.

The strike was more or less total in all the Paris engineering plants, and the department of Nord. The engineers in eastern France had presented their list of demands, and a strike was not far off. The Federation of Engineering Workers chose this moment to wake up and courageously decide to 'shoulder its responsibilities'!

The most important unions, then, were making strenuous efforts to regain the leadership of the working class during 6 and 7 June. The workers were masters of the storage depots, the factories, shops, and sites, all of which they guarded with cheerful tranquillity. But boredom could cause evil counsels to prevail . . . the workers needed distractions, and the workers' papers set about providing them by launching appeals for 'artistes, singers, and musicians'[23] to place themselves at the disposal of the municipal *Maisons de la Culture*.

What to do?

As for the government, during 5 and 6 June the impression given to all observers was one of complete impotence.

Salengro attempted a vain bluff with his communiqué of 6 June which identified 'a growing feeling of détente'. He was soon obliged to acknowledge the continued and extensive growth of the numbers on strike, and the movement's spread to the whole of France.[24] Both right and left wings of Blum's parliamentary majority called on him to intervene as mediator — the Radicals took fright naturally enough at the violations against 'property' and were particularly upset by the strikes among agricultural workers. Through the pen of Vaillant-Couturier, the Communists called for a rapid resolution of the conflict. 'Discussions must be resumed,' wrote the Communist deputy.[25] 'The government must lean heavily on the employers' organisations . . . to get them to recognise the justice of the workers' cause. The present situation, brought about by the employers' selfishness and obstinacy, if it continues, can only threaten the security of the French people.'

But the government could no longer play an effective mediating role in each of the strike-bound industries in turn. The most they could do was attempt to mitigate the effects of the strikes in the areas causing the most urgent problems — for example by distributing the army's fuel to doctors and bakers, or by exerting pressure on the market wholesalers to get them to resolve the deadlock at *les Halles*. Their desire to set themselves up as arbitrator was undermined by the extraordinary dynamism of the workers' upsurge, the generalisation of which called into question the whole relationship between labour and capital.

The urgent problems provoked by the workers' demands could now be resolved only at a national level, involving all industries together, not simply one at a time. The government moved on to this national and inter-industrial plane at midday on 7 June, when it published a new communiqué:

> Following the vote of confidence by the Chamber, the Prime Minister has appealed to the CGPF and the CGT. He has informed them that parliament has expressed its desire that there should be an immediate re-establishment of contact between the two organisations, with an urgent examination of conditions which would permit a return to work without delay. A meeting will take place today at 3 o'clock at the *Hôtel Matignon*.[26]

5

THE MATIGNON AGREEMENT

THE CIRCUMSTANCES surrounding the arrangement of the meeting which led eventually to the signing of the Matignon agreement during the night of 7 and 8 June only became known during Léon Blum's trial at Riom.[1] Indeed, Blum's statements to his Vichy judges provide us with some very interesting details about an initiative which had previously been unanimously attributed to the government. Here is what Blum had to say:

> As early as the morning of 5 June, Mr Lambert-Ribot,[2] who had been a friend of mine for many years at the Council of State before entering the service of the employers' organisations like all too many former university or public administration officials, Mr Lambert-Ribot, with whom I had always preserved friendly relations, approached me by means of two mutual friends, two separate intermediaries, to request that at the earliest possible occasion, without wasting a moment, I attempt to establish contact between the two sides: leading employers' organisations and the CGT.
>
> No doubt I would myself have attempted what is now called the Matignon agreement. But I am compelled by respect for the truth to say that the first initiative came from the employers' leaders. So, I repeat, as early as Friday morning, through two mutual friends — I can name one of them, Mr Grunebaum-Ballin, honorary president of a section of the Council of State — Mr Lambert-Ribot contacted me with a request to bring the two sides together as speedily as possible on the basis of an across-the-board wage increase in return for the ending of the occupations . . . That is how the Matignon agreement came about.[3]

Before this account was published it was generally supposed that Blum himself had been the instigator — some said the guiding spirit — of the meeting at the *Hôtel Matignon*. The account given by employers' leader M. Duchemin certainly gives that impression.[4] A triple motive may be discerned in the CGPF leader's willingness to let this myth of the government's initiating role go unchallenged. First of all was the employers' desire to avoid admitting to the workers the extent of their weakness and fear. Indeed it is inconceivable that negotiations carried out in the circumstances of 6 and 7 June could lead to other than the employers' capitulation on all points at issue. The pressure from below was too strong, and the employers could easily imagine how their open opposition to any one of the workers' main demands might provoke a movement threatening to destroy the basic principles of the existing economic order. Secondly, by attributing to the government the initiative of an agreement favourable to the workers, the employers would help to reinforce the government's sagging authority, and the personal prestige of Léon Blum. Finally, and this third preoccupation was shown to be justified the day after the deal was signed, the employers' leaders knew that if their actions were seen to be dictated by circumstances they would become the target of criticism and reproaches from some of their own members. These reproaches were indeed made, and later led to important changes in the French employers' organisations.

The affair having begun in this way, Léon Blum hastened to act on the employers' suggestions. On the evening of the 5th, about 10.30 pm, he received the leadership of the CGPF — Richemond, Dalbouze, Lambert-Ribot and Duchemin — and acquainted them with his point of view. The situation was alarming and the most serious element in it was the government's ignorance of where the workers' explosion had come from, and where it was going. The parliamentary bills would be presented on Monday (8 June). The only point at issue with direct bearing on the employers' organisations, therefore, was the question of wages. Here it was desirable to reach a general agreement which would achieve an end to hostilities and the evacuation of the factories. The government refused to consider the use of force. Were the employers prepared to meet the CGT and join them in a search for agreement on the wages question?[5]

The employers gave their assent, on condition that the evacuation of the factories be expressly included in the written terms of the deal. With this proviso, and if the sovereign body of the CGPF gave its approval, a meeting could take place on the Sunday.

The next day, 6 June, at three o'clock in the afternoon, the central council of employers' federations met and 'unanimously authorised its representatives to take part in negotiations with the CGT'.[6] Armed with this agreement in principle, Léon Blum turned to the unions. Salengro himself went to the *rue Lafayette* on Sunday morning 7 June where the *commission administrative* was meeting, as it did at the same time every day.

'That morning', runs the account of a participant,

> Jouhaux had just said yet again that the only position to adopt was as if the CGT had not lost control of the workers, and that it alone could reimpose order once satisfaction on the wages question was received. Somebody came to tell him that the Minister of the Interior wanted to see him immediately. He left the room and returned a quarter of an hour later . . . Almost without discussion the *commission administrative* agreed . . . to send a CGT delegation to a meeting which was to take place that afternoon at the *Hôtel Matignon* . . . with the CGPF leaders.[7]

On 7 June at three o'clock in the afternoon there sat down at the same table along with Blum: on the one hand Jouhaux, Frachon, Belin, Semat, Cordier, and Milan, and on the other Duchemin (president of the CGPF), Richemond (president of the Association of Engineering and Mechanical Industries), Dalbouze (president of the Paris Chamber of Commerce) and Lambert-Ribot (representing the *Comité des Forges*).

The CGPF at that time stood for much the same on the bosses' side as the CGT did on the union side. It was the supreme body composed of representatives of the various industrial and commercial federations. But it is important to recognise two important facts about the structure and behaviour of the CGPF before June 1936.

On the one hand the employers' organisation was not very centralised; the various industrial federations had a large degree of autonomy and not all the employers' organisations — especially the commercial ones — were members of the Confederation. Furthermore, until June 1936, the CGPF had largely concentrated its activities in the fields of finance and commerce. Representation at governmental or parliamentary level on general problems facing the various sectors of industry and commerce, problems relating to production, prices, taxes and tariffs — this was the area of competence of the CGPF, presided over by Mr Duchemin. 'Social' problems, that is wages and conditions, were left to the various federations. Only the very biggest of these, Engineering, and the *Comité des Forges*, had any kind of organisation and specialised staff to deal with such questions. The employers' organisations existing in June 1936 had never had to confront a general offensive by the working class; social struggles had always been sectional, and the degree of organisation by the bosses in each industry generally speaking mirrored the strength of the unions and the level of worker-militancy opposed to them.

What was in the minds of the men who now found themselves facing Léon Jouhaux and the other representatives of the CGT? For the first time they had to assume the task of representing the entire French bourgeoisie. The responsibility weighed on them, and they had no illusions about the difficulties of their position. They knew how much was at stake in the struggle that was in progress, and that to preserve what was essential it might be necessary to compromise on incidentals, that is on whatever did not call into question the existing ownership of the means of production. They were ready to accept anything if they could obtain the evacuation of the factories, whose occupation was a violation of the single most important of the principles on which the whole of capitalist society was built. At the same time they doubtless hoped that if the working class could be satisfied by the promise of immediate material gains, it would be possible to win back piecemeal at a later date what was given up 'en bloc' under duress.

And they were all the more disposed to make concessions when they recognised in their adversaries the same uncertainty, the same fears, the same need to put an end to the workers' agitation. A policy of concessions would allow the CGT leaders to pose as victors and to regain control of an ever more precarious situation.

Six representatives of the CGT made up the workers' side. Beside the secretary-general, Léon Jouhaux, and the assistant secretaries, Benoît Frachon and René Belin, the *commission administrative* had delegated Cordier from construction and Milan from hat-making, both former CGT militants, and Semat from engineering, formerly CGT-U.

As they arrived at the prime minister's residence, the workers' representatives were not entirely sure that agreement was possible.[8] This uncertainty as to the possible outcome of the negotiations may seem surprising. It is readily explained, however, if we look at the ambiguity in the positions of Jouhaux and his senior colleagues. All their power was vested in the irresistible mass movement, but they were made vulnerable by their inability to rely 100 per cent on a movement which they were following rather than leading, which they had been attempting to hold back for more than a week, and whose every new development caught them unawares.

Another element of weakness in their situation lay in the fact that they were closely tied to the government despite their protestations of independence. The connections lay in the Popular Front programme, in political links as well as in personal relations. It was true that this connection worked both ways, and that they could count on Blum's support in negotiations with the bosses. But this support would not go beyond the political programme which the Popular Front government had set for itself, and as yet no member of the workers' delegation had contemplated by-passing these narrow limits and relying on the very dynamism of the working-class explosion.

Meanwhile the working class, while daily carrying the struggle to ever higher levels, gave evidence of its confidence in the CGT leaders by the soaring union recruitment figures of which the latter were now beginning to be able to give details. In the course of the strikes the unions' workplace branches were gaining hundreds of members. The peacefulness of this immense strike involving hundreds of thousands of workers would now be strengthened by the discipline which comes from membership of a trade union.

The above observations are an attempt to sketch in the ambiguity in the positions of the employers and the union leaders. But they could not, of course, obscure the essentials of the situation. After a 'courteous, difficult and painful discussion,'[9] 'they' gave in 'on all points'.[10]

The Matignon discussions

The Matignon discussions extended over two sessions. The first session lasted from 3 o'clock until about 8 o'clock. After a few hours break, the talks began again at 11 pm and the agreement was made known to the press at about twenty minutes to one in the morning. We can now trace the development of the conversation by reconstituting the whole from the accounts given by the various participants.[11]

Léon Blum opened the proceedings by reading the agenda. He recalled the matters which came within the competence of the law (paid holidays, the length of the working week, the principle of collective agreements). On these matters parliament would within a short time be called upon to give its sovereign verdict, while the general clauses of any collective agreement, and the question of wages, fell into the realm of contract. It was accepted by all sides that wages were too low — the principle of an across-the-board increase could be settled here and now; minimum percentage increases could be decided; and the government was prepared to arbitrate in cases where agreement could not be reached.

There ensued a dialogue between government and employers on the principles of the reforms which were about to be implemented. The CGPF stressed the burden which would be imposed on the French commercial and industrial entrepreneurs. It was the old familiar song — the bosses' difficulties, international competition, the crisis and so on, and the need to re-establish order.

Léon Blum had his reply ready: the purchasing power theory. Only an increase in purchasing power could revitalise the French economy, which had been almost suffocated by the deflationary policies of previous governments. If, as a result of the new 'social laws', certain firms found themselves temporarily embarrassed financially, the government would make available whatever financial facilities were required to give the national economy the desired boost. As for law and order, it could only be guaranteed by allowing the working class some measure of relief from its poverty-stricken condition. The employers were finally obliged to accept that parliament would decide, and that they would bow before the law.

Once these elaborate preliminaries were over they got down to business. Jouhaux at once raised an important point: any agreements reached should not jeopardise gains which had already been conceded by some firms to their staff. These should be retained in their entirety. Agreement was fairly easily reached on this point, but it was specified, at the owners' request, that wage increases granted since the beginning of the strikes should be seen as advance-payments on whatever increases were agreed as a result of the present discussions. However, if in certain cases workers had obtained results better than those provided for by agreement between the two confederations, these would be allowed to stand.

Discussion was brief when it came to collective agreements. A lot of the ground in this area had already been covered by discussions between the two sides in the engineering industry. The same applied to the question of recognition of workers' delegates. As well as defining the delegates' role, methods of election were determined. Union recognition, and the promise that there would be absolutely no victimisations of strikers, were agreed relatively easily, and the bosses obtained in return the inclusion of a paragraph on the exercise of union rights which stipulated that this 'must not involve acts which are against the law'.

Finally they came to the question of wages, which according to the union men had two aspects to it. On the one hand, an across-the-board increase was necessary and it should not be less than between 10 and 15 per cent — which a considerable number of firms had already conceded anyway. On the other hand there existed throughout France various firms and establishments which habitually paid starvation wages. Each of the union delegates quoted numerous examples of hourly rates at less than 2F.

The employers made a show of stupefaction which Léon Blum later recorded thus:

> On the subject of raising abnormally low wages, I heard Mr Duchemin say to Mr Richemond, on seeing with his own eyes the evidence of certain wage-rates frightening for their extreme modesty, 'How is such a thing possible? How could we allow this to go on? We have failed in our duty in allowing such a state of affairs.'[12]

This show of human emotion and its accompanying *'mea culpa'* did not, however, cause the employers to lose their heads. They resisted the CGT proposals for a general wage rise of between 10 and

15 per cent, proposing instead that increases should be calculated by taking account of the situation in each industry, with a general ceiling of between 7 and 10 per cent.

There followed a long and abrasive discussion, of which Léon Blum recounted certain highlights thus:

> I remember all the incidents . . . I can still hear the voice of Benoît Frachon when wage-increases were discussed. Mr Lambert-Ribot said: 'What, you're not happy with such rates? But tell me, when have French workers ever had such a general increase in their pay?' And Benoît Frachon replied: 'Tell me when you have ever seen a workers' movement in France of such breadth and size?'[13]

With no agreement in sight, the government proposed their own arbitration. Each of the parties asked to be allowed to consult their colleagues before agreeing to this, and a further meeting was arranged for 11 o'clock.

Jouhaux and the other CGT delegates returned immediately to the *rue Lafayette* where the members of the *commission administrative* were waiting for them. Unanimous approval of the bosses' concessions was a foregone conclusion.

The employers' representatives were deliberating at the same time. First, at nine o'clock the engineering employers met at the Horticultural Hall, listened to a report from Richemond, and, with one dissenting voice, authorised him to sign in their name the points on which agreement had already been reached, and to accept governmental arbitration on wages. At ten o'clock the CGPF central council adopted broadly the same point of view, but with reservations from the representatives of the banks, insurance companies and big stores, who wanted to conduct their own negotiations on wages.

While these various federations and union meetings were going on, an immense crowd gathered at the *Vélodrome d'Hiver* stadium and on the *boulevard de Grenelle*. Several tens of thousands of people had come to hear speakers from the Popular Front. Léon Blum had promised to appear, and l'**Humanité** announced across its whole front page in poster-sized letters that Communist Party leader Maurice Thorez would speak. Loud-speakers were rigged up under the overhead railway lines where the crowds unable to get into the auditorium were massing to listen to the speeches from the Radical, Socialist and Communist leaders.

Léon Blum referred to the discussions in progress, and said among other things: 'I would like to pay tribute to the understanding of the situation and the spirit of conciliation displayed by the employers' representatives in the course of the debates.'

The spectators, including numerous contingents from strike-bound factories, marked the intervals between speeches with rousing choruses of the *Internationale*, and became almost delirious when Blum and Thorez applauded each other. Outside the same enthusiasm reigned, and the crowd called for the speakers to appear on the balcony; but Marceau Pivert had to announce: 'Comrades, don't expect to see Léon Blum — he is hard at work.'

Unable to wait until the end of the meeting, Blum had indeed already returned to the *Matignon* where, with his assistants, he was drawing up the terms of the compromise deal. When the new session was under way, and the two sides had given their assent to the principle of arbitration, he gave his verdict: a general wage-rise of between 7 and 15 per cent, the total wage-bill for any firm not to be increased by more than 12 per cent.

The CGT representatives returned once more to the question of the so-called 'abnormally low' wages, and secured a special clause providing for a separate adjustment prior to the general increase. The bosses in turn asked for assurances concerning the return to work and evacuation of the plants, which they wanted to take place on Monday 8 June. The CGT men were cautious. Evidence from two quite different sources helps us to understand why.

First, assistant secretary Benoît Frachon, at the CGT *comité confédéral national* of 16 June:

> The bosses were keen for us to return to work on 8 June. We were unanimously against. We had no desire to discredit ourselves in front of the masses. We proposed direct contacts between strikers and managements. The bosses wanted something more — this is how we arrived at the wording in the agreement.[14]

Secondly, the explanation given by Léon Blum:

> In return for the gains made by the workers, the question of ending the occupations was raised. The CGT representatives said to the representatives of big business: 'We will undertake to do everything in our power, but we cannot guarantee success. With a tidal-wave like this, the best thing is to give it time to run its course. Maybe now you will start to regret using the years of deflation and unemployment to weed out systematically all our union militants. There are hardly any left to exercise the necessary influence on their workmates for our orders to be carried out.' And I can still see Mr Richemond, who was sitting on my left, bow his head, saying: 'It's true, we were wrong.'[15]

With these verbal reservations a text was drawn up which envisaged a return to work as soon as each factory management had accepted the general agreement.

It was now half past twelve midnight. The agreed text was signed by each of the delegates and initialled by Léon Blum. It was immediately made public, and appeared in the newspapers of 8 June. We have thought it worthwhile to include here in its entirety.

Article 1: The employers' delegation accepts the immediate institution of collective contracts of employment.

Article 2: These contracts should include articles 3 and 5 hereafter referred to.

Article 3: Since observation of the law is the duty of every citizen, the employers recognise the freedom and the right of workers freely to join and to belong to a trade union constituted within the meaning of book 3 of the *Code du Travail*.

— The employers bind themselves not to take into consideration the fact of belonging or not belonging to a union in making decisions concerning hiring of labour, the organisation and sharing of work, disciplinary measures, or the dismissal of labour.

— If one of the contracting parties should contest that the motive for dismissing a worker is in violation of the right to union activity described above, the two parties shall make it their duty to seek out the facts and bring about an equitable solution to the case in question.

— This procedure shall not infringe on the rights of the parties to obtain redress in a court of law of any wrongs caused. The exercise of the right to union activity must not involve the commission of any acts contrary to the law.

Article 4: The real wages in force for all workers as of 25 May 1936 shall be adjusted, from the day of returning to work, according to a diminishing scale, starting at 15 per cent for the lowest paid and falling to 7 per cent for the highest paid.

— The total wage-bill of each establishment being increased in no case by more than 12 per cent, any wage increases agreed to since the above-mentioned date shall be deducted from the readjustments defined above. Nevertheless, these increases shall remain in force for any part by which they exceed the aforesaid adjustments.

— The negotiations, to be begun immediately, for the fixing of minimum wage-rates by region and by occupation, shall in particular be concerned with the necessary adjustment of abnormally low wages.

— The employers' side undertakes to make any adjustment necessary to maintain the accepted relation between remuneration of office-staff and hourly-paid employees.

Article 5: Notwithstanding special cases already regulated by the law, in each workplace employing more than ten workers, after agreement between union organisations, or, if there are none, between interested parties, there shall be two (designated) or several (designated and provisional) workers' delegates, according to the size of the workforce. These delegates shall have the function of presenting to management any individual claims which have not been directly satisfied, in pursuance of the application of the law, of regulations of the *Code du Travail*, of agreed rates of pay, and of measures relating to health and safety.

— Eligible to vote are all working men and women aged 18 years and over who have completed three months service in the workplace at the time of the election, and who have not been deprived of their civic rights.

— Eligible to stand as candidates shall be electors as defined above, of French nationality, aged at least 25 years, having worked in the establishment for one year without interruption, excepting that this length of service must be reduced if its observation would reduce to five the number of eligible candidates.

— Workers engaged in retail trade, of whatever kind, either in their own name or in the name of their spouse, are not eligible to stand as candidates.

Article 6: The employers' delegation undertakes to ensure that there shall be no disciplinary measures arising from the act of going on strike.

Article 7: The joint workers' delegation shall ask the workers on strike to return to work as soon as the plant management shall have accepted the terms of this agreement, and as soon as negotiations relating to its application shall have been started between management and personnel of each workplace.

Form and scope of the Matignon agreement

Analysis of the legal form, validity and implications of the Matignon agreement does not seem useful. The document initialled by the employers and the CGT men had not, in the strict sense of the term, any legal bearing. It created no civil or commercial obligations for the parties. At the most it could be described — if one is not too fussy about the strict legal meaning of the words — as a pre-contract, or rather a promise to contract, the two parties undertaking to recommend to their affiliates the conclusion of collective agreements based on the 7 June compromise. But the Matignon agreement had a greater importance than any contract could have, since it was at once a factor in the social struggle and a political act.

First of all, it was a translation into legal terms of a certain balance of forces between the classes. Its terms bore witness to the fact that French capitalism was obliged to grant the working class certain material concessions, which it would never have considered granting of its own free will; it summarised the bosses' weakness in the social struggle.

But if it bore witness to the state of the class struggle, it was also an attempt to stabilise the social relations which had resulted from the conflicts in the workplace. Its object was to halt the workers' struggle by establishing new legal relations between the owners and the workforce, by giving a legal sanction to what were in fact workers' conquests, won in battle at the height of a wave of strikes. So the tendency of the Matignon agreement was to bring to an end the inequality in the balance of class forces which it highlighted, just at the moment when the strike wave was tending to accentuate the inequality to the detriment of the factory owners.

The Matignon agreement was, in addition, a political act by a government which called on the two sides of industry to adopt its economic and social programme before the two houses of parliament had debated it, a political act which proved that in the particular circumstances of June '36 agreement between the conflicting parties carried more weight than a parliamentary division.

Any question of a legal, contractual side to the agreement made under Blum's auspices was rendered even more doubtful by the complete absence of any sanction applicable to its non-fulfilment by either one of the parties. No arbitration procedure was laid down, and no power of conciliation given to the state. Furthermore, there were many who thought that the importance of the 7 June agreement went beyond its actual terms, as it implied tacit acceptance by the employers of the whole social policy of the government, including its intentions concerning the length of the working week.[16] Finally, the way the articles were drafted — suffering from the haste which motivated the negotiators — left the door open to a number of arguments about the interpretation of the clauses dealing with wages; hardly a normal occurrence in a contract of employment!

One of those who signed the accord, Mr Lambert-Ribot, the delegate of the *Comité des Forges*, in a statement to **le Temps** the following day, denied any contractual sense to the document bearing his initials, and invoked the constraint under which the CGPF had had to operate:

> The employers have no illusions about the consequences of the experiment which is being imposed on us, and to which we are obliged to submit. We could do no other than accept arbitration by the government which, from now on, must assume all the responsibilities of the new situation, which is both dangerous and false. The employers made the most pointed reservations in accepting the government's proposals.[17]

Meanwhile, and this was not the least paradoxical aspect of the business, the trade union representatives could be heard emphasising the most formal aspects of the Matignon deal, and trying to attach a binding contractual quality to an essentially political document. This was in fact the central argument of the CGT leaders, who multiplied their appeals for a return to work in the days following the agreement. The CGT, they argued, had, in the fullness of its own sovereign independence, made certain undertakings which the working class now had to respect. The Matignon agreement was supposed to have consecrated the workers' victory, and a return to work would be the natural sequel to this victory.

Was it a victory?

The three workers' dailies proclaimed the Matignon deal with enormous headlines on the morning of Monday 8 June, the word 'victory' recurring constantly in editorials concocted hastily during the night.

L'Humanité's headline, covering the whole front page, trumpeted 'Victory is Ours!'. **Le Peuple** had 'Victory over poverty — eight million workers get satisfaction.' Meanwhile the editorial in **le Populaire**, entitled 'Victory to the working class', observed, 'Victory! Victory! The bosses have capitulated! . . . The bosses, which bosses? All of them! . . .

> A victory? Better . . . a triumph! In twenty years of struggle the working class has never achieved, perhaps never hoped to achieve, as much as this. A triumph for the independent action of the working class . . . a triumph for the Popular Front government, whose quick and clear decisions have broken through the bosses' unwillingness and hesitations. A triumph for trade union organisations, whose temperate but bold attitude has been justly rewarded. Now the victorious workers can again take up their tools. They will stay on their guard, and strengthen their workplace organisation by massively joining the unions. The Popular Front government, the government of their class is even more than ever assured of their support.

The same refrain could be heard in Frachon's speech to the *comité confédéral national* on 16 June:

> I consider this agreement a great victory . . . I wish to acknowledge the total backing given to the workers by Léon Blum's government, and we want our attitude to be known outside the union movement as well.[18] . . . All the gains have been made thanks to the Popular Front, and to its government, as well as to the efforts of the union movement.

It was left to Léon Jouhaux, in his radio broadcast of 8 June, to give the most penetrating analysis of the accords which he had signed the day before:

> The victory won during the night of Sunday and Monday marks the beginning of a new era . . . the era of direct relations between two of the great organised economic forces of the country. In the fullness of their independence they have debated and resolved the problems which form the basis of the new organisation of the French economy. For some time people have been talking of the need for a new formula. This has

been found in completely free and equal discussion of various claims, and the exchange of different points of view. All the decisions have been arrived at without the slightest compulsion, under the aegis of the government, the latter ready, if necessary, to fulfil its role of arbitrator corresponding to its function of representative of the common good.

For the first time in the history of the world, a whole class has won an improvement in its condition at the same time . . . There is an important lesson here . . . These events prove beyond doubt that there is no need of a dictatorial and authoritarian state to achieve the elevation of the working class to its rightful role of collaborator in the national economy. This can be achieved by the normal functioning and extension of democracy.

As we mark our first success we workers must honour our signature, the CGT's signature, and do everything to fulfil our side of the bargain as honestly as possible, and in this way we can win the new forces and develop the greater understanding which we shall need in the struggles yet to come. Victory and hope . . . this is the meaning of the agreement signed on 7 June.[19]

The last part of Jouhaux's speech was echoed in the joint communiqué issued by the CGT and the *Union des Syndicats de la Région Parisienne*, published the same day:

The CGT having signed, and the *Union Syndicale* having approved this agreement, we ask all union organisations to help explain its great importance, to help our national confederation to respect its signature by returning to work wherever local managements sign a local agreement and are willing to open negotiations with a view to concluding an agreement at national or regional level.[20]

This was indeed the procedure agreed at Matignon: in each workplace the strike was to be halted if the boss gave a declaration of willingness to abide by the decisions of 7 June, and was ready to begin negotiations either with a view to signing a local agreement, or (if the agreement was to be a regional one) with a view to solving the particular problems of the workplace. The CGT had formally pledged itself to encourage this process of pacification.

The second Matignon agreement

A few days later, however, on 10 June, a second meeting proved necessary. The CGT's assistant secretaries, Belin and Frachon, were called in by Léon Blum at the request of the CGPF, and found themselves face to face with their erstwhile antagonists. Firstly, it seemed there were problems of interpretation relating to the government's arbitration on wages. 'For 24 hours,' wrote Mr Duchemin later, 'we had found ourselves assailed with demands for increases to take effect *before* the overall adjustment of between 7 and 15 per cent, not on the basis of increases for abnormally low wages, but on the completely new basis of the demand for a living wage.'[21] The government sided with the employers, specifying that the expression 'abnormally low wages' should be interpreted restrictively, and was intended to apply only to hourly rates similar to those quoted during the discussions of 7 June.

The second matter of concern was the question of the return to work. Faced with numerous cases of refusal to end an occupation, the parties to Matignon confirmed that a return to work must take place as soon as negotiations for a collective agreement had started, as soon as the local management had accepted the terms of the overall agreement.

It is easy to see why this 'second Matignon' had become necessary. Workers still on strike were attempting to go beyond the gains of 7 June, and were therefore ignoring the union directives; but this time the government set its face against the workers' demands.

6
THE CRUCIAL DAYS:
7-12 JUNE

MANY WRITERS who have briefly sketched a picture of the June
events as part of their memoirs generally locate the first stage of
'pacification' on the day after the Matignon deal. 'The Matignon
agreement restored control of the movement to the CGT,' writes
Delmas,[1] and Léon Blum declared before his judges at Riom: 'There
is no doubt whatsoever that after Matignon the movement went into
decline.'[2]

These remarks do not take account of a decisive period — the
days 7–12 June — which is in our opinion of very great importance.
During these days the strikes spread and were transformed, taking on
new features which persuaded Trotsky to write: 'The French Revolution has begun.'

We shall take the strike wave region by region, and in most cases
we will give a break-down of the main industries caught up in the
struggle. It will be apparent that we have concentrated our account
principally on the Paris region and the north, the most industrialised
regions in France and those where the workers' action was at its most
dynamic. It is noticeable, and we shall return to this fact in the next
chapter, that the provinces, apart from the north, joined the movement some days after Paris and its suburbs, and that although these
regional outposts underwent experiences quite comparable to those of
the capital, this was always after a delay of a number of days which
remained more or less constant, up to and including the dying down of
the movement.

The Paris Region — Engineering

There is an apparent contradiction between the positions taken
on 6–7 June by the assembly of strikers' delegates in the Paris region,

and by the national council of the engineering union. The debates among the strikers' delegates, along with the national council's communiqué, allow us to judge the workers' mood in this industry — which was now completely paralysed.

The assembly of delegates from factories on strike, which took place on Saturday 6 June — the day before Matignon — opened with a report from Gauthier, one of the union secretaries, who summarised the situation to date. The employers had not yet agreed to resume talks; in the factories, where perfect order still reigned, the workers were looking for new ways to force the management to concede. Declared Gauthier:

> From all sides, our comrades insist that we make approaches to the Ministry of Aviation, the Ministry of War, and the Post Office [to get them to put pressure on the employers]. 'If not,' they tell us, 'we shall personally assume control of production.'

The delegates from numerous workplaces, Citroën-Javel and Rateau in particular, returned to this theme in their contributions from the floor. 'We can easily organise the work without the bosses,' declared the Rateau delegate. Various delegates from small firms described their bosses' attempts at blackmail: they claimed to sympathise with the workers, and to be willing to meet their demands, but in the employers' organisations they were exposed to influence from the big firms, who pressurised them to stand fast against the workers' claims. Others used the usual bankruptcy — and redundancy — blackmail: if we meet the workers' demands, suggested the owners of many small and medium-sized firms, we shall be forced to close our doors and lay people off, otherwise we shall rapidly go bankrupt.

All delegations were unanimously in favour of continuing the strike until complete satisfaction of all demands. The resolution proposed by Gauthier and adopted unanimously expressed this agreement, and continued:

> Given that the forty-hour week, paid holidays, and national collective agreements will shortly be the object of parliamentary legislation, we resolve, on the basis of this new situation, to seek negotiations for a return to work on the basis of the wage-claims put forward in each factory.

The next day, Sunday 7 June, an extraordinary session of the national council of the engineering union having decided, as we have noted, 'to assume our responsibilities, and to co-ordinate the strikes to give them maximum effectiveness and discipline,' then adopted a resolution in which we read as follows:

While it is true that the forty-hour week, paid holidays, and collective agreements belong to the legislative sphere, it is nonetheless true that the engineering workers cannot wait for parliament to press laws to force all the employers to meet out demands. We also consider that the proper formulation and application of the proposed laws depends on the specific and independent actions of trade union organisations . . .

From these texts it may seem that the federal engineering secretaries had taken a more radical position than the delegates of striking factories. We shall see that it was nothing of the kind.

No dramatic events marked Sunday 7 June in the factories. Strikers' families came to chat at the gates with the captive workers. Dances and concerts were organised, radios were installed in many of the factories thanks to assistance from small shopkeepers. Parisians diverted their habitual Sunday walks to the industrial districts, and their children regarded with curiosity the usually sombre buildings where today some kind of party seemed to be going on. The middle class, deprived of petrol, were unable to get their cars out, and remained shut up indoors. They discussed the latest alarmist articles to appear in the **Écho de Paris**, and the catastrophic news from the Stock Exchange. The boldness of the workers' paper sellers, who that morning had come right up to the church doors to chase away the vendors of the semi-fascist **Action Française**, seemed to them symptomatic of the general revolutionary atmosphere, and they consulted each other on the chances of sending their children to the country.

On the morning of the 8th the striking workers learned of the Matignon agreement. There was great joy in the factories, but it wasn't always easy to see how to put the bosses' concessions into practice locally. Delegations made contact with management and put forward their lists of demands. But where wages were concerned, these demands went considerably beyond what was envisaged in the government arbitration, and no agreement was possible.

At Hotchkiss there was a meeting organised by the strike committee which included representatives of 33 neighbouring factories, as well as an invited spokesman for the engineering union. A communiqué was issued, which later appeared in **l'Humanité**:

Two main points were discussed. 1) The workers' demands, and 2) The situation inside the various plants. All delegates paid tribute to the union for its activity . . . They expressed satisfaction with the Matignon accord, and on the wages question stressed the need to reach agreement on the guaranteed minimum straight away. Finding this first meeting useful [the delegates] decided to hold another on the following Thursday, 11 June, and expressed a wish to set up a central committee where delegates from all firms and the engineering union would be represented.[3]

Meanwhile, at regional level, Lebas, the Minister of Labour, had organised a meeting between employers and workers. It was agreed to carry on negotiations from the point they had reached on 4 June. A meeting of sub-committees was arranged, including one dealing with wages, which would meet the next day.

On Tuesday 9 June, at 8.30 in the evening, 700 delegates from factories on strike assembled in the *salle Mathurin Moreau*. Gauthier, in the name of the union, asked the delegates to make a definite statement on a return to work. The employers had accepted the Matignon agreement.

> No doubt, the agreement between the CGT and the CGPF does not contain everything that the engineers would like to see in it. But we must not forget that we are now operating in new conditions, so we can consider a return to work as long as we remain on our guard.[4]

Poirot spoke in similar vein, and the meeting was opened up to the floor.

A large number of delegates indicated that they wished to speak, and their contributions all stressed the same points. Delegates from Ducellier, the *Comptoirs de Montrouge*, Brandt, Chaboche, and other firms, gave voice to their fears that the new working conditions would not measure up to what had been included in their lists of demands, and all were united in demanding increases in low wages before the agreement accepted by the CGT was put into effect. The strikes should continue until these demands were met. There were still 17 workers waiting to speak when Doury interrupted proceedings as the union delegation had a meeting with the bosses at 11 o'clock. There would be another report-back meeting the following afternoon at three o'clock.

On the morning of the 10th a communiqué issued by the employers showed the degree to which the representatives of capital were pained by the engineers' refusal to implement the Matignon agreement.

> The establishments affected are deeply concerned by the information, confirmed in the course of yesterday, that the hourly-paid staff have not committed themselves fully to the agreed bases for resolution of the conflict which were decided at this arbitration [meaning the Matignon agreement], whereas the employers' side have unanimously demonstrated their willingness to abide by these decisions.

Their anxiety was all the more acute in that the theory that the workers were being misled by irresponsible elements could hardly stand up in the present circumstances. A certain Mr Harlé made this somewhat wounding discovery, when, attempting to speak to 'his' workers without the intermediary of the strike committee, he was obliged to take to his heels before a forest of clenched fists, while all the workers chanted 'Out! Out! Out!', and his exit was crowned with a burst from the *Internationale*.

The plenary meeting of the conciliation committee got nowhere, since the employers were unwilling to go beyond the concessions already made by the CGPF. So, on the 10th, when Gauthier made his report on the state of the negotiations before 700 delegates, there were angry mutterings in the hall. The factory delegates' dissatisfaction was symptomatic of the mounting tension amongst the strikers, who were impatient for action. They insisted that the struggle must go on until complete satisfaction was obtained, and adopted a resolution which contained an ultimatum to the bosses:

> The delegates . . . keeping in mind the special conditions of the Paris region, the abnormally low wage-rates paid in numerous factories, cannot accept implementation of the Matignon agreement without a prior and significant increase in wages. We believe that our efforts to resolve the conflict are not being matched by the employers; . . . [we] resolve to set a limit of 48 hours for agreement to be reached, that is until 12 June at 6 o'clock in the evening. If this deadline is not met we shall demand
>
> 1) nationalisation of armaments factories, and all those working on state contracts, normal operation of the plants to be maintained by the workers and technicians under overall control of the relevant ministries;
>
> 2) that all legal means be used to oblige the other firms to sign a collective agreement. Nevertheless, the delegates believe that it will not be helpful to resort to these means, and that the collective agreement will be signed within the time-limit stipulated.

As on the previous day the meeting had to be cut short, even though delegates from 28 factories had not been able to speak, to allow the union representatives to meet the employers at 5 o'clock.

Gauthier and his colleagues delivered the workers' ultimatum to the leaders of the Paris Region Engineering Federation . . . and the bosses gave in. They gave in on the main points concerning minimum wage rates, after an extremely long and stormy meeting in which Minister of Labour Lebas had to deploy all his talents for conciliation. The collective agreement was ready for signature; the only thing left to do was to secure ratification by both sets of delegating bodies.

A further meeting of strikers took place the next day, 11 June. Frachon took the chair, while Hénaff, Timbaut and Costes were also present. Gauthier reported the concessions made by the employers, but the factory delegates still found the guarantees unsatisfactory, and demanded that their representatives obtain further guarantees on four points: that the bosses concede completely on minimum wages; that the law relating to paid holidays be written into the agreement; that payment should be demanded for the days lost in strikes; and finally that the workers' delegation should expressly declare that the workers were in complete solidarity with the technicians and office-staff, who should obtain the same conditions, validated by a collective agreement.

The tone of the strikers' contributions grew more heated, and the report of the proceedings given by **le Peuple** explained their anger in these terms:

> It is quite evident that the contempt shown by the employers up to now has provoked the workers' deepest resentment. If today we see the workers taking their chance to press their demands, the fault must lie with the blind arrogance of the exploiters who for more than ten years have refused to take any account of the smallest claims for consideration presented by any group of workers, be they organised or not.[5]

When the delegates had finished, Frachon, Timbaut and Costes each made interventions designed to soothe their anger. They spoke to the audience, 'in a language full of common sense and reasonableness.'[6] But it was impossible to sign the collective agreement, and when the joint committee met again at 7 o'clock that evening, although the employers had obtained the complete approval of their organisations, and declared themselves ready to sign, the workers' delegation recounted the objections raised by their comrades, and the conclusion of the discussion had to be postponed until the next day, Friday the 12th.

So on two occasions the assembly of strikers' delegates had rejected the terms of an agreement put forward by their union. In so doing they were articulating the demands of the workers still bottled up in their plants, who were growing impatient of the bosses' resistance. On the evening of 11 June the rumour could be heard in some quarters that the engineers were talking of leaving the factories en masse to descend on Paris.

Paris — the construction industry

The order for a general strike in the building industry, to which we have referred already, took effect on 8 June. The stated aims of the strike were the abolition of payment by the job, piece-work, and piece-rate bargaining, observances of the usages and customs of the industry, and a wage-rise. The negotiations which got under way were pursued separately in each of the trades operating in the construction industry.

On the morning of the 8th the strike was total, but that hardly changed the situation from what it had been on the 6th, as the stoppage was already more or less general. Various sites were occupied; half-constructed buildings and the sites of roads under construction were decorated with placards and flags. Work on the Exhibition site was halted, with complete solidarity between foreign workers, North Africans and Frenchmen. In the streets the drivers of buses, taxis and lorries gave the clenched-fist salute to striking road-menders; while sometimes the latter occupied themselves by supplementing the thin ranks of the police and were to be seen directing traffic on the edges of their sites as the roads filied up again after the fuel depots returned to work.

The navvies employed at the Exhibition site very quickly won their demands, and after an imposing demonstration through the centre of Paris they assembled at Japy to approve the collective agreement, signed on the evening of the 8th.

There was greater difficulty concerning the other trades and the Paris Regional *Union des Syndicats* had to dampen the ardour of some of the strikers who tried to pull out public service workers.[7]

Numerous meetings attracting considerable numbers of workers were held throughout both the 8th and 9th. Cabinet-makers, brick-layers, locksmiths, carpenters, heating engineers, roofers, plumbers, cement-workers, floor-layers, painters, stone-masons, ceiling-insulators, they assembled in their hundreds or their thousands to list their particular demands or take stock of the progress of negotiations.

On the 9th, the ornamental stone-masons ratified a collective agreement. But not all the assemblies which took place on the 11th were ready to accept the deals drawn up as a result of discussions which had gone on throughout the previous day. Demolition workers, locksmiths and road-menders accepted new agreements and a return to work. On the other hand, the glaziers rejected the employers' offer on wages, regarding hourly rates of 5.65F to 6.40F as insufficient. On the same day, 8,000 cement workers marched from their sites to assemble at Japy. The delegations entered the concert-hall singing the *Internationale*, and heard speeches from Bourcier, Launay and Arrachart.

Since the union leaders were engaged in a meeting with the bosses, it was decided to wait for them; singers and musicians improvised a concert at the microphone while in another part of the hall delegates hung in effigy the symbolic caricature of a jobbing labourer. Then the union delegation arrived and straightaway announced the bosses' concessions: 1) abolition of the system of payment by the job, and of piece-work; 2) wage-rise of from 0.50F to 1F per hour; 3) washing-up time to be paid by the boss.

Arrachart immediately underlined 'the importance of the gains made',[8] but the workers raised the question of payment for the days lost through the strike. The announcement of the bosses' resistance on this point 'brought new life to the debate',[9] and it was decided to stay out.

The next day, the 12th, the painters' delegates rejected the bosses' terms with two votes in favour. All the other building trades likewise continued their strikes.

Paris — department stores on strike

On 8 June the strike was more or less total in the big department stores, along with *Uniprix*, the shops selling the latest clothing fashions and so on. It was the first time joint action had ever been taken by the workers in this industry where trade union organisation was particularly weak. During the 8th the hairdressers at the *Galeries Lafayette*, *le Printemps*, and *Bon Marché* joined the movement, and the locked-out white-collar workers of *la Samaritaine* turned up in their thousands for a meeting at the labour exchange. They declared their solidarity with the strike which so far had been pursued only by the manual grades, and decided not to return to work until they had obtained complete satisfaction. The same day the various branches of *la Semeuse* also ceased activity.

Salengro did his best to find a solution to the conflicts. On this, the day after the Matignon agreement, he arranged a meeting between representatives of the owners, and Botherau and Capocci, general-secretary of the *Fédération des Employés*. After a five-hour meeting, with no agreement in sight on wages, the two sides parted with no progress recorded, and on the 12th they were no further forward. In this industry unaccustomed to strikes, where the employees traditionally turned up their noses at the usual forms of working-class struggle, the owners were still hoping they could win through, and their resistance was all the more bitter. But the workers showed admirable solidarity and discipline. They swarmed to the meetings which the CGT organised on the spot or in various halls throughout Paris.

These strikes usually evoked particular sympathy from the public, who were stupefied to learn of the starvation wages in force when they read the posters displayed at the shop entrances.

We can note here in passing that the unions of the Catholic union federation CFTC did not take part in the negotiations, but Salengro met their representatives to inform them of the progress of talks.

Paris — the insurance companies

On 8 June strikes broke out almost simultaneously in the offices of the insurance companies *le Nord*, *l'Abeille*, *la Préservatrice*, *la Paix*, *la Prévoyance*, *le Patrimonie*, *La France*. Pickets were organised straightaway but not all the employees took part in the occupation of their workplaces. At *le Nord* only a hundred strikers stayed overnight on the 8th, although there was a payroll of 700. On the morning of the 9th several other firms ceased activity, and there were soon more than 50 companies under occupation.

The managers of these firms, used to the habitual docility of their employees, had never dreamed of a day when they would see their well-behaved staff camping on the pavement in front of their office doors, and at the very first meeting, which took place on the 9th at the Ministry of Labour, under the chairmanship of a civil servant whose departmental responsibility was insurance, they agreed to sign a deal based on the following points.

1. Application of articles 3 and 5 of the Matignon agreement.
2. Establishment of formal relations between unions and employers' organisations.
3. Security of employment for all employees aged 22 and over.
4. Setting up of disciplinary committees equally representative of employers and staff, which must give unanimous consent in every case of dismissal of an 'established' number of staff.
5. 10 per cent pay-rises for all those currently below 12,000F per year (men), or 10,000F per year (women); rises of between 4 per cent and 10 per cent for all those earning between 12,000F and 18,000F (10,000F and 15,000F for women); minimum annual wage rates to be fixed at 10,000F and 12,000F, plus the traditional annual bonus of one month's pay.
6. Talks aimed at the drawing up of a collective agreement would begin immediately after the return to work.

On the same evening the union offices for CGT and CFTC white-collar staff issued communiqués asking the workers to 'approve the agreement we have signed, to end the occupation of offices and return to work'.[10]

However, le Temps announced the next day: 'In insurance, the situation is unchanged. The agreement signed between employers and unions does not seem to have received the assent of all the non-union members',[11] and le Peuple published the following communiqué:

> The text of an agreement relating to insurance staffs which we published yesterday morning was simply a draft which was subject to ratification by the strikers. The latter have not accepted it as it does not go far enough. Negotiations have been suspended temporarily.[12]

On 11 June there were developments. Strike pickets at l'Abeille were assaulted by individuals who were suspected of belonging to the Croix de Feu. On the same day an agreement was signed at the Union Vie insurance company which brought about a return to work in the afternoon, but it was a paltry deal which did no more than record the bosses' promise to apply any collective agreement which might be accepted by the industry, and to examine particular local grievances 'within a reasonable lapse of time'. In all the other firms the strike continued.

Banking and the stock exchange avoid the strikes

The evening papers of the 7th had announced that bank employees would stop work the next day, and that it was likely that the Stock Exchange would be prevented from trading. This alarmist information was immediately refuted by the Ministry of Finance. What had in fact happened was that Mr Lehideux, president of the Union of Bank Workers, had asked for a meeting with the Minister of Finance, Vincent Auriol, and requested his intervention to assist in arriving at an amicable solution. There was a serious threat of a strike and the CGT bank and stock exchange committee issued an appeal for calm,

> inviting all the bank staffs to remain cool and calm and assuring them that their interests will be and are already being defended. A meeting has already taken place at the Ministry of Finance in pursuit of their claims and those of the savings societies' staff.[13]

On the 8th, Auriol chaired a meeting where both CGT and CFTC were represented. It was established that regular and official contacts would take place between the two sides, that all problems would be dealt with by a collective agreement for which negotiations would begin on the 10th, and that without waiting for this to be signed, minimum rates of pay were to be fixed at 12,000F for men and 10,000F for women for established staff over 22 years of age.

The CGT organised a meeting for bank-workers' delegates on the evening of the 9th, but the union's communiqué recommended that the choosing of delegates should take place 'in the calmest possible surroundings, and without disturbing the rhythm of work'. Negotiations proceeded rapidly, and after arbitration by Vincent Auriol, agreement was reached on wages on 12 June without any stoppage of work having occurred. On the 13th, 8,000 bank employees applauded the CGT at a huge meeting where Buisson, a member of the confederation's *bureau confédéral* took his chance to remind those present:

> The CGT has always been 100 per cent behind you. But you have not always been with the CGT. You usually showed limitless admiration for your bosses, who paid you with . . . polite words of encouragement.

Paris — strikes in the cafés, hotels and restaurants

On Sunday 7 June, the union of café, hotel and restaurant workers took stock of the progress of negotiations in their industry.

The bosses had already accepted the abolition of caution money and stoppages from pay for breakages or big cleaning operations. Conversations were still in progress. 'During the negotiations we ask all members to be patient and to avoid going into dispute with their own management.'

The hostelries on strike were quite numerous, in many different parts of Paris, and the movement began to spread by a process of osmosis. Talks went on throughout the 8th, and ended on the evening of the 9th with an agreement which encouraged **le Peuple** to announce the end of the strike. Under the aegis of Marx Dormoy a scale of minimum wage rates had been fixed; the daily rate for workers in cheap snack bars and *prix fixe* restaurants should not be less than 30F, and café waiters should earn at least 25F per day. It was also agreed that 'if an establishment should find itself in financial difficulties, its situation will be examined by the two sides.'

But this agreement was not followed by a return to work, and the union was quickly obliged to renege on its signature of the day before. 'Given the mounting agitation amongst our members,' the union 'asks everyone to disregard rumours concerning the negotiations in progress', and a little later, on the evening of the 10th, it issued a call for a general strike, allegedly provoked by the employers' 'bad faith'. Nevertheless, the union announced that it would bring out a poster authorising those establishments which had agreed to the demands to stay open.

On 11 June about 8,000 blue- and white-collar workers from the hotels and cafés formed a series of processions which wound through the main boulevards of Paris to arrive at an immense meeting. Towards evening there were incidents on the terraces of the cafés which were operating normally under the cover of the union poster. The strikers pulled out those still working, a step which occasionally provoked conflict with the management or police. A few of the demonstrators were arrested. On 12 June, the great majority of cafés, restaurants and hotels were closed. The big hotels such as *le Scribe* or the *Astoria* bid farewell to their last customers.

Paris — some other industries

It is impossible to draw up a full list of the different trades and professions on strike. We may note, anyway, according to the CGT paper of 10 June, that there were general strikes in each of the following: *patisserie*, confectionery, woodwork and furniture, making of military and public service uniforms, leather and water-proof clothing, shirtmaking, cap-making, apprentice hat-makers, footwear, leather goods, car-washing, the water authorities, cinema (production, distribution, and auditoria) and publishing.

The next day were listed 2,000 workers in dress-making, white-collar workers in the fashion salons and new clothes shops, several pharmacies, stable-lads at the race-tracks, and butchers. Agreement was reached in the food industry and in the *Wagon-lits* company, but 65 commercial travellers for Potin, 80 employed by Hoover, and 200 franchise-holders of the sewing-machine company Singer stopped work; the union of *concierges* presented a list of demands. On the 12th, workers in bakers' shops, the *Urbaine* cleaning company, and Paris boat-workers went on strike, the latter setting up a barrage of canal-boats which blocked all traffic on the river Seine. Railwaymen presented their lists of demands, and agitation was rife amongst Paris bus and tram workers.

The evening of the 11th and all day on the 12th brought a rash of sweet disturbances. In the 16th *arrondissement* of Paris some *Croix de Feu* members attempted to form an auxiliary police force to safeguard the 'freedom to work'. Strikers' processions criss-crossed the streets and boulevards. Paris was in the grip of feverish excitement.

General strike in the north of France

The situation in the departments of Nord and Pas-de-Calais quickly became as tense as in the Paris region. **Le Temps** of 9 June reported that 80 per cent or 90 per cent of firms were on strike there. The stoppage was total in textiles and mines — to which we shall turn in a moment. These two industries, along with engineering, where every workshop was under occupation, provided the great bulk of strikers in the north of France. But every other industry was affected in some way.

We have already noted that the engineers, as in Paris, were the first to down tools. On 2 June the 2,700 workers at Fives-Lille stopped work at 10 o'clock, and on the same day at the end of the afternoon, 2,000 railway workers from the Hellemmes workshops marched past the factory in a solidarity demonstration. Joining the movement on the following day were 1,100 engineers from Five-Lille's Lille Engine Company, *les Etablissements Kuhlmann*, the three Lesquin factories (2,500 workers). And from then on, with no sign of a halt, the movement began to exert a more and more powerful stranglehold on all economic activity.

The Lille newspapers failed to appear, and when the *Messageries Hachette* firm tried to recruit unemployed people to distribute news-papers coming from Paris, strikers seized and destroyed them at the station exit.

Boatmen at Bouchain formed more barrages with their canal-boats, which interrupted all traffic between the north and the Paris region; the docks at the Ile Jeanty were blocked shortly afterwards. Cafés, hotels and restaurants were closed. Then, on 8 June, as the strike in construction became general, the important port and dock industry joined the fray. At Dunkirk, where the port opened in the morning, the dockers occupied the wharves and an hour later, at the given signal of a blast from a hooter, 2,000 workers walked out of the ship-building yards. After them water-workers, tramways, sawmills, oil-plants, sewage workers each in turn ceased activity.

It is noteworthy that throughout the north the municipal public services were quite seriously affected. At Lille, where Salengro was mayor, now Minister for the Interior, a strike of tramworkers was narrowly averted, which was not the case at Dunkirk, nor at several other towns, where gasworks and power-stations were also closed down.

It seems to us not particularly interesting to list all the urban centres where the situation was similar to Lille and Dunkirk. It is more interesting to trace the stages in the development of the strikes in the region's two main industries, mining and textiles.

The miners' strike and the Douai agreement

We have already described the circumstances in which the regional Miners' Federation launched the general-strike instruction for Monday 8 June. This step did indeed have the intended pacifying effect. The Paris papers of 9 June, from **le Peuple** to **le Temps**, published the same agency despatch:

> The general impression is that the strike has become more uniform, and that the unions, who were in danger of being swamped, have taken the situation in hand.

On the 8th, an agreement in principle was signed in Paris under Ramadier's chairmanship, between the miners' union, the *Fédération du sous-sol*, and the mine-owners' *Comité des houillères*. This provided for the calling of regional meetings which would draw up regional agreements in the framework of the Matignon deal. The relevant meeting for the Nord and Pas-de-Calais coalfield took place on the 9th at Douai, where an agreement was signed immediately. This gave an increase of 1F on the minimum basic for an underground worker, taking it from 26F to 27F, and an increase of 12 per cent in the enhancement to basic rate.[14]

The principle of an immediate return to work was included in the deal, which was not, however, put into effect everywhere. On the town square at Lens on 10 June, after listening to a speech by the deputy and mayor, Maes, appealing to them to return to work, 15,000 miners decided to carry on the strike.[15] The eastern part of the coalfield stayed out solidly, while it went on unevenly in the centre. The union organised a plethora of report-back meetings to try to win a vote for a return to work, but the miners' passive resistance blocked all their efforts.

Negotiations in the textile industry

In textiles the strike began on 3 June at the Leblanc works. At 1.30 in the afternoon, 'a solid picket cut off the electric current thus stopping the three plants', and the Hellemmes factories were affected immediately afterwards. In a few days the strike was general, supported by 80,000 workers. The ardent union activist, Martha Desrumeaux, in seeming contradiction with the Communist Party's general orientation, was unsparing in her efforts to co-ordinate the strikes and organise solidarity. The engineers, especially from the Fives-Lille company, sent delegations to the mills to offer help based on their previous experience of strikes; railway workers organised teams prepared to help the women guarding the gates outside their occupied plants.[16]

The textile owners, among the best-organised and most vicious where conditions of work were concerned, refused all discussion up until the Matignon agreement. On 9 June Mr Ley, secretary of the employers' organisation, finally agreed to meet a workers' delegation, and informed them of the decisions taken by the respective national bodies. A return to work was a prior condition before discussion of a collective agreement could take place, which the employers nevertheless accepted in principle. Mr Ley was of the opinion that wages in the northern textile industry were higher than in other regions. Therefore, in order to avoid difficulties vis-à-vis their competitors, the northern industrialists demanded, firstly, that there should be an inquiry at regional and national levels into the wages paid in different branches of the textile industry, and secondly that the government should pass a law establishing a national minimum wage for each of the textile trades.

With these reservations, an increase of 10 per cent on all wages was granted. The workers' representatives declared themselves in agreement and undertook to deploy every effort to ensure that work would start again on the following Thursday.[17] Until this date the mills in fact remained under occupation, and the rare plants still working ceased activity.[18]

Attempts at pacification by unions and government

The trade union leaders, in their majority formerly of the CGT tendency, and the local political leaders, mostly Socialists, pooled their efforts to maintain order in the region, where the strikes seemed even more dangerous than in Paris since public sector workers were on strike along with their comrades in private industry. The Socialist municipalities sent delegations to the factories to exhort the workers to remain peaceful. In the absence of newspapers, the Lille unions availed themselves of the assistance of local taxi drivers to distribute the text of the Matignon agreement in a leaflet.[19]

On the 10th Salengro returned to Lille to hurry along the negotiations and make a radio broadcast to the strikers in which he warned them against 'elements which have nothing to do with the trade union movement', who were inciting them to prolong the strikes even though an agreement had been signed. He announced impending vigorous measures against anyone speculating on price-rises, and, in the name of the government, thanked the working class for their calmness, which showed evidence of 'great political and industrial maturity'.[20]

On the 11th, at Lille, the secretary of the *Union Départementale des Syndicats*, Dumoulin, called a meeting of delegates from all the strike-bound factories in the region. He told them:

> You should honour your signature. If not, you will be the ones to suffer. We have to look at the situation as a whole, with all the possible consequences, and it is not over yet. This great movement of ours has been fighting the capitalists for a long time. What we are seeing today is an episode in that struggle, which will be fought in an orderly, calm and disciplined manner.

Le Temps reported that the government had deployed several squadrons of riot police to the periphery of the working-class districts.

The Lyons Region and the Bollaert agreement

On 10 June, the union officials of the *Union Départementale des Syndicats du Rhône* and the representatives of the Lyons employers signed a regional Matignon-type agreement in the office of Bollaert, prefect of the department. The Paris agreement had already become a dead letter: building, chemicals, clothing manufacture, dyeing, tanneries were all on all-out strike. Only engineering, in patches, had returned to work; the Berliet plants at Vénissieux carried on alone — for these engineering workers it was the second strike in the space of a few months, for they had already fought a hard three-week long battle in April. The Bollaert agreement added nothing to that of 7 June. It was simply a confirmation of it, and recorded the two sides' commitment to respect every point of the national convention between the CGT and the CGPF. The next day the strike spread to Villeurbanne.

Marseilles and the south-east

On 8 June, after Matignon, there were no more than 17 enterprises to be found on strike in Marseilles. These included the *Forges et
Chantiers de la Méditerranée* engineering group, the sugar refineries,
the *Compagnie Générale* oil undertaking, Kuhlmann's chemical works,
dockers of the Fraissinet company who were occupying the ships due
to sail for Corsica, and labourers from the municipal parks.

On the 9th the Kuhlmann workers won a 5F-a-day increase over
and above the provisions in Matignon, and went back to work. But the
number still out reached 13,000 as the construction industry and
Messageries Hachette had stopped work. The wives of strikers at the
Forges et Chantiers de la Méditerranée marched in a demonstration to
the prefecture to demand intervention by the civil administration.
Near Cannes, the *Aciéries du Nord* at la Bocca were occupied.

From 10 June onwards occupation-strikes spread rapidly to
construction, chemical works and shipyards. Taxi-drivers ceased ply-
ing for hire, and the local newspapers failed to appear. The big stores
gave their staff a paid holiday and closed their doors. The correspondent of **le Temps** sent the following cable:

> The movement seems to have escaped the CGT's control. Although a
> general agreement has been reached between the managers of several
> firms and the workers' representatives [the strike is spreading] . . . Yet
> the *Union Départementale des Syndicats* has promised to ask the workers
> to end their occupations immediately and to go back to work.

Two million on strike

Bordeaux was one of the rare French towns where the strike was
unknown before 8 June. But **le Peuple** of 9 June noted, 'The workers
of the Gironde are waking up to the struggle', and the last oasis of calm
disappeared. The whole of working-class France had entered the fray.
On 11 June the figure reached two million on strike.

The *département* of Seine-Inferieure was typical of many in
provincial France. Here, the coalyards, engineering and textile
plants, dockers, paper-mills, the river authority, textile plants in the
Barentin valley, dustmen and tram-workers were all out. Also included were, in the centre, the big battalions of Peugeot, Dunlop,
Bergougnan, Michelin; at Toulouse construction and the trams; at
Saint-Nazaire construction and the shipyards; at Nancy the footwear
factories, engineering and chemicals; the miners of the Loire coalfield; at Mulhouse the Alsatian mechanical engineering company, the
Charles Mieg textile mill, the Dolfuss Mieg plant, and, again, the
trams. In the *département* of Aisne, river-traffic was halted; at Belfort
electricity and gasworks were crippled. At Orléans, engineers won a
rapid victory and returned to work. In the countryside, thousands of

agricultural workers were on strike and occupying the farms, for example in Seine-et-Oise and Seine-et-Marne, where the strikers numbered 10,000. The farmworkers' strikes spread to north Africa, where serious disturbances were not slow to follow.

The government's response

The parliamentary debates provided an opportunity for moderates and right-wing deputies to give vent to their anxieties about a situation which was running more and more out of control. 'Paris gives everyone the impression of a rudderless ship', declared Paul Reynaud.

These worries echoed the hundreds of messages sent to Léon Blum by the representatives of the propertied class. The 'Federation of small shareholders' expressed the fears of the 'savers' democracy'. The assembly of presidents of Chambers of Commerce vouchsafed their regret that 'no measures have been taken to assure the protection of civil liberties', and recalled that 'business confidence is dependent on public order'. The national veterans' organisation, referring to their 'well-known concern for the social good', described the situation as revolutionary. On 12 June, le Temps editorialised, 'It is quite obvious that there is a a problem of authority, that it looks less and less likely to be resolved, and that there is a serious risk that it will shortly become insoluble', and the newspapers asked the question 'What do the Radicals think of these events?'

What the Radicals did indeed think of the state of affairs can be judged from the laconic nature of their utterances. On 10 June the bureau of their executive committee held a long session ending with a short communiqué: 'The bureau has proceeded to an exchange of views on the political and social situation.' The meeting of Radical deputies on 12 June listened to some 'very anxious' contributions, particularly from Campinchi, and a vigorous intervention by Daladier was required to secure a motion of confidence in the government. In the Senate, the powerful 'democratic left' group was in a state of agitation, and the senators anxiously questioned Léon Blum in the corridors when he appeared amongst them.

Government activity was frenetic. Night and day ministers and their deputies performed arbitrations or chaired committees charged with working out the details of various agreements, while Léon Blum pushed the new social legislation through the two houses of parliament, at break-neck speed.

Speedy passage of the 'social laws'

Immediately after the signature of the Matignon agreement, in a letter dated midnight, 7 June, Léon Blum wrote to Léon Jouhaux in terms which amply demonstrated the government's anxiety to see the basic elements of its social programme passed rapidly into law.

> My dear friend, here is written confirmation of my intentions as described to you. The bills relating to the 40-hour week, paid holidays and collective agreements will be put before the house the day after tomorrow — Tuesday.
>
> Since the parliamentary committees are not yet constituted, and will not be before the 16th, I will ask, in the name of the government, for the election of a special committee, and this can be arranged in the course of Wednesday.
>
> I will ask it to meet and get down to work as a matter of urgency.
>
> I should think that the bills can be passed on Thursday or Friday. They will be sent immediately to the Senate where the government will bring all pressure to bear to insist that they are debated and voted on without delay. I hope the bills will pass the Senate before the end of the week. In any event I am absolutely counting on the final vote by the two houses towards the middle of next week.
>
> fraternal greetings — Léon Blum.

On 9 June the bills were introduced into the lower house and Léon Blum appealed to its members to avoid any actions which might cause delay, for 'we are in a situation where every minute counts.' The special committee of the house, chaired by the Socialist Serol, ratified the texts during the night of 10–11 June, and on the 11th the deputies voted in quick succession the laws on paid holidays, the rescinding of the decrees which had imposed public employees' wage-cuts, and the law on collective agreements. On the 12th it was the turn of the law establishing the 40-hour week, which was immediately sent to the Senate while Léon Blum brought forward a second series of measures dealing with an amnesty for political offenders and the raising of the school-leaving age.

The CGT

We have already looked at the activities of the main CGT federations during these difficult days. Reinforced by the realisation that they now had more than two million members, the Confederation leaders redoubled their appeals for calm and discipline. A typical example was a communiqué from the Paris regional *Union des Syndicats* (USRP):

> Given the impossibility of getting in touch individually with all the members in the Paris region involved in the current strikes, the USRP reiterates that in all factories where agreement has been reached between management and workers on the basis of the Matignon accord, there should be a return to work when ratified by the unions concerned. Of course all these local agreements should include the following proviso:

'The . . . company and their staff accept the terms of the Matignon accord, and undertake to apply . . . all the clauses of any collective agreement which may be elaborated in pursuance of its provisions.' The USRP appeals to the sense of discipline of all members to see that its instructions are carried out without hindrance, and reminds members that they should accept orders only from duly mandated union delegates.

Similar considerations were at work in a communiqué of 11 June, which

stresses that only those issued with an official mandate are empowered to speak in the name of the CGT. All affiliated unions must provide their delegates with a mandate . . . In all workplaces where disputes have been settled with some sort of agreement, work must continue normally if the employers are observing the agreed terms, notwithstanding interference by elements without mandate or responsibility; [the CGT] is confident of speaking for the wishes of all workers in asking that everything should be done to preserve the ordered and disciplined framework of the movement.

Security measures taken by the government

The same theme of interference by elements hostile to the trade union movement was the government's primary pretext for various dispositions involving the forces of 'law and order'.

At the government's request, the national committee of the Popular Front decided on 10 June to cancel the huge victory demonstration which had been planned for 14 June in Paris, and voted for a resolution declaring that it would concentrate all its efforts on 'the organisation, on 14 July, of a monster demonstration to celebrate the electoral and the industrial victories at the same time.'

The government meanwhile judged that the situation required certain precautions. As Léon Blum explained to the Chamber:

It is true that since yesterday [11 June] things have begun to look a little different. We have the impression that dubious groups are at work, which have nothing to do with trade unionism. The government can and indeed must affirm that we are perfectly resolute in our intention to preserve order in the streets.

Le Temps announced with relief that public order 'seems at the moment to engage the administration's attention, and particularly that of its head,'[21] and in fact a communiqué announced on 12 June:

In view of the intrusion into the conflicts between employers and workers of elements which have nothing to do with the movement, a meeting took place yesterday evening at the *Hôtel Matignon*. All appropriate measures have been taken to prevent disturbances on the public highway.

Troops and squads of riot police had been directed towards the Paris region, and were already in place in northern France and in the regions affected by the farmworkers' strikes. The Communist Party protested against these police dispositions. After its meeting on 9 June the Communist parliamentary group published a communiqué supporting 'our representatives in the *Délégation des Gauches* [the left parties' parliamentary caucus] who proposed that a delegation be sent to the Ministry of the Interior to demand an explanation of the rumour that troops and riot police were being concentrated in the capital.'

Finally, on the evening of 12 June, the government seized at the printworks all copies of the Trotskyist newspaper, **La Lutte Ouvrière**, and announced legal proceedings against the leaders of this leftist organisation.

Could Thorez succeed where Jouhaux and Blum had failed?

During the decisive days following Matignon, the Communist Party's political line did not change from the one we have described already: unconditional support for the strikes, limitation of the various movements to the framework of the Popular Front demands, neutralisation of any revolutionary element in the movement. The minutes of the politbureau meeting of 10 June showed the ambiguity of this position:

> The politbureau expresses its solidarity with the strikers; recognises with pleasure that through their legitimate action the workers are putting into practice the Communist Party's slogan of reconciliation between the French people. We send warm greetings to all Catholic and *Croix de Feu* workers who are fighting in their factories, workplaces and offices alongside socialists and communists, under the red, white and blue of our forefathers, and the red flag of the future, reconciled by the Communist Party . . . It is not true that the employers have made great sacrifices . . . the party will fight the exploiters of the people, who are trying to organise a crusade for high prices . . . The politbureau does not believe that the riot police and the army are hostile to the workers in struggle.

The continuation of the strikes when the employers had given in to the workers' main demands posed new problems. Here was a possible source of conflict with the government. The party had to choose — either support the new demands emanating from the workers, develop a new programme to direct the workers' energies towards further gains, maybe even raise the question of state power, or, on the other hand, stick to the existing parliamentary pact with the Radical and Socialist leaders and ask the strikers to return to work, limiting their gains to what had been granted by the Matignon deal.

The party's general secretary, Maurice Thorez, explains in his autobiography **Fils du Peuple** the position which he adopted at that time:

> The strike movement reached its highest point during the week 7–14 June. Alarmist stories spread discontent in the countryside. Despite the Matignon accord there were several employers who refused to sign agreements with their workers. There were several incidents involving the police; suspicious elements, both Trotskyist and *Croix de Feu*, infiltrated the movement in the hope of causing it to degenerate into an adventure harmful to the workers' interests. Our party had supported the strikes. . . . This active solidarity imposed new responsibilities on us . . .
>
> There was a risk that the Popular Front might break up. Was the working class about to cut itself off from the mass of the people in struggle? We were haunted by the memory of the tragic events of June 1848 and May 1871. At all costs we had to prevent the re-emergence of such a situation. We remembered Lenin's teaching — Patiently explain. He had written to the French workers in 1920: 'A regular source of a lot of trouble in France has been anarchist phrase-mongering.' On 11 June, in the feverish atmosphere of the capital, we organised a mutual information meeting for party members.[22]

The 11 June report

As Thorez recorded in **Fils du Peuple**, l'**Humanité** of 11 June called all party members in the Paris region to a meeting at the Jean Jaurès gymnasium. The Communist Party general secretary's long report began by recalling the Popular Front programme, some of whose demands could be achieved only by direct action by the working class. The struggle for these demands was the source of the admirable strike movement whose unprecedented form — occupation — demonstrated the Parisians' flair for originality, and whose calm and dignity foretold the birth of a new order. The strike movement was characterised by the entry of new layers of the working classes into struggle, and by the effective reconciliation of all French people around the red flag and the tricolour. The Matignon deal was an important gain; nevertheless it left something to be desired as far as wages were concerned, and it was important to get acceptance of the principle of the minimum wage.

The Communist Party members had been able to play a role in the forefront of the strikes, but they did not aspire to be the leadership, because it was the role of the unions and the strikers themselves to lead, and no agreement should be signed without referring to them. Successful leadership of an industrial struggle was impossible without workers' democracy. And if it was important to know how to lead a strike, 'it's important also to know how to end one.'

'There is no question of taking power at the present time.' The party's aim was still soviet power, but that was not something to be achieved this evening, or even tomorrow, for the conditions were not ripe, in particular:

we have not yet got the rural population behind us, with us, determined like us to go the whole way. In certain cases it is even possible that we run the risk of alienating ourselves from sections of the petty-bourgeoisie and the peasantry. So what next? . . . *So, we must know how to end a strike when satisfaction has been obtained. We must even know how to accept a compromise when all demands have not yet been met but victory on the essential points has been achieved.*

Everything is not possible for the moment, said Thorez.[23] We must not risk breaking up the cohesion of the masses and of the Popular Front. We must not allow the working class to be isolated. Party members must argue against the ultra-leftist tendencies in the movement:

The battle on two fronts is not only an internal battle. It is often — and rightly so — a struggle involving the whole politics of the party when we are dealing with an ultra-left argument. I'll give an example. If all the main demands of the comrades in engineering are met, if the lowest wages have been adequately raised . . . if the highest-paid grades have had increases of the agreed amount, if paid holidays are included in the agreement, we can, indeed must, sign an agreement which brings the current dispute to an end.

Another ultra-left tendency — building workers directly employed by a Communist municipality — went on strike, said Thorez. But the comrades had realised their mistake and returned to work that morning.

It was also necessary to look at the effects of certain strikes. Thorez quoted the lorry-drivers' strike at *les Halles* which, had it continued, might have alienated the petty-bourgeoisie and small peasants who would have had to face the prospect of their produce rotting by the roadside.

There was to be no question of saying that 'now wage-related questions slip into the background, and our task now is to take possession of the factories and institute direct workers' control of production.'

We must on no account compromise the government's work, Thorez continued, which was why he was worried by the government's recourse to police action, and by the pronouncements of Salengro, who was against the *Délégation des Gauches* support for the strikes.

Thorez concluded his report with a summary of the astounding growth of the party in the previous few days (membership had now reached 146,000), and with a call for the education and training of the new recruits 'in the image of Martha Desrumeaux.'

The application of the line enunciated by Thorez

L'Humanité's front page on 12 June carried the essential passage of the report[24] (which we have placed in italics). The party's central committee, meeting on the 13th, formally approved[25] the political line enunciated by Thorez, who again took up the same theme in a speech at Lille on 14 June.

'We must know how to end a strike' became the *leitmotif* for all speeches by Communist leaders from 12 June onwards. This was the secretary-general's effective response to the political problem facing his party, and at the same time to the challenge thrown at him in the Chamber on 6 June by the rightist deputy René Dommange:

> Since the Communist Party's reason for not wishing to join the government was the fear of provoking panic among the middle classes, it is certain that, if Léon Blum wishes, the Communist Party will help him in every way to ensure that the strikes do not spread and that the factories and workshops are freed from occupation.

The press was unanimous in greeting the Communists' new orientation with rapturous relief, while Thorez' declaration was described by one journalist as 'simple, obvious, calm and reasonable truth'.[26] 'This political wisdom,' Thorez concluded in **Fils du Peuple**, 'soon brought its fruits. Collective agreements were signed by the hundred, while the victorious workers marched out of the factories with music playing and flags flying.'[27] After 13 June, '*détente*' was more or less the order of the day.

7
THE WAVE RECEDES

ON 11 JUNE the entire French economy was paralysed by the strikes. The factories were under workers' control. The unions, overwhelmed by the mass movement and the scope of the problems it posed, were unable to fulfil all the tasks which fell to their lot. Could the working class continue its offensive and, through its own independent action, call state power into question?

The end of the conflict in the Paris engineering industry was the turning point. The movement was still spreading in the provinces, but the main tendency from the 12th and 13th onwards was downwards. Solutions were found to the key points in dispute; the strikes became patchy and localised. As the fire died down, occasional bursts of flame would spring up again, signifying the state of tension which still reigned, but the numbers on strike were dropping and by 14 July the traditional Bastille Day demonstrations took place in towns which had resumed their tranquil, ordered and workmanlike atmosphere.

The end of the struggle in engineering

On 11 June the engineering workers' delegates had once again rejected the proposed peace terms and demanded new guarantees. On the 12th, the day after Thorez's speech, a new delegate assembly took place which 'almost unanimously' accepted the terms on offer, and mandated the union representatives to sign the collective agreement. This was ratified at 10 o'clock the same evening.

The strikers' delegates had accepted a compromise, and their representatives had realised they would not be able to demand payment for days lost during the strike. This important point having been accepted, the Minister of Labour, Lebas, recommended an ex gratia payment as follows: no payment for two of the days lost; payment to

be made for a maximum of six of any remaining days at the rate of 10F
per day to single people, 15F per day to married workers, and 20F per
day to those married and with children. The return to work would be
on Monday 15 June. 'Victory for the engineers!' blazoned **le Peuple**,

> After three weeks of struggle the workers are to go back. No more low
> pay for women (2.40F an hour at Panhard): the minimum is now 4.90F.
> No more low pay for tradesmen (370.45F for 100 hours at Lancia); the
> minimum will be 7F an hour. No more low pay for labourers (3.50F on
> average): the minimum will be 5F. No more child exploitation (100F a
> week): they will earn between 3F and 5F an hour![1]

The employers admitted that they had given in to pressure from
the workers, and Mr Villey of the engineering industries group
declared:

> As we have already made known, we do not have any illusions about the
> seriousness of the modifications to the wage rates for certain grades.
> The problem was raised during the group's general assembly yesterday
> evening, and it was accepted by the members that our main considera-
> tion had to be to re-establish order and end the thoroughly abnormal
> situation. This consideration in fact outweighed any question of analysis
> of the economic situation.[2]

The breaking-up of the occupations began on the evening of the
13th. Processions formed up and traversed the streets of the various
districts of Paris, finally dispersing without incident. Towards the
end of the afternoon an immense procession assembled at Renault
while the entire local population filled the streets and squares. At the
head marched the Socialist Party senator and mayor, Morizet, with
the local councillors and aldermen, and the Communist deputy,
Costes. They were followed by a lorry-load of musicians alternately
playing the *Marseillaise* and the *Internationale*; the musicians wore the
traditional patriot's bonnet of 1792. Behind the band came a float
constructed by the pattern-makers. It carried busts of Léon Blum,
Alfred Costes and Marcel Cachin, together with a placard bearing a
portrait of Edouard Herriot.[3] Then came the workers, grouped
according to their workshops, some of them preceded by flower-laden
floats.

For two hours more than 20,000 workers circled the Boulogne
district amid indescribable exultation. In front of the town hall the
whole procession marched past the councillors, who were clutching
enormous wreaths in their arms, while the most original banners were
presented to the authorities, including one which featured the statue
of liberty brandishing a 4lb loaf. Dispersal took place before the
factory gates, and the stewards made it their business to ensure that
the demonstration did not carry on into Paris itself. Soon there were

only a few engineering plants still under occupation, and on Monday 15th all but a few thousand workers were back at their workbenches.

Settlements in the main industries

On 12 June, fourteen collective agreements were signed, covering engineering, abattoirs, cement workers, bricklayers and plasterers, stonemasons, crane-drivers, heating engineers, cabinet makers, fuel merchants, printing, hairdressing and corsetry. On the 13th, seven more followed — footwear, telephones, electrical engineering, granite-cutters, carpenters, roofers and contracting electricians. As can be seen, the majority of these agreements concern the building trades, which all returned to work except for the painters.

But not all problems had been solved. The cement workers had accepted an agreement along with all the other unions, even though discussions of payment for the duration of the strike had not been concluded. **Le Peuple** announced on 13 June that all the union meetings for the building trades were cancelled, and a general meeting was laid on instead on the grass of the *Bois de Vincennes*, 'to demonstrate satisfaction with our victory. Members should cause as little disturbance as possible in arriving at the meeting. There are to be no street processions.' In the event, several tens of thousands of workers assembled to applaud the speakers from the building federation.

In the printing industry, the settlement between the Book-workers Union, and the Master-Printers' Federation brought a slight adjustment to the existing national agreement. The deal allowed for new clauses to be added to the contracts between individual firms and their workers, granting a wage-increase based on the cost of living, the costs of production, and the state of the market in each locality.

The agreed aim was a substantial improvement in the standard of living throughout the country compared to what it had been before the 1914–18 war; wages would not therefore be adjusted only according to the current rate of inflation, but were to include a sizeable once and for all increase over and above that adjustment.[4] In each area where there had been no new agreement since 25 May, wages should rise by a percentage to be fixed locally, but not lower than 5 per cent or higher than 15 per cent according to the movement of wages in the district involved. This maximum of 15 per cent could be exceeded if a skilled worker's wage was less than 30F per day. Finally, for the determination of the increases at local level, a system of arbitration involving one delegate from each of the two sides was agreed.

This national agreement came into force immediately in Paris. In certain provincial centres the workers occasionally resorted to strike action again during the course of the arbitration procedure.

15 June was also the day on which work restarted in the insurance firms. That morning a mass meeting decided to return to work the same day, accepting that the outstanding clauses dealing with wages should go to the Ministry of Labour for arbitration. This arbitration was delivered the same evening, and, although the workers had not asked for payment for the duration of the strike, the owners' representatives declared that if work was begun straight away, the strike days would be regarded as paid holidays, and, providing the workers were of good behaviour, this holiday would not be deducted from the normal annual leave.

Meanwhile the glaziers had once again rejected their employers' offer. In this industry the workers had broken an agreement in force for 15 years, which included a sliding-scale clause. The employers offered increases from 5.05F and 5.70F to 5.80F and 6.60F, in line with the Matignon agreement, along with the maintenance of the sliding-scale. The workers demanded 7.50F an hour, and a compromise eventually brought agreement on 17 June.

The strike in the factories making electric lamps was ended by an additional clause in the engineering industry's agreement. This was followed by the signature of a collective agreement for dressmaking and tailoring, while provisional agreements in dyeing and bleaching, chemicals and signwriting brought about returns to work in those industries, and home-workers in the Paris rag-trade chose just this moment to declare a strike. For the first time this particularly exploited group of women workers won a guaranteed minimum wage in an agreement signed on 22 June.

In cafés, hotels and restaurants, a new, and this time decisive, agreement was finalised during the night of 12–13 June. The compromise signed under Dormoy's chairmanship confirmed the agreements of 6, 8 and 9 June, and minimum wages were fixed at 30F, 35F and 40F a day, while a monthly minimum of 700F was agreed for hotels. Marx Dormoy announced government plans for the abolition of tipping and to regulate casual employment. The union committee lost no time in calling for an immediate return to work, 'which must be accomplished without disturbance. The victory which we have just won constitutes a great step towards the complete regulation of all sections of our trade.'

The return to work did not go altogether smoothly, for the bulk of the small workplaces were prey to a multitude of individual quarrels and conflicts. On the 19th, the union and the employers' organisation made a joint appeal for conciliation, asking, on the one hand, for disciplined behaviour at work, and on the other that no penalty be imposed for having gone on strike.

Similar difficulties arose in the barbers' shops. Numbers of small-scale bosses refused to apply the industry's agreement, or threatened to sack their workers. The result was a certain amount of social tension, giving rise to the fear that the strike might break out again at any moment.

Another small incident — a strike by the lower ranks of workers at the American hospital at Neuilly — provoked a protest from the American Embassy. Arbitration by the Paris prefect of police resolved the conflict less than 24 hours after it had begun.

On 16 June the Ministry of the Interior announced that the number of strikers in the department of Seine had fallen to 62,000 and on the 26th Salengro was able to tell the Chamber that still unresolved conflicts involved less than 10,000 workers. Between the two dates, the dispute in the department stores had come to an end.

The strike in the department stores

This struggle, involving more than 32,000 workers, had begun on 5 June and lasted until the 20th. We have already mentioned the reasons for the employers' particularly strong resistance in this industry, where trade union activity was previously unheard-of. *Bon Marché* had, for example, no more than ten union members amongst its staff when the management decided to close the store to prevent its occupation. Daily meetings in Salengro's office had no effect. There were two contentious issues: wages, and the workers' demand for joint disciplinary committees which they hoped would end the bosses' customary arbitrary behaviour.

A joint strike committee of all the shops involved met daily in the basement at *le Printemps* and soon received the unconditional backing of the CGT's *bureau confédéral*. The CGT leaders attached great importance to outright success in this industry. On the one hand they wanted to make sure that trade unionism took root among the shopworkers, and on the other hand they wanted a well-publicised victory for the last mass struggle in the Paris region. They drew heart from the fact that in this industry there was very little chance of unruliness or of the strike escaping from union control. Jouhaux and the other *bureau* members personally visited the stores in order to exhort the workers to continue their resistance. Order and discipline were admirable, not a single case of vandalism or theft being reported. The workers cleaned and maintained the premises as normal, so that their dances and theatrical productions took place in impeccably neat surroundings.

The workers' papers accused the stores' owners of intransigence. The latter replied by claiming that they had agreed to pay the same wages as the banks.[5] A communiqué from their representative body declared:

> The department stores are anxious to inform the public of the true situation. We have offered minimum rates which mean that no man over 21 would earn less than 1,000F, and women not less than 800F per month. The minima for sales and office staff, at 1,100 F and 900F, are comparable to what Mr Auriol [the Finance Minister] awarded in a recent arbitration. Where in all this is 'the employers' intransigence'?[6]

When negotiations got under way firm by firm, the owners of *le Louvre* were the first to concede defeat and agree to minimum rates between 1,000F and 1,200F for sales staff, as well as the setting up of a joint disciplinary board. During the night of Saturday 20th and Sunday 21st an agreement involving the bulk of the firms was reached with the help of an element of arbitration by Salengro. The main points were:

1. Immediate introduction of a collective agreement for the industry.
2. Free exercise of union rights in the workplace.
3. Election of workers' delegates.
4. No sacking for going on strike.
5. Payment for the days lost in strike.[7]
6. Application of the legal right to paid holidays, with staff working in the basements to get one week extra.
7. Monthly payment for workers in the clothing departments, and rapid establishment of a minimum wage scale for workers under 17 years of age.

The Minister of the Interior's arbitration set up a joint disciplinary board which had the right to be consulted if management wanted to dismiss any worker. He also fixed the minimum wage-rates, with proportionate increases on a scale from 25 per cent to 5 per cent.[8]

It was agreed that the occupations should be ended immediately, and the return to work would be on Monday 22 June. In the event, the workers abandoned their strongholds during the day of the 21st, not without inflicting further indignities on their employers. Thus the top management of *Bon Marché* arrived at their premises that Sunday morning to be met by pickets who accompanied them to their offices, where the strike committee was in session. The bosses' demand for an immediate evacuation was refused on the grounds that the workers needed the rest of the day for cleaning and tidying up. A second refusal met the demand for a return to work on the Monday morning. The delegates decided on one o'clock in the afternoon. By now the *Bon Marché* union branch numbered more than 1,800.

The strike at *La Samaritaine* comtinued for a few more days until the owners surrendered.

In all industries in Paris where provisional agreements had been made, negotiations for an industry-wide collective agreement were continued. The working class remained on the alert, but peace returned to the streets and workplaces. The employers and the government now turned their anxious attention to the provinces.

The movement on the wane in the north

The strikes began to die down in northern France from about 13 June onwards. Engineering and textiles returned to work. Pressure from the union full-time officials finally overcame the miners' resistance when the last two pits on strike, at Anzin, began production again.

The one remaining important strike centre was Dunkirk, where the director of the electric power station was imprisoned in his home by the workers, while engineering, textiles, docks and the construction industry were all still under occupation. Electric power was restored thanks to an agreement of 14 June. Engineers went back to work, but the dockers refused arbitration by the Minister of Labour, declaring that they would decide themselves on any offer made to them. This dispute was resolved only at the end of June.

The numbers on strike in the two departments of Nord and Pas-de-Calais decreased steadily, from 60,000 on 16 June to 40,000 on the 18th and 30,000 on the 25th. But new struggles broke out, for example in Lille in printing, the National Assistance Board and the *Galeries Lafayette* department store.

The dispute affecting river-transport, which was particularly important in the north, deserves special attention. It involved more than just the classic confrontation between employer and wage-worker within the river navigation companies and the ship-owning firms. In addition there was the rivalry between the small-scale employers among the boatmen, and the big firms whose fierce competition threatened their very existence. It was the former who organised the barrages across the main canal and river routes, stopping all traffic for several weeks.

On the 16th the big companies and the small employers' representatives reached agreement on the basis of a prohibition of all traffic during certain times of the night, and the institution of a roster for all contract haulage. Negotiations succeeded in removing the barrages, and normal activity was resumed when the workers' demands were met.

The situation in the north was therefore reverting more and more towards normal, despite the persistence of one or two isolated conflicts. One of these which deserves particular attention was the

strike at the firm of Delespaul-Havez, a chocolate and biscuit manu-
facturer employing 650 workers at Marcq-en-Bareuil. On 4 July, after
nearly a month on strike during which the owners refused all negotiations, the workers decided to run the factory themselves. Reinforc-
ing their security arrangements, they prepared the workshops for
production, and ran the machines throughout the morning of 4 July.
At one o'clock production halted when the electric current was cut
off. The authorities became agitated. Salengro was despatched to
Lille, where, faced with the workers' determined resistance, he
maintained the existing sanctions — no electricity, and a conspiracy of
silence on this experiment in workers' control. The following day
workers adopted the following resolution:

> After the press comments about our action on Saturday, undertaken
> against intransigent employers who are pushing their barbarous beha-
> viour to the point of starving hundreds of workers' children . . . Faced
> with this inhuman behaviour we appeal to the whole working class to
> support us in this great battle to run the factory ourselves. To foil the
> bosses' plans we have decided, given the enormous quantity of goods
> which are liable to be spoiled, to make a free distribution to the town's
> poor after a lapse of 48 hours, for otherwise, and we declare this for all to
> hear, these goods would only be given to pig-farmers.

This resolution was put into effect as soon as the 48 hours had
elapsed, and the workers in fact carried on working, making bread for
their own consumption as best they could with the means available to
them.

The Lyons and St Étienne regions

On 17 June the numbers on strike in the Lyons region rose from
7,000 to 20,000 with the entry into struggle of building sites, the
Gerland fuel depots, pharmaceuticals workers, and fruit and vegetable
traders. On the 18th, however, there was evidence of a certain slowing-
down of the movement, a tendency soon reversed on the evening of
the 21st when a strike broke out on the trams, soon followed by a
complete standstill in construction, dyeing, and artificial fibres. The
situation was a source of grave concern to the employers, expressed in
a letter to Léon Blum by the president of the Lyons Chamber of
Commerce, who stressed that the Matignon agreement no longer
commanded respect, 'for the strikes are continuing to spread, often
without warning.'

Edouard Herriot, who besides being president of the Radical
Party, was mayor of Lyons, had great difficulty in averting the threat
of a strike by council workers; cafés and restaurants shut their doors;
while textile workers abruptly ceased activity. On 23 June strikers'

demonstrations led to street disturbances, and before the day was out the council manual workers had struck 'in breach of their engagements'.[9] We should mention also the strike by bakery workers which began on 12 July.

The longest-running dispute, and the most difficult to resolve, was that in the construction industry, which lasted until 29 July. A collective agreement had been in force since 1935 in the Lyons building trades, and there was a wage increase provided for on 13 May 1936, which among other things took the bricklayers' rate to 6.25F an hour.

On 16 June Mr Rousseau, president of the Chamber of Building Trades Employers, informed the *Union départementale des syndicats du Rhône* that the Matignon agreement did not apply to the Lyons construction industry. This exclusion was at first verbally accepted, but when various sectional strikes broke out a list of demands was put forward including a claim for an increase of 0.75F an hour. There was a meeting between the two sides, in the course of which Mr Rousseau observed that the workers were reneging on their signatures by breaking the collective agreement of 13 May. His final offer was an hourly increase of 0.50F. The CGT delegates explained the bosses' offer to a mass meeting, which threw it out and voted for a general strike.

After the failure of an attempt at conciliation by the prefect, the two sides went to Paris, where they were met by Léon Blum. The prime minister supported the workers' interpretation of the Matignon agreement, holding that it applied to industries which had already won a collective agreement before it was signed. Mr Rousseau was then invited to confer with union leaders Jouhaux, Arrachard and Nocaudie, secretary of the Lyons building trade unions. He promised a reply by 24 July.

But the Lyons workers would not accept this delay, and instead organised a demonstration outside the offices of the building employers' federation. Workers' delegates sought out the employers' leaders, demanded an immediate reply to their claim, and threatened that if they did not get one they would not let them out of the building. Rousseau announced that he would accept arbitration by the prefect. Three bosses were left behind as hostages, and the two sides went on to the prefecture, where the prefect, Mr Bollaert, appointed the First President of the Court of Appeal as arbitrator. The judge's decision, made public the following day, found in favour of the workers, and wages were raised by 0.75F an hour.

On the following day, 25 July, the committee of employers' organisations issued a communiqué in which they noted the absence of official CGT representatives at the demonstration, which had been organised by certain ring-leaders whose past histories leave a lot to be desired . . . If it should turn out, as a consequence of more demonstrations like that of yesterday, that the economic and social experiment in progress amounts to a veritable civil war . . . then the employers wish it to be known that we do not intend to abdicate.

The president of the Chamber of Commerce informed Léon Blum of the affair, and demanded that measures be taken to 'ensure the freedom and safety of all firms and their managements.'

In the St Étienne area, which was affected by strikes in the building and steel industries, there was a similar confrontation involving the Loire Mines company. A regional agreement covering the mining industry was signed on 10 June. Despite pressure from their union, 2,000 miners at Montrambert refused to ratify it. Two hundred strikers went to the Monterras pit in an attempt to bring out the workers there. For a while there was a danger of a conflict with delegates at this pit who tried to uphold their right to work, and a compressor was sabotaged. However, interventions by the union and the authorities succeeded in calming the situation, and order was re-established from 13 June, even though strong resistance to an immediate return to work made itself felt in the other strike-affected industries.

Disturbances in Marseilles

The Marseilles newspapers had still not re-appeared by 13 June and the street vendors had joined the workers of *Messageries Hachette* on strike. The number of strikers was still growing, and Henri Tasso, mayor of Marseilles and Minister for the Merchant Navy, addressed the Marseilles workers over the radio:

> What I am asking now of the workers is that they do not allow their triumph to be spoiled by elements who only want to exploit it . . . Respect for the right to work, adherence to the contracts signed and agreements made, these are the tasks for the workers of Marseilles — you have an important role to play, which should not be spoiled by the slightest provocation.

Engineers and dockers returned to work on the 16th, but the cinemas were closed and the strike spread into the surrounding areas, to Toulon, Cannes, and Nice, where the Casino was occupied, and even as far as Corsica. On the 17th the situation in Marseilles appeared somewhat difficult. Cafés, hotels, restaurants, construction, and taxis were still out, while new struggles were still breaking out after agreements had been signed. The president of the Chamber of Commerce 'asked all Frenchmen to display the tricolour', in reply to the profusion of red flags which had blossomed all over the town.

The prefect conferred with the union leaders to try to discover ways of persuading the workers to accept the agreements already made. The appeal from the president of the Chamber of Commerce provoked demonstrations resulting in violent clashes on the Canebière between strikers and fascists. Thorez arrived in Marseilles to repeat his appeal of 11 June.[10]

The various disputes were on the way to being resolved when the seamen walked out on strike. Their list of demands had been put forward some time before, and a collective agreement was being elaborated in Paris. There remained four points at issue which were to be handed over to Merchant Navy Minister Tasso for arbitration when, on 22 June, the Marseilles seamen asked for discussion of the special working conditions in the great Mediterranean port.[11] The masters asked for time to consider the claim, but the strike broke out the same afternoon. Ships were occupied and the red flag run up despite intervention by some groups of officers. The latter were forced to leave the ships by the seamen's declaration that they would no longer recognise their authority. Ships at sea were invited to join the strike at their next port of call. The strike spread to Rouen, but Tasso's mediation eventually brought an end to the dispute.

The Bordeaux region

As well as the by now classic strikes in engineering, docks, construction, and the big stores, Bordeaux was affected by strikes in the oil refineries,[12] by seamen, and in the wholesale produce markets. The employers' representatives, coming together in the Chamber of Commerce, and

considering the strong feelings aroused by acts of vandalism . . . inter-ference with individual liberty and the rights of property . . . request the government to put an end to the illegal occupations and invite our members to remain calm and display the national flag.

An agreement with the oil companies on 20 June was rejected by the strikers, who broke with the chemical workers' union and decided to set up an independent union to continue the strike.

On the same day the tramworkers' union, whose committee had made every effort to avoid a strike, was forced by its members' intense desire for action into declaring one. The depots and head office were occupied, the only vehicles continuing to operate being those supplying the strike-bound Dambes oil refinery.

This latest confrontation in municipal transport hastened the conclusion of talks being held in Paris at the Ministry of Public Works. A national agreement was signed on 21 June and immediately transmitted by telegraph to the mayors of the major cities. Before it could be brought fully into effect, some local disputes continued for several more days, notably at Bordeaux.

Special features of the strikes in North Africa

We should summarise briefly the special conditions in which the strikes in North Africa took place.

Firstly, conflicts in industries where European labour predominated normally remained calm, and followed the same pattern as the strikes in France. This was particularly the case in Algiers, where contruction, footwear and the big stores were all affected.

But, secondly, this was not the case for strikes involving only indigenous workers, especially strikes by agricultural workers, which rapidly produced serious incidents, clashes with the police, the gendarmes or the army, during which shots were often fired. The European settlers who lived in the interior organised themselves into militias for self-defence against the strikers, while aircraft were mobilised to help keep the countryside under surveillance. It is not possible to describe all the occasions where confrontations led to violence, but they included the Ouenza mines at Constantine on 29 June, Algiers, Mostaganem and Oran on 30 June, Geryville on 3 July, and Oran again on 4 July.

Thirdly, the demands put forward by the African workers were not the same as those of their French comrades. One example will be enough to illustrate this. When the workers of the phosphate fields at Kowiga in Morocco went on strike, they demanded an eight-hour day and the institution of health and safety representatives, demands which the *resident-général* was obliged to concede.

Demonstrations by the unemployed

On 13 June at Lyons, while a thousand unemployed people were outside the town hall of the sixth *arrondissement* waiting to sign on, there was an improvised street meeting accompanied by lively agitation. The claimants managed to get into the offices and decided to occupy them until their demands were met, demands which they then proceeded to draw up and put down on paper. The occupation lasted for several hours, at the end of which, after lengthy negotiations, the occupiers agreed to leave.

On 15 June at Lambres, in the department of Nord, the town hall was invaded by unemployed workers demanding the abolition of the obligatory three-hours' work to which they were subject. After intervention by the prefect, the municipality agreed. The same day at Herin there was a similar demonstration around demands for the abolition of signing-on, and the arbitrary ceiling to the amount of benefit paid. Elsewhere there were protests demanding the re-establishment of an unemployed fund (at Loon-Plage), increases in benefit and so on.

At La Rochelle on 17 June 300 unemployed who had been given work on municipal construction projects stopped work to win an increase in their hourly payment from 3F to 4F. At the same time they demanded paid holidays and the 40-hour week. Sometimes the municipal authorities became personally involved in these demonstrations, finding themselves blockaded in their offices.

The disputes still running on 14 July 1936

It has not been possible to do more than sketch the rise and breaking of the great wave of strikes, and we have not been able to give a summary of even all the biggest struggles. Thus we have left out the strike in the mining and steel industries of Lorraine, the long-running strikes in Haut-Rhin, the tanneries strike in Strasbourg, strikes in Colmar, Tarbes, Toulouse, Avignon, Grenoble, Rouen, Nantes, and Saint-Nazaire, disputes in the departments of Oise and Finistère, occupations at Rheims, and repeated strikes in the potassium mining industry.

We would have liked to follow each stage in the development of the occupation strikes in each town and industry, as we have done for the Paris region. But we have not even been able to mention many of the diverse incidents which contributed to the overall character of June '36, being concerned above all with the struggles involving the biggest battalions of workers.

We could have related the misfortune of a certain Popular Front deputy from Bar-le-Duc who was obliged to close down his firm in order to avoid a humiliating strike and occupation. Or the battle at Joze in the Puy-de-Dome between workers from Clermont-Ferrand, who had arrived to picket out the workers at the local cement factory, and the local peasants who took umbrage at their action. Likewise, we can mention only in passing the demonstrations by big farmers at the Amiens prefecture in the Somme, protesting against occupation of their farms.

Let us open l'**Humanité** of Tuesday 14 July, with its appeal for support for the great Popular Front demonstration in Paris. Industrial disputes take up no more space than the report on the 29th stage of the *Tour de France* cycle race. According to the Communist daily paper, what were the disputes in progress? In Paris, the conflict in the department stores had burst into life again. The men and women who worked in these stores' mass-production clothing workshops, having

THE WAVE RECEDES ■ 123

still not obtained monthly payment despite the bosses' promises, had stopped work at *Réaumur, le Printemps*, the *Galeries Lafayette*, and *Bon Marché*. The workers at *Belle Jardinière* and *le Louvre* had won their demands, while white-collar workers at *la Semeuse* had been on strike continuously for 37 days.

Parisian office workers employed by the Vichy Water company won their struggle after 29 days on strike. Negotiations for a collective contract for technicians in the engineering industry were still going on. The partial stoppage at the Paris gas company was drawing near to its end on 15 July, 'developing towards a successful conclusion', according to l'**Humanité**.

In the provinces, Marseilles saw the end of the 32-day strike in the textile industry, while building workers at Vesoul won a 35% increase after 12 days out. There was victory for the 150 workers at the Jourdain factory at Troyes after 31 days. Nîmes saw the return of its bonnet-makers, with only boot and shoe-workers, carpenters and painters staying out; the latter, however, were victorious at Alès. In Nice, 800 hairdressers were still on strike; in the Haute-Vienne the union of ceramic workers declared a general strike. There was a general strike also by Lyons bakery workers, while 300 building workers walked out at Chaumont. Finally a solution was thought to be near in the dispute at the Penhoët dockyards in Saint-Nazaire, which had been under occupation for 16 days.

The Popular Front and the end of the strike-wave — *Reform*

As we have seen, the members of Blum's government, especially the Socialists, were running hither and thither trying to mediate in the various disputes, both in Paris and in the provinces. Interior Minister Roger Salengro simultaneously carried out negotiations with the big stores and mediated in the north. Vincent Auriol settled the disputes relative to his government department — banks, insurance, and the Stock Exchange, while Merchant Navy Minister Henri Tasso was at Marseilles, Blancho at Nantes and Saint-Nazaire. Salengro was in continuous contact with the prefects, in order to get them to align their attitudes with that of the government in Paris. On 20 June he sent a circular to all departmental authorities, warning them that

> individuals with no authority are passing themselves off as CGT deleg-ates. If such an event should occur in your department, you should seek out those responsible, make a careful investigation of the situation, and, where necessary, have them brought before the courts.

Meanwhile, in line with Blum's promises to Jouhaux, the government sent to the Senate the bills encapsulating their social reforms, after these had passed through the lower house. The Senate debated them in committee on 13 June, and in full session on the 16th. By the 17th the senators had passed the bills dealing with civil servants' pay, pensions for war veterans and paid holidays. The following day the law on collective agreements was carried by 284 votes to 5. Finally, after an unusually long debate, lasting until one o'clock in the morning, the upper house passed the law on the 40-hour week by 182 votes to 84. The timetable laid down by Léon Blum had been followed, albeit with a few days' delay due to the cumbersome parliamentary procedures.[13]

During the parliamentary debates on the new social legislation, Léon Blum was constantly called upon to deal with the disputes still going on, and to spell out the government's attitude to them. He repeated for the Senate's benefit the assurances he had given to the lower house on the subject of law and order. Meanwhile the Chamber of Deputies gave its attention to a debate on financial policy which was Auriol's first opportunity to draw the balance sheet of his predecessor's activities and make known his plans. He drew attention to the drain on the gold reserves caused by the flight of capital which had been unchecked in the past few weeks, and to the speculation on the fall of the franc which had caused the collapse of government stocks and of share-values. At the same time he was full of expressions of moderation designed to reassure the 'class of savers'.

Two motions in particular resulted in significant debates. In the lower house, the disturbances in Marseilles were raised during a debate in which the socialist deputy Vidal made a sharp attack on the Communists. He was immediately disowned by his party and by Léon Blum. In the Senate, in the course of a debate on law and order, Salengro gave a detailed account of the security measures and orders given to the police during the strikes, for which he was responsible as Minister of the Interior:

> In the whole of France there have been 2,438 interventions by the police, of which 1,382 were in the department of Seine, and 1,303 arrests, including 819 in Paris alone. 491 cases were referred to the courts, including 196 in Seine. 1,106 expulsion orders have been issued since the elections in May, of which 467 were during our government. As a result of incidents arising out of strikes, the prefects of Doubs, Isere and Moselle have issued eight expulsion orders. In the department of Seine, 14 foreigners have been the subject of attention from the *Sûreté Nationale*, of whom six are to be expelled.[14]

As the strike wave gradually receded, parliamentary activity returned to its normal routine, with laws providing for a political amnesty, raising of the school leaving age, nationalisation of certain arms firms, and the creation of a Cereals Office all being enacted in July and August 1936. We should mention finally the decrees ordering the dissolution of the fascist leagues, which were promulgated at the end of June.

The CGT and the last disputes

The CGT's *commission administrative*, meeting on 14 June, unanimously passed a resolution celebrating the workers' victories and the imminent passage of the social reforms. They considered that

> both the principles of the Matignon agreement, and the government's undertakings concerning abolition of the decree laws,[15] the fight against poverty and unemployment, and for national economic revival, are all well on the way to being fulfilled . . . A new social policy has been born, which can only grow to maturity in an environment of public order and hard work.

The CGT leaders considered that the strike movement should not stray from its proper domain. They called on all workers, and the leaders of those still on strike, to have nothing to do with people from outside their industry, or with demagogic provocateurs who might try to extend industrial struggles into non-industrial domains or attempts to lead the membership into untimely and dangerous street demonstrations.

On 15 June CGT leader Jouhaux read this resolution over the radio, saying that it reflected the CGT's sense of its and the working class's new responsibilities which neither the union nor the class would evade. The same themes ran through the report with which he opened the first session of the next CGT national confederal committee on the 16th:

> Today we are more than 2,600,000. The increase in our numbers will continue for a while, and then we must expect a certain relapse. But our task now is to look for ways to keep and to teach discipline to those drawn towards us in this period of enthusiasm. It will be easier than in the past because the trade union movement has the prestige of success and real achievement behind it. But we have to maintain this prestige and that is why the department stores' strike must succeed.

The unanimous final resolution reiterated the confederal committee's

> total solidarity with all workers still fighting for better working conditions, and for the free exercise of trade union rights, and especially with the shop workers still in struggle . . . We thank the government for the sympathy they have shown towards the workers' cause, and its unfailing

impartiality in helping to resolve the social conflicts produced by intolerable conditions to which the workers have been subject for several years . . . We fully support the Matignon agreement of 7 June, and call on all affiliated unions to take the fullest advantage of its provisions.

Finally, on 21 June, in response to the announcement of the seamen's strike, the CGT's *commission administrative* passed a resolution in the form of an appeal to the workers. We reproduce this here in total, for this text amounts to a summary of the general position adopted by the CGT during the whole movement of May and June 1936:

The CGT once again congratulates the workers on the admirable orderliness and calm of their immense industrial struggle.

We remind everyone that this order and this calm could not have been maintained if the government had not broken with its predecessors' usual methods of anti-working-class repression.

The CGT reaffirms its steadfast hostility to those irresponsible organisations which have tried on several occasions in various places to prolong disputes unnecessarily with the aim of fomenting disorder.

We declare that the employers' organisations have a duty to avoid the outbreak of new conflicts, and to help bring to an end those strikes still in progress, by prompt application of the Matignon agreement and sensitivity to the general situation.

Having made these general observations, we repeat the guidelines we have already proposed for dealing with the current disputes.

We cannot stress urgently enough that the workers recognise the absolute necessity for the trade union movement to maintain the strictest order throughout the country. We ask all workers who have not yet benefitted from the Matignon agreements to present a list of demands to their local management before entering into dispute, and to refrain from going on strike unless they are met with intransigence or refusal to negotiate by the employers.

We declare that the agreements made must be strictly adhered to by all concerned. In any cases of failure to fulfil undertakings made, the procedure to be followed is for the union to make an immediate appeal to the authorities, in an effort to avoid if at all possible any further stoppages of work.

The CGT stresses yet again that everything must be done to ensure that adequate supplies of foodstuffs are available to the people. The workers, for their part, have already understood the importance of this, for they wish to keep the full support of public opinion. It is much to be desired that the same concern for the interests of the common people should be in evidence on the employers' side.

As far as public services are concerned, the CGT notes that the efforts of the government and the municipal authorities should not be hampered by ill-considered actions whose effects would be to weaken the position of the Popular Front, and make it easier for disruptive elements to do their work.

The CGT asks all our federations, our unions and our members, and all workers to heed this appeal. We are counting on the French working-class, with its discipline and good sense, to understand the reasons for these guidelines. Scrupulous observation of them is an essential condition for the defence and extension of the gains we have already made.

The demonstrations of 14 June

The celebration of the Popular Front's victory at the polls, fixed by the Front's national committee for Sunday 14 June, was the occasion for grandiose demonstrations throughout France. In every town and village hundreds of processions took place without the slightest disturbance. They overflowed with the people's delight in the new national political alignment, and in the successes of the Parisian workers' struggle. These demonstrations doubtless had a decisive effect in encouraging the later mass strikes in the provinces.

As we have seen, in Paris itself the demonstration had been cancelled because of the state of tension in the capital. In the north, particularly in Lille, the demonstrations provided occasions for the Popular Front leaders to issue their most urgent appeals for calm and hard work; Thorez contributed a repetition of his 11 June speech.

The fascist and reactionary organisations in France offered no opposition. This was not the case in Algeria, where the ranks of demonstrators, which included a lot of indigenous workers, were attacked by fascist groups, notably at Sidi-bel-Abbès.[16]

The Battle of the Flags

The centenary of Rouget de Lisle on 19 June gave the Parisian right-wing groups their first opportunity to mount some kind of demonstration. In the courtyard of the Invalides, more than a thousand musicians and singers performed a concert ending with a rendering of the *Marseillaise* which the massed audience took up with such vigour that the security forces judged it wise to invite President Albert Lebrun and those ministers present to leave by the back entrance.[17]

The right's next tactic, following the appeal of the president of the Marseilles Chamber of Commerce, was the ostentatious display of the national flag. The right-wing newspapers took up the slogan which had been directed towards the residents of Marseilles, and asked their readers to hang the tricolour from their windows, in reply to the red flags adorning the entrances of the occupied factories and building sites. The appeal met a wide response, notably in Paris, where the apartment buidings in the bourgeois districts were soon alive with flags in amongst which were mingled a few small blue and white streamers, the colours of the deposed French monarchy. This demonstration went on for several weeks and had very little impact in Paris.

But the battle of the flags was soon overtaken by the battle of rosettes, which at any moment was liable to provoke scrimmages and exchanges of punches in the streets, in the Latin Quarter of Paris, and even in the school-yards, where the supporters of the left themselves began to display small red handkerchieves. It was doubtless because of some contested rosette that fights broke out on the *Champs Elysées* in Paris on 21 June. The next day at the Saint-Lazare station at rush-hour there were violent clashes, lasting more than two hours and eventually spreading to the *Salle des pas Perdus* and the nearby streets. Demonstrations were repeated on the following Saturdays and Sundays on the *Champs Elysées* and later in the Latin Quarter, while the concourse of Saint-Lazare station became a regular battle-ground for opponents, who returned each evening until the fascists wearied of the continual beatings and finally gave up. Similar clashes occurred in the provinces, especially in Marseilles, Lyons, Toulouse, Toulon and Bordeaux.

One million Parisians at the Place de la Nation on 14 July

On Tuesday 14 July Paris was in its turn invited to celebrate the electoral and industrial victories. Two processions were formed. The first, starting from the *Boulevard de la République* and the *Boulevard Beaumarchais*, passed to the left of the *Place de la Bastille* and followed the *fauborg St Antoine*. The second began from *rue de Rivoli* and *rue St Antoine*, took the right-hand side of the *Place de la Bastille*, and joined the first column at the *Place de la Nation* after traversing the *rue de Lyon* and the *Boulevard Diderot*. The two columns mingled on the *cours de Vincennes*, from which point they later dispersed.

A large body of stewards lined the whole route. Big crowds watched from the pavements, while hundreds appeared at their windows. Practically every window in the *fauborg St Antoine* was draped with flags, banners and placards displaying Phrygian caps (the traditional symbol of the French republic), the three arrows of the Socialist Party, or the hammer and sickle.

At 2.30 pm the two processions joined together. Walking arm-in-arm across the front of the first were Thorez, Paul Faure, Frachon, Cachin and Jouhaux, who went to take up their positions on the rostrum at the *Place de la Nation*, where they were joined later by Léon Blum. At the head of the second column were the members of the CGT *commission administrative*. The Young Socialists' contingent, marching in step, stood out with their impeccable turn-out of blue shirts and red ties. So too did the company of youth-hostellers, in shorts and rucksacks. In the Beaumarchais section the CGT federations had rigged up floats symbolising their trades, and one could pick out the various provincial delegations — the miners, the butcher-boys in their aprons, and cleaning-ladies each carrying a broom.

All of working-class and petty-bourgeois Paris was there, rapturous and joyful as never before: the office-workers, beginning to learn the words of the *Internationale* as they had learnt the ways of the class struggle; engineers, applauded by the crowds; technicians with only one slogan — 'Collective contract, now!' The *Carmagnole* and the *Jeune Garde* were sung as well as the *Marseillaise* when it came over the loud-speakers.

And when everyone came out into the *Place de la Nation* it was more the emotion of the occasion than the desire to listen to speeches that silenced the songs and chants. Tongues were briefly stilled by pride and happiness at the sight of this whole city on the march; activists forgot for a moment the new responsibilities weighing on them and thought back over the years of struggle and setbacks which seemed at last to be ending with the fulfilment of their dream.

The march lasted until after ten o'clock at night, but not a single participant deserted the last contingent; during the whole evening the taxis, tubes and buses were full of happy, exhausted, hoarse-voiced returning demonstrators who on reaching home would reverently put away in a drawer the small red Phrygian cap, the symbol of republican France, which had adorned every button-hole.

8
THE OCCUPATION TACTIC AND ITS REPERCUSSIONS

LET US dispose first of all of two pseudo-problems.

Firstly a question of terminology; Léon Blum in parliament contested the exactness of the word 'occupation', saying that 'no factory had been occupied from the outside — it was rather a question of workers installing themselves in the factory by remaining behind when the day's work was finished.'[1]

Secondly, a juridical problem — the legality or illegality of the occupations. All who have written on this subject have agreed in recognising the illegality of the factory 'installations' which are regarded as an attack on the hallowed right of property.[2] We will look no further into this question of legality, recalling only that all the achievements of the working class have involved methods operating either at the margin of the law, or in clear opposition to it.

Some historical precedents

After the Russian revolution the Italian working class was the first to use factory occupations in the class struggle.[3] The workers of the Franchi and Gregorini factories seized their plants in March 1919; in February 1920 the workers of the Ansaldo concern at Sestriponente took over their factory and set up a management committee, a step rapidly imitated by engineers in Naples and Turin. But the height of the great Italian workers' struggle was from the end of August until October 1920 when 300,000 engineers seized their plants in response to an appeal from the central union confederation.

The Italian occupations had certain specific features. First of all, the workers were armed and their factories were turned into fortresses which the Giolitti government made no attempt to conquer, despite pleas from the owners. Secondly, the Italian engineers tried to run the plants themselves, but quickly ran up against insuperable problems stemming from the hostility of the managers and technicians, lack of raw materials, and the impossibility of obtaining credit.

There were repeated bloody clashes between the 'red guards' and the police. The political nature of the strikes was clear, and the question of state-power was inevitably posed. Despite the encouragement of Lenin and the Communist opposition in Italy, the Italian union federation (CGIL) and the Italian Socialist Party backed away from their political responsibilities, doing their best to restrict to a purely industrial domain a movement which raised the question of the ownership of the factories. The government enacted various measures on workers' control and the CGIL came to an agreement on wages with the employers which eventually led to the evacuation of the occupied premises.

This rapid exposition is enough to show that 'the Italian ocupations of 1920 amounted to a real revolutionary upsurge . . . It was only when this was checked, an event for which the leaders of the movement alone were responsible, that its political character disappeared and the so-called strictly economic aims of the occupations were proclaimed.'[4]

After the events in Italy, workers in France, Poland, Spain, Britain and the USA all had some experience of occupation strikes.[5] But only the Italian events were comparable in scale to the movement which took place in France in June 1936.

Characteristics of the French occupations

We can define the special features of the French occupations by comparing them with the Italian experience.

Firstly, the French workers were not armed. Guards were on duty at the factory gates but in practice their role amounted more to checking the comings and goings of their own comrades than mobilising against fascist or police operations. It is certain, however, that the workers were mobilised to a very high degree, such that the slightest alert would have transformed their seemingly benign and peacefully-organised workshops into impregnable fortresses.[6]

Secondly, the occupations were not accompanied by attempts at production under workers' control. Stocks of raw materials remained intact, hence problems involving finance and money did not arise.

And thirdly, violence was the exception, not the rule. Any damage caused, usually purely accidental and amounting to no more than the odd broken window, was made good on the spot. There were no reports of thefts of tools or raw materials, nor of misappropriation of retail goods in the shops.

These negative definitions are not enough to bring out all aspects of the French occupations. The workers turned to them first of all as the most effective means of pressing their economic demands. They were also a way of making the bosses understand that the era of their iron-fisted rule was over. Finally, they gave the workers the chance to test their own discipline and organisation.

ONE: We have already noted that the main obstacle to success in winning economic strikes during the crisis years was the permanent existence of a large body of unemployed. For the employers, the soldiers of this reserve army of labour amounted to a trump card — often desperate, and ready to accept pitiful wages in an effort to redress their poverty. The workers were afraid of this competition and therefore hesitated to undertake any risky course of action which had every chance of ending in defeat.

The first occupations of engineering plants were in response to these considerations. If the factory remained in the workers' hands, the boss would be unable to hire substitute labour.

But the occupations were also an exceptionally powerful tool for exerting pressure on the owners. In the normal run of strikes, the employers' resistance was liable to lead to violent reactions from the workers, up to and including street demonstrations and bloody confrontations with police or scabs. Now the employers were obliged to fear the consequences which a provocative attitude on their part might have for their own property, for the workers controlled their buildings, their machines, their records, in short, everything which made a reality of their title of ownership.

TWO: An occupation conceived as a method of defence and a means of exerting pressure quickly loses its original character when the movement starts to become general. What was clear, given the social and political climate in France since the end of May, was that the owners could no longer have recourse to their normal battle-tactics. As far as strictly economic struggle was concerned, the occupations seemed an almost unnecessary precaution.[7] They spread, however, until every industry and every region were in some degree affected.

People have spoken of 'contagion', but the word does not adequately explain the phenomenon. One author has written: 'The French working class was seized by a great collective feverish escapism.'[8] The expression has a good ring to it, but we must be precise. Was it a question of escape from work, or an attempt to escape the proletarian condition itself?

Contagion, imitation, certainly played a decisive role in a large number of cases. The very novelty of the undertaking was a source of attraction, with its creation of a whole set of new situations — the feeling of escape from the routine of everyday life, the breaking-down of the barrier between private lives and the world of work, transformation of the workplace into a place of residence, fulfilment of the desire for action, of the need to 'do something' at a time when everyone felt that important changes were coming. All these elements played a part in the spread of the occupations and helped to account for participants' universal enthusiasm and cheerfulness.

But a feeling of revenge against the bosses was no less essential. The workers felt a need to stand up and say that relations between the classes should never again reflect the bosses' omnipotence, their right to make the rules as they wished. On the contrary, now worker should be able to face owner as an equal, even take his or her turn at laying down the law. The desire for symbolic assertion of this new dignity explains the numerous strikes which broke out in factories where all the workers' demands had already been met.

We shall return to these developments to show how in certain cases the workers were led to skip over this stage and consider taking over the firm completely.

THREE: There was exemplary order and organisation. All observers are unanimous on this point. Here again it was the engineers from Paris and the *Nord* who established the characteristic features of the occupations. In fact, right from the earliest days the occupations' standard pattern was clear. We shall attempt to trace it by making use of various witnesses' accounts.[9]

At the entrance to the plant, a picket — a few men smoking and chatting amiably. A few flags fixed to the gate — tricolours and red flags invariably decorated with the insignia of the Popular Front parties. At the entrance, a poster, '*n*th day on strike', inviting passersby to throw a few coppers into the strike fund. In many places there was a list of the workers' demands alongside the scale of wages in operation before the strike, for comparison.

Inside the workplace, all power was in the hands of the strike committee, subdivided into sections each with its own leader. The names of the section leaders were usually posted up on the premises. Typical functions were: internal discipline, that is, distribution of exit permits, enforcement of a strict code of conduct including a ban on wine and spirits, and strict observation of conventional morality; organisation of pickets; safety and maintenance, that is, fire prevention inspections, checks on the teams responsible for keeping the premises clean and for maintaining the machines; provisioning, and liaison with the local Popular Front committees who were most often responsible for providing the elements of subsistence; leisure, that is the organisation of daily dances and shows; and, finally, management of the strike funds.

There was a daily mass-meeting where the leaders reported on the state of the talks with the employers and gave the latest instructions on internal organisation. The women returned home every night,[10] and in theory every striker had one day off in four. Some, especially at the beginning, taking advantage of the first exit permits they were given, did not return. In other cases, workers tried to make off as the occupation got under way, but this was fairly rare, and many later returned to the plants to take their places. When the second strike began at Renault some of the strikers followed fleeing workers actually into the trams and forcibly brought them back to the plant. In some cases, the escapers' desire to return home was motivated by fear of conjugal recriminations.

There were a variety of pastimes: cards, bowls, amateur dramatics. An accordion or harmonica were enough to improvise a dance, while the more well-endowed plants boasted a record player or wireless. The orchestras from the strike-bound cinemas offered their services; singers, comedians and balladeers were everywhere. Impresarios appeared who seemed able to mount theatrical or music-hall performances with whatever materials lay to hand.

When the women had left, the men stayed on in the yards to take advantage of the warm June evenings before bedding down in the improvised dormitories between benches or machines, while those on duty remained alert the whole night. What with strike committee meetings, liaison with neighbouring plants, union meetings, meetings of central strike committees where these existed, mass meetings of strike delegates, there was little time left for relaxation, especially if one adds the nervous tension resulting from the new responsibilities which the militants had assumed. They also had to cope with the problem of reconciling their comrades' ardour with the official union calls for moderation.

FOUR: How did the rank and file exert control over the leaders? Did workers' democracy really operate, and what forms did it take? And were the leaders in fact elected?

In the very great majority of cases the answer is no. The strike committees were mostly formed by an admixture of the more dynamic trade-union and political activists, those who had been the most prominent in the original decision to stop work, or towards whom the other workers turned after the walk-outs because they were known for belonging to some workers' organisation. As the strike progressed the strike committees co-opted those workers who showed themselves to be the best organisers. And of course there is no doubt that the strike committees remained in very close contact with the rank and file for the whole duration of the occupations. Decisions to approve or reject terms of settlement were the subject of votes at mass meetings, and we have mentioned several occasions when the delegates' recommendations were rejected.

In the big plants wall newspapers were created in order to inform the strikers on all matters affecting them. However in the factories, shops or sites employing the biggest numbers of workers contact was more tenuous, and control was exercised by means of intermediate layers. Simone Weil,[11] who was able to get inside Renault during the strike, reported that her conversations with the workers revealed widespread ignorance of the state of negotiations with the bosses. No doubt the complexity of the various contacts between the two sides at regional level caused some confusion. But there was always vigilant and effective control of all aspects of the organisation of the strike and of the particular issues in each factory.

FIVE: Let us leave it to Simone Weil, then, to describe the high spirits reigning in all the occupations:

The very act of striking is a joy. A pure and unalloyed joy.

Yes, a joy. I have been to see my pals in the factory where I worked a few months ago . . . What joy to enter the plant with the smiling authorisation of a worker guarding the gate. What joy to find so many smiles, so many friendly words of welcome . . . Joy to roam freely through the shop where we were once chained to our machines . . . Joy to hear music, songs and laughter instead of the pitiless din of machinery . . . Joy to walk near the foreman with our heads held high . . . Joy to live the rhythm of human life in amongst the silent machines . . . Of course, the old hard existence will begin again in a few days, but no one is thinking about that now . . . At last, for the first time, different memories will haunt these heavy machines, souvenirs of something other than silence, constraint, submission. Memories which will keep a little pride in our hearts, which will breathe just a little human warmth into all this cold metal.

Relaxation is complete. There is none of that fierce nervous energy, that determination mixed with pent-up anxiety so often associated with strikes in the past. We are determined, certainly, but no longer anxious. We are happy.

SIX: Finally, it should be stressed that the factory occupations contributed, paradoxically, to the maintenance of order. 'The established social order,' remarks Delmas, 'has perhaps benefitted from the workers' use of the factory-occupation tactic, which has so mortified the defenders of the *Code Civil*.'[12] Léon Blum several times voiced this idea. First of all in the Chamber, where he declared:

It is possible that, from the point of view of public order, these acts [the occupations] present less serious dangers than those street battles we are used to seeing in the generality of industrial disputes, than the clashes between pickets and workers desiring to go back to work, where the police have to defend the right to work, all that taking place around padlocked factory gates.[13]

Blum returned to the subject with more precision during his trial at Riom:

> It should be noted that from the point of view of public order this form of strike has incontestable advantages. The workers occupy the factory, but it was also true that the factories occupied the workers. The workers were there and not elsewhere. They were not in the street. While they were all assembled in their factories they were not forming those processions with chants, red flags, etcetera, which would inevitably have come up against police blockades.[14]

The employers and the factory occupations

Although the employers tried to refuse negotiations, even when their factories were occupied, they never demanded forcible evacuation. Léon Blum several times insisted on this point, thus confirming the declaration by former prime minister Albert Sarraut which we have already recorded.[15] However the employers' organisations developed a procedure according to which, as soon as a workplace was occupied, they informed the authorities and registered a complaint with the *Procureur de la République*. The aim of these formalities was to secure compensation for any damage caused, in line with the law on 'responsibility of the local council in case of riot'; they had no other practical importance.

It was only when the strike wave receded that the owners or their spokesmen accused the authorities of having failed in their duty. Léon Blum had to remind his Riom judges of how the bourgeoisie had panicked in June '36, a memory which had somehow been effaced by the reassuring presence of Hitlerite bayonets and the Vichy militias.[16]

The generalisation of the strikes

Here we reproduce the statistics of the Ministry of Labour, noting that not too much importance must be given to them, given the inevitable inaccuracies.

1. Strikes from January to May 1936

	Strikes	Lock-outs	Numbers involved
January	50	1	8,739
February	39	2	9,142
March	38	1	12,127
April	32	0	12,784
May	65	0	13,727

Causes	January	February	March	April	May
Wages	15	10	19	12	33
Resistance to wage cuts	13	7	8	4	2
Working conditions	9	7	7	1	5
Resistance to sackings	5	6	3	8	12
Various	8	8	2	7	13

Results	January	February	March	April	May
Compromise	10	5	11	10	3
Victory	7	4	4	3	4
Defeat	9	8	6	2	4
Results not known, or disputes still running	24	21	18	17	54

2. June 1936[17]

	Number of strikes	Number of strikers	Number of occupation strikes	Total of disputes settled
TOTAL	12,142	1,830,938	8,941	9,473
Seine	1,286	337,685	1,262	1,236
Seine-et-Oise	762	68,722	514	711
Seine-et-Marne	360	16,764	141	314
Nord	2,400	335,359	1,929	2,171
Pas-de-Calais	595	140,399	456	429
Rhône	505	69,085	442	323
Bouches-du-Rhône	111	71,945	98	14
Gironde	288	29,581	236	163
Seine-Inférieure	335	64,907	289	311
Loire	195	41,471	174	173
Alpes-Maritimes	329	26,881	147	176
Haut-Rhin	108	30,540	66	106
Moselle	56	47,567	44	32
Aisne	189	17,323	169	158
Oise	274	22,672	274	235

3. July 1936

	Number of strikes	Number of strikers	Number of occupation strikes	Total of disputes settled
TOTAL	1,751	181,471	639	1,500
Seine	91	9,252	90	72
Seine-et-Oise	348	5,096	14	386
Seine-et-Marne	17	1,903	8	55
Nord	42	1,944	28	246
Doubs	31	23,167	26	36
Moselle	17	16,485	17	40

It is interesting to examine the degree to which the strike became general in each industry. We have several times stressed that the only important industries where an official general strike was called were the mines, in the departments of Nord and Pas-de-Calais, and in construction and cafés, hotels and restaurants in the Paris area, and that the unions launched these strike calls when the strikes were already effective and all but 100 per cent.

In the Paris engineering industry no strike order was ever given, and the union never opposed isolated returns to work. Far from it. When certain medium-sized firms returned to work after agreeing terms with the management, the workers' newspapers congratulated themselves on the victory, and if it happened that a new sit-down strike took place — whether for solidarity with the rest of the industry still in struggle, or because the gains made were thought to be insufficient when compared with the demands put forward by the bulk of the industry — the Engineering Union was never the source of this new action.

In the construction industry several unions were opposed to separate negotiations firm by firm; but this was as much in order to prevent the lodging of excessive demands, so-called 'demagogic brinkmanship', as to co-ordinate the negotiations in this very decentralised industry.

We will try to summarise some aspects of the spread of the strikes under three headings.

Firstly, there was no *national* general strike covering the whole of France by a single group of workers, even those whose negotiations were carried on at national level, for example the seamen and tram-workers.

Secondly, at local or regional level the strikes were usually general strikes limited to a particular industry or branch of industry, and the element of generalisation was spontaneous. We can trace a typical schema of the stages of development of these industry-wide strikes: beginning of the movement in one or several firms; negotiations at factory level; spontaneous generalisation to all similar firms in the town or region; negotiations at town or regional level; town or regional agreement; return to work after settlement of problems specific to each firm.

Thirdly, the spread of the 'contagion' to small establishments sometimes employing fewer than ten workers was one of the characteristics of the 1936 strikes. This brought about important changes in working relationships to which several authors have referred:

> There are in France hundreds of small firms where it was the custom for the owner's wife herself to take a set of baby-clothes to the home of a woman worker who was about to have a child, and where if the boss was ill the workers came with tears in their eyes to ask for news. In June they went on strike and occupied the workshops along with the rest. The bewildered *patron* felt as wounded as a father who suffers the revolt of an ungrateful son.[18]

Absence of inter-industrial strikes

The only case of a general strike mounted at a local level by a *union départementale* was the 24-hour general strike at Avignon in July called to support the demands of building workers on strike for several days. And even this strike, which was decided by a large majority of delegates from different trades, was immediately reduced in scope by the officials, who excluded from the action the public services and workers in the food distribution industry, public health and so on. The development of regional general strikes was a phenomenon of spontaneous combustion, but there was not a single case of an organised across-trade or inter-industrial liaison. Although demonstrations of solidarity were numerous, they were always limited to good wishes, resolutions, and financial contributions.

However, these remarks might lead one to conclude that the various movements were largely sectional in nature. We have dwelt deliberately on the formal separation of the strikes in order to contrast this with the movement's profound unity. Everywhere there were the same methods, the same hopes, the same desire for change mixed with the same illusions; the same complex attitude of defiance and confidence towards the leaders. Whatever the political affiliation or social origin of the strikers — manual workers and office staff, proletarians and petty-bourgeois — all were fighting the same battle.

No strike — no sense of victory

Every workplace, in every industry affected by the movement, wanted to have its 'own' strike, even if an agreeement had already crowned the achievement of their demands. This was another highly important aspect of that contagion and imitation which helps us to put our finger on the real meaning of the 1936 workers' struggles. They went a great deal further than a simple demand for immediate material benefits. There was a human meaning on a much higher level which has been described as 'a complex of self-betterment and conquest'.

> The self-betterment complex involved first of all a judgement: none of us is any longer a slave, and we will find our leaders amongst ourselves; secondly, a feeling: the breaking of bonds; finally, a type of behaviour, namely, in negotiations speaking as firmly as the employers' representatives. The conquest complex also involved a judgement: since the tools and equipment are instruments of labour, they ought to belong to the workers; a feeling — a new respect for the machines, which were no longer foreign to them; and a new type of behaviour — strike with occupation.[19]

When their comrades' struggles had allowed them to glimpse this new dignity, the majority of workers wanted to discover and to conquer it for themselves, even if their strike was of only a symbolic nature.

It is right then to ask ourselves whether the strike-wave was a movement in the direction of the complete emancipation of the proletariat.

Revolutionary implications

The above words can have a general sense or a precise meaning. For the employers and the bourgeois press every strike is a revolutionary act because it is a threat to the unfettered power of the owners of the means of production. In June '36 the leader writer of le Temps discovered dangerous revolutionary manoeuvres in the workers' every step. Naturally, we do not share his opinion. We understand by 'revolutionary tendencies' all those actions and attitudes of the working class which disclosed an intention of disputing the capitalists' right to own the factories. For us, such aspirations are revealed by all those actions which hinder the normal functioning of existing political institutions, and are in evident contradiction with their spirit, even when no conscious revolutionary aims have been formulated.

In this sense we can point to a number of significant individual events, some of which we have already described in the preceding chapters. We shall mention others in due course, without even remotely exhausting the list of examples available. But we shall give our main attention to the general tendencies involved, these being the more important.

We have described the attempt at direct control of production by the workers of Delespaul-Havez in the *Nord*. We have also related the events in Dunkirk, Lyons and Marseilles, and shown how in Paris on 11 June the strike spilled over in the streets, mainly through the demonstrations by builders and café/hotel/restaurant workers. A few further examples should be mentioned here.

First of all, Salengro revealed in the Chamber that 'in the Lille suburbs the workers armed themselves with their tools, or improvised weapons in order to defend themselves against a supposed fascist threat.'[20]

Secondly, restraint and confinement of factory managers was rife, especially in the early days of the strikes before the CGT intervened vigorously at the behest of Sarraut. These were confinements without physical violence, but revealed the workers' desire to inflict some kind of humiliation on their bosses which would deflate their arrogance.

Thirdly, the workers' struggles were often brought into the strictly political arena when it came to the question of banning right-wing demonstrations. Several senators gave numerous examples during the famous session of 7 July.[21] A certain Mr Dorman complained, for example, that on 6 July the Popular Front supporters had opposed the holding of a reactionary meeting at Etampes whose only object was to 'explain to the public what the effects of the new laws will be, and even, perhaps, to encourage people to conform to them.' Mr François Saint-Maur related how at Nantes pressure from below had forced the prefect to ban a monarchist banquet, with worker-activists supplementing the police efforts to supervise the dispersion of the royalists. Finally, Mr Henri Haye, senator, and mayor of Versailles, complained about the popular demonstrations of 14 June, in which soldiers in uniform participated, so that a visiting general who had arrived in order to attend a military parade was obliged to distribute his medals in undignified haste in the barrack square!

The first general revolutionary tendency, however, was the huge number of cases of reluctance to return to work or of hesitation to accept collective agreements, which for a while swamped the union officials. Walter, for example, notes that the Matignon agreement

> was far from satisfying all the workers of the occupied factories in equal measure. Some of them, displaying an exemplary sense of corporate discipline, obeyed CGT recommendations, and went back to work. Others, on the contrary, announced that they had been betrayed, and demonstrated their discontent. They had expected something better

. . . and Jouhaux was once again accused of betraying the working class. Only this time to his name was added that of Benoit Frachon, who had been closely involved with the drawing up of the deal in question. Workers' delegates came to the CGT to press their demands. They were not all Communists. Some were not even union members. Hénaff, who had to deal with them in his capacity as secretary of the *Union Départementale de la Seine*, described them as big-mouths and windbags.[22]

These events were of some concern to the government, and Léon Blum at the dispatch-box frequently used the term 'overrun'. The CGT were no less worried:

It was clear that our members everywhere found it impossible to lead the strikes, to control their extension, or predict their consequences. The Communists themselves, who tried to pretend that they were more in control than anyone else, admitted in private conversations with fellow militants that the workers' upsurge made a mockery of all their slogans, and the wisest course was to let oneself be carried along by the torrent of enthusiasm in order to give the impression of leading it. It is absolutely exact to say that the leaders were following the men without knowing how this adventure would end.[23]

To support these observations we can recall the stubbornness of the Parisian engineers who kept deferring the signature of their collective agreement; the votes of the Paris cement-workers, the insurance company staffs, the northern miners, the Dunkirk dockers, and the attitude of the oil refinery workers of the Gironde and Rouen. In Marseilles, the socialist deputy R Vidal, assistant to the mayor, redoubled his efforts at mediation, but

each time we negotiate the end of a strike, ten more are born out of it; or even the strike we have succeeded in stopping breaks out again a few days later.[24]

There was, then, a distinct tendency for the masses to pursue strikes beyond the objectives originally assigned to them. But this tendency was no more than half-fulfilled, for no new slogans were raised in the absence of a new leadership which could give a political expression to the workers' aspirations.

In these circumstances the efforts of the Hotchkiss workers of Levallois were of the greatest importance. We have not been able to discover whether the originators were fully conscious of the scope of their initiative. But it gave birth to a new organ of power, closer to the workers, more sensitive to their needs, an organism capable of opposition to the union leaderships, even of replacing them, an organism ultimately capable of welding the workers' struggles more tightly together and giving them an added strength. The decision to bring together in a factory-yard the strike committees of all the different local firms was in itself a demonstration of mistrust of the union leaderships; a CGT representative was admitted to the committee as an advisor, but not as guide or non-controllable spokesman.

The Hotchkiss initiative, in other words, was an attempt at *soviet*-style organisation, in the original meaning of the term.[25] The spread of this form of organisation could have raised the struggle on to a new and higher level, could have reinforced and implanted this second focus of power which so worried the bourgeois press. But the Hotchkiss workers' step was the only one of its kind — nothing was to come of it.

It was no accident, of course, that Thorez, in his 11 June speech, made a direct link between the tendency of the unions to be swamped by events, the attempt to give a *soviet* form of organisation to the strike, and his slogan, 'We must know how to end a strike . . .'

A tendency towards the appropriation of the factories was the second of the revolutionary tendencies inherent in the occupation strikes. All commentators have referred to it. The discipline and orderliness of the movement and its extraordinary passivity were its classic characteristics. This, perhaps more than anything else, was what terrified the bourgeoisie. A few outbreaks of violence would have discomfited them less than this anguished waiting, disturbed them less than the masses' breathtaking composure, which kept alive for several long weeks the threat of total dispossession. The anxious care of the machines, the guarding of their product, these were not only the workers' way of asserting their dignity and exhibiting their conscientiousness — they were also a simple demonstration of collective appropriation.

But here again it was a case of a tendency not clearly or fully formulated. The engineers, in the speeches of their delegates, did call for direct production by the workers alone. But the texts of the resolutions which they adopted in the end came down to calls for the requisition and running of the plants under ministerial authority. Those who had translated the workers' aspirations into these ambiguous terms played on the confusion caused by the existence of a Socialist-led government sympathetic to the working class.[26]

The same idea of recourse to the state was behind the Rouen oil workers' declaration that they wanted to continue their strike 'until nationalisation'.

Thirdly, however, this inclination to turn to the state was nevertheless accompanied by growing evidence of mistrust of the parliamentary system. Indeed many were struck by the opposition between legal forms of power and real power. The most important social reforms ever debated by parliament were hastily enacted, but the procedural machinery seemed to be working in a vacuum — the members deliberated amidst general indifference. At the same time, outside, workers' power imposed its own reforms *in the real world*. Refusing to rely on parliament and the government, it was satisfied only by the concrete gains which it succeeded in forcing into the various agreements signed with the employers.

Fourthly, when the workers returned to work they felt as if they and the life of their factory would never be the same again. Though they returned to the same jobs, to stand at the same machine or behind the same counter, they felt that they had taken the first step towards a wider emancipation. They remained ready for action, and put their trust in men who they thought would soon lead them into further battles. They had glimpsed the solution of previously insurmountable problems in the new-found unity of all sections, petty-bourgeois or proletarian, manual worker or technician, and the unity won in the strike lived on in the fusion of their hopes and aspirations.

Fifthly and finally, in a sense it is pointless to try to list the revolutionary tendencies inherent in the mighty struggles of 1936. In reality the strike-wave itself, taken as a whole, was a revolutionary upsurge which fitted the precise definition we have given of the word. It was an unofficial general strike, forging new organs of power, laying down its own laws, groping for new slogans and new forms of struggle, only to abandon them and go on to yet others, mobilising hundreds of thousands of workers in efforts which would be largely unnecessary if their goals were purely economic. A strike of this kind is usually the classic overture of a revolution.

Proletariat and middle classes

One proof of the sympathetic response which the workers' demands and their strikes evoked from the middle classes was the fascist groups' demagogic attempts to retain their audience among the petty-bourgeosie. Some, like de la Roque, went as far as to proclaim 'our ideas have taken power'. Their efforts were in vain. Small shop-keepers, clerks, technicians and administrative types were all beginning to turn to a working class on the march.

On the one hand, without the active support of small shop-keepers and the general sympathy of the whole population, the strike-wave would have lacked some of its most typical features. Ordinary people agreed with the workers' demands, while the traders had hopes that business would pick up if wages were increased. The shopkeepers helped the strike committees and strikers' families with gifts, offers of credit, and big price reductions. In the factories the workers posted up notices showing which traders were sympathetic to the cause and which were not.

On the other hand in each workplace manual workers, clerks, technicians and administrative grades all struck together. The administrative types did not conceal their admiration for the organisational abilities and self discipline of the manual workers; and they profited from the lesson in solidarity which the latter gave them by often refusing to return to work until the technicians' demands had been met, even though the technicians themselves had in the past not always resisted the bosses' divide-and-rule tactics.

It is true that about the same time various managerial staff associations were formed which declared themselves 'neutral' in the struggle and denounced the occupations. But these organisations mostly involved only the higher management, whom the workers regarded as blind followers of the owners, and whom they had in the same way either chased out of the plants or trapped and held prisoner in their offices. The main thing was that

the folly of 6 February is gone forever; the shop-workers, the technicians who announce that they have no special demands to lodge but simply want to demonstrate their solidarity with their worker comrades, the women, the young girls so full of fight, the staffs of the insurance companies, the stock exchange and the banks, they all now understand that there is only one fight.[27]

And they were ready to follow the path beaten by the industrial workers.

Repercussions outside France

The events of May–June 1936 had immediate repercussions abroad. The Popular Front newspapers made frequent references to the effects of the movement in Italy and Germany, but we have not been able to find any hard information to support their reports. The workers' struggle in Spain had already burst forth when news of the mass strikes in France gave them a new vigour. In Britain we have found one case of an occupation strike by civil servants during June.

But it was above all in Belgium that there arose a vast industrial struggle closely linked to the French movement. It began on Tuesday 2 June when a general strike by dockers in Antwerp came in the middle of a political crisis caused by a general election in May. At first disavowed by some union organisations, the strikers' 100 per cent solidarity eventually won them full support. They were demanding a 28 per cent wage increase (14 Belgian francs per day), and were soon joined on strike by public transport workers. Next came 2,000 diamond workers, and then the Liège miners, who occupied several pits. The miners were, however, immediately thrown out by the police, after the caretaker government, which included Socialists, had unanimously approved the use of tear gas for this purpose.[28]

On 15 June the Belgian miners' strike became general. The Antwerp dockers were still out, and as many as 30,000 engineering workers were on strike. The next day quarrymen came out, the number of striking engineers was up to 85,000, while in Liège the big stores and public services were paralysed. The movement spread daily, without occupations, it is true, but not without violence. On 17 June a general strike was declared in the Brussels region, where 48,000 textile workers walked out, and in the Borinage the miners dug up paving stones to build barricades. These were charged by the gendarmes, and bloody clashes ensued.

On 19 and 20 June the movement spread still further, but intervention by Vandervelde and Pierard succeeded in calming the agitation in the Borinage. In the whole country there were more than 400,000 on strike. Negotiating committees got down to work; the employers were ready to compromise on wages, but refused to budge on the 40-hour week. Agreements were signed on 20 and 21 June, conceding pay increases of between 5 and 10 per cent and paid holidays. On Monday 22 June the downturn set in. The Antwerp dockers, the engineers and miners all returned to work, and pacification continued with the same uneven rhythm as in France.

9
THE WORKERS' ORGANISATIONS AND THE STRIKES

The Communist Party: The Villeurbanne Congress of January 1936

FIRST we will attempt to summarise the main themes in Thorez's report[1] to the Communist Party congress which preceded the 1936 elections and the strikes.

Many people found it hard to understand the situation in France, explained the general-secretary. Our country was rich, 'endowed with abundant natural resources, and French industry has a very large productive capacity which is technically very advanced.' But the country was at the mercy of a very serious economic crisis. 'The French people ask: but how can this be . . . how can we have unemployment, scarcities, and poverty in such a rich country?' It is because workers and peasants do the work, explained Thorez, and a handful of rich owners get the benefit. These are

> the heads of the two hundred families who dominate the political and economic life of the nation . . . They have the power to frustrate the plans of the elected government and to dictate their own wishes. They have the power to bring down ministries and violate the will of the people expressed by universal suffrage, the power to impose on the French people governments which will do the capitalists' bidding.

The consequences of the crisis and of the policies imposed by the 200 families were penury for the working class, impoverishment for the middle classes, ruination for the small peasants, a fall in the birth rate, corruption, 'a decline in moral standards . . . decadence in art and literature.'

Throughout the country protests were mounting against Laval's reactionary and anti-Soviet policies. Strikes by workers, demonstrations by the civil servants, the peasants' coalition against governmental seizures of their property, these were all part of the people's struggle against reaction and fascism. The Communist Party had formulated a plan to save France. It had fought for a battle-alliance between the working class and the salaried middle classes. The Communists had been alone in calling for a fightback on 9 February 1934, and their martyrs' blood had spelled 'no they shall not pass!' on the Paris pavements. Their policy of the United Front, decided at the Ivry conference in June 1934, had led directly to the pact of unity in action and the formation of the Popular Front.

The Communists fought for a decent standard of living by supporting the demands of all types of workers; they also fought for the unity of the French people, for 'we love our country,' and we want 'to help it grow prosperous, so that there is work, happiness and peace for everyone.' If there was to be any chance of saving the country, the most urgent need was to unite the forces of the working class, and Thorez explained what was meant by the United Front:

> The United Front must not be limited to a meeting once a year. It must be rooted in the workers' everyday political and economic struggles. The United Front should be able to initiate and help to carry through even quite small disputes. It should also be able to guide the working class towards higher forms of struggle, even including the preparation of a *political mass strike*, whether for the purpose of a possible response to new fascist attacks, or as a method of supporting workers' demands of a general or national nature.[2]

The Communist Party in fact wanted more than a united front, for it wanted 'one class, one union, one party'. At the same time, to unite working class and middle classes, the Communists had desired and were helping to build the Popular Front.

What did the Communists want to get out of the Popular Front? It was not, insisted Thorez, a temporary, passing tactic.

> It is a fundamental element of our politics, an application of the ideas of Marx and Lenin on the need for an alliance between the working class and the middle classes *to the very end*,[3] not only to defeat the fascists, but to have done with the capitalists' exploitation . . . Our party refuses to consider all the bourgeois parties as if they were a single reactionary mass . . . The Communist Party, leading the working class in the pursuit of its natural demands and aspirations, has given itself the task, difficult though it may be, of building an alliance with the peasant masses and the democratic petty-bourgeoisie to prevent the triumph of fascism in France and transform the balance of power in the international arena in favour of the working class . . .
>
> Sometimes people say that the Popular Front is nothing but the old *'cartel des gauches'* extended to include the Communists. In the *cartel des gauches* you had a section of the working class dragged by a policy of class-collaboration into the camp of a section of the bourgeoisie, for the

benefit of capitalism. In the Popular Front you have the working class, by its own activity, influencing the salaried middle classes, and drawing them into the fight against the bourgeoisie, against capitalism and fascism.

And it was only in this context that the formation of a Popular Front government could be envisaged.

In a situation of worsening economic crisis, general paralysis of the bourgeoisie and increasingly revolutionary working-class activity, a Popular Front government would get rid of the fascist menace by disarming and effectively dissolving the armed gangs. It would be a governent to *make the rich pay* . . . and in order to complete this double task it would have to rely on mass activity outside parliament, organised by the Popular Front committees.[4]

It would be a government preparing the ground for the taking of all power by the working class. The Communist Party would never consider participation in a bourgeois government, and as long as there was no possibility of a Popular Front government 'of the kind which I have described', the party would support in the Chamber any left government 'whose programme was in conformity with the interests and wishes of the French people,' that is, including the necessary steps 'to safeguard the franc, bring a rapid end to speculation, protect the interests of the working population, defend democratic rights, disarm and dissolve the fascist leagues and work for peace.'

The Communist Party policy, enunciated by Thorez, thus had two aspects to it. On the one hand, given the Popular Front pact, the Communist Party would support governments attempting to implement the common programme. But on the other hand the use of the Popular Front tactic, as they saw it, ought to encourage the development of a mass movement and grow towards assumption of power by the working class.

Were these really, as Thorez claimed, simply two sides of the same policy, or might events show that parliamentary support for a left government would lead the Communist Party to neglect the importance of working-class action?

The Communist Party and the Popular Front after the elections, May 1936 to the Arles Congress of December 1937

We have already described the position taken by the Communist Party in the Popular Front national committee when the programme was first drawn up. Their moderation at that time hinted at a tendency which became more clearly defined as time went on, despite the apparent contradictions in the party's attitude to both the Popular Front and the strikes.

Although part of the Popular Front, the Communist Party continued to act independently in parliament by putting forward bills on subjects which were not mentioned in the joint programme. This was the case, for example, with its measure 'to make the rich pay', which was nothing less than a wealth tax. On the other hand they campaigned for the 'democratic widening' of the Popular Front, that is the transformation of local and factory Popular Front committees, which had been reduced to meetings of party representatives, into bodies composed of bigger numbers of party members as well as members of no party.

This campaign, which was in fact carried out more by contacts with the other party leaderships than by grass-roots political agitation, came to nothing. Thorez explained its failure in these terms:

> We have not been able to overcome the hostility of the Socialist and Radical leaders, who were opposed to the election of Popular Front committees in every factory and village, nor could we convince them of the need for a national Popular Front Congress composed of delegates elected by meetings of the rank and file . . . The Popular Front has become a simple summit agreement.[5]

Others made a more searching self-criticism, and stressed the Communists' own responsibility for their failure:

> The Communists carried to such a point their concern to do nothing which might hinder the achievement of working-class unity, they so underestimated their own initiating role in the formation of the Popular Front, that they often thought it necessary to subordinate everything in the prior approval of the Socialist leaders, and gave in too easily to a veto from the likes of Blum and Paul Faure. We should add that the euphoria caused by the left's electoral victory and the magnificent strike movement of May–June 1936 pushed into the background a mistrust which in fact was more than justified. Heads were turned by the successes achieved, and by the improvements in the living standards of the humbler sections of the population, which had been won by their own tremendous efforts . . . Our party let itself get bogged down in endless discussions about the conditions of our participation in the government. We spoke of nothing but 'unity between the Popular Front parties' . . . from the beginning we did not orientate ourselves strictly and consistently enough towards the masses; we did not leave enough room for action from below. These are the reasons for the collapse of a magnificent movement which was undermined more from within than from without.[6]

The Communist Party programme was in effect put into cold storage. The campaign to 'make the rich pay' was pushed only inter-mittently, while the appeal to the Popular Front's mass support was to all intents and purposes abandoned. On the other hand, there was still 'unflinching support' for the Blum government, as confirmed by several communiqués from the party's politbureau which we have already quoted. 'They always supported Léon Blum with their votes in the Chamber, and even when they were dissatisfied with him on account of the events in Spain they went no further than abstaining from the vote,' noted one observer.[7]

Equally significant were Thorez's speech on 30 October 1936 in which he examined the different points of the Popular Front programme and the degree to which they had been achieved, together with his report to the 1937 Arles Congress. The Communist Party declared its complete support for the government's record, which it undertook to defend before public opinion. What was more, the widening of the Popular Front was no longer conceived as a way of reaching still more deeply into the masses, but rather as a broadening of the political range of the parliamentary majority. Thorez was now floating the idea of the 'French Front':

> French Front for the defence of law and order, protection of the economy, for the freedom and independence of our country . . . Our opinion is that on these three points we can meet halfway with people who do not accept the Popular Front as a whole, without asking them to give up the rest of their ideas.

Inevitably, the logical conclusion of this political development was participation in the government. On two occasions, the Communists declared themselves ready to accept ministerial appointments. First in June 1937, when the first Blum government was about to fall, and subsequently in March 1938 when Blum was trying to form his national unity government 'from Thorez to Louis Marin.'[8]

The Communist Party during the strikes

The evolution of the Communist Party's political line helps us to understand its attitude during the decisive weeks of June 1936.

The central committee meeting of 25 May 1936 was the last occasion on which a 'left' tendency within the party's ruling circles attempted to make a stand. Ferrat advocated a break with the Blum government in order to take the head of the movement and lead an onslaught

> which is vaster than anything we have seen since 1919 . . . We should say to the workers: you will only get what you are prepared to take by class action. At this time of all times we should not even dream of underwriting the government's good intentions, of linking our fate with theirs, or of accepting responsibility for their actions, and in no way should we appear to the masses to be doing so.[9]

But his was a lone voice, and the resolution adopted by the central committee simply repeated the party's central slogan: 'Everything for the Popular Front, everything by the Popular Front,' and stressed its total solidarity with the government then being formed.

Some people have tried to see hidden designs and Machiavellian tactics in this resolution, since it included a mention of the masses' impatience with the long-drawn-out parliamentary procedures. But, placed in its context, this was proof only of the Communist Party's usual care to make sure that they stayed in close contact with the class and were able to give expression to its aspirations, irrespective of the general drift of the party's politics. The workers had expected Blum to assume office immediately on winning the elections, and they were palpably impatient with his respect for the formalities.

It was the same concern to keep in touch with the masses once they had moved into action which led the Communist Party's polit-bureau to declare their total solidarity with the strikes at each stage of the movement's development. But of course we have mentioned already that their declarations were always informed by a desire to avoid appearing to break the unity of the Popular Front. Sometimes they justified their support for workers on strike by referring to Socialist Party congress resolutions; they at all times insisted on the strictly economic character of the strikes.

Thorez's appeal of 11 June remained the essential point, the strict instruction to Communist Party members to know how to end a strike when the main demands had been won. This appeal put an end to any possibility of a 'double game' which some people attributed to the Communist Party, and in fact the Communist deputies played an extremely active role in the pacification of the movement.[10]

It does not seem to us that the Communist Party had had any different attitude at the beginning of the strikes, nor that the date 11 June marked a particular turning point in the party's policy. The party had in fact at all times thrown its weight into an effort to contain the strikes in a strictly economic framework, and to prevent the upsurge from escaping from the trade unions' control. A few months after the June strikes the Communists were to go as far as advising against occupations, for, according to Thorez, 'given the development of campaigns by the right, which are a source of worry and doubt amongst ordinary people, it is better not to employ this form of struggle.'[11]

The Communist Party's justifications and explanations

Thorez justified the Communists' attitude to the June strikes by the need to protect the alliance between workers and petty-bourgeoisie, and he referred several times to the lessons of 1848 and 1871:

> We were right . . . in our attitude to the strikes when we said, 'we have to know how to end a strike,' when we explained to the workers that they must not go too quickly for the country as a whole, and so run the risk of being cut off from the rural population, succumbing to isolation and provocation by the reactionaries. That is the lesson of 1848, when, having brought the republic into being in February, the workers were isolated, and then forced to give battle in June . . . The lessons of 1871 were the same. Marx wrote that the heroism and audacity of the Communards could not overcome the fact that the Commune was isolated and so condemned to defeat. We do not wish to be responsible for an adventure. We wish to progress steadily towards our goal, taking the mass of the people with us towards a better life, avoiding both adventurism and demagogy.

Most observers are agreed that the Communists themselves did not in fact accept this justification of their policy by the lessons of history, but preferred the explanation given by Gitton: 'Given the Nazi menace, a policy which involved risks for French national security was impossible for us.' The Communists felt obliged to avoid doing anything which might weaken the military potential and diplomatic weight of France, simultaneously an ally of the Soviet Union, and the supposed pivot of the Western democracies' defensive strategy.

It was on this central question of the defence of the 'democracies' allied to the USSR against international fascism that the important Communist turn had already taken place in 1934. Their behaviour during the 1936 strikes and the following months was only the logical extension of their acceptance of the Stalinist strategy of the defence of the Soviet Union.

Communist Party members during the strikes

The official figures given by the Communist Party leaders show the extraordinary growth in the party's membership:

	Total (including Young Communists)	Young Communists
25 May 1936	163,000	38,000
(Thorez — report to central committee 25 June 1936)		
30 May 1936	170,400	40,200
(letter from the Communist Party to the Socialist Party Congress)		
4 June 1936	173,900	40,800
(l'**Humanité** — article by J Duclos)		
18 June 1936	200,600	46,000
(declaration by Gitton)		

	Total (including Young Communists)	Young Communists
8 July 1936	246,000	63,000
(Thorez in l'Humanité)		
11 July 1936	252,200	65,000
(Gitton, at Communist Party national conference)		
6 August 1936	303,000	78,000
(Thorez in report of the same date)		
28 August 1936	330,200	86,000
(Gitton, in l'Humanité of 29 August)		
6 September 1936	336,500	87,000
(l'Humanité of 7 September)		
2 October 1936	363,000	93,000
(l'Humanité of 3 October)		
29 October 1936	380,000	100,000
(l'Humanité of 30 October)		

The rapid growth in party membership during and just after the strikes showed two things. On the one hand, the Communist activists had played a very active role in the strikes. Their organising abilities and tireless devotion to the cause carried them into positions of responsibility, where their example was a powerful pole of attraction to other workers. This helped recruitment, and the extension of the party's influence over wide layers of workers, as was evidenced by the increased circulation of the Communist Party papers. On the other hand, those workers who stood out as the most dynamic and the most class-conscious during disputes, who were thus propelled by their workmates into the leadership of the strike committees were, to begin with, simple union members, but as the situation evolved they inevitably began to come to grips with the political aspects of the strikes, and they turned towards the party which seemed to them to offer the best promise of the revolutionary solution for which they were groping.

The Socialist Party and the Popular Front

From 4 June onwards there was no longer such a thing as a Socialist Party policy independent of the government. **Le Populaire** became a kind of official newspaper which in all circumstances displayed irrepressible optimism and blind faith in the 'comrade (or citizen) ministers'. Leaving aside the special situation of the revolutionary tendency inside the party, the *Gauche Revolutionnaire*, an examination of the Socialist Party's politics is therefore necessarily primarily a study of government policy. This was itself based on a fundamental ambiguity whose elements we shall attempt to unravel.

It is easy to contrast the Socialist Party's political orientation at the time when the Popular Front programme was worked out with its attitude to the formation of the government. The party's representatives on the committee in charge of drawing up the action programme were more intransigent than the Communists, and wanted to include a series of nationalisations in the reforms to be laid before the verdict of the electorate. This was not simply a question of rhetoric, or a desire to embarrass the Communists. There is no doubting the good faith of the Socialist Party leaders or their sincere desire to bring about the nationalisation of credit and insurance. But the policies of French social democracy have always consisted of a broad reform programme devoid of the means of implementation.

Thus it is not surprising that, when they were put to the test, the Socialist leaders became more mindful than anyone else of the pact's more modest proposals and followed to the letter the twists and turns of parliamentary formalism.

The aim of the Blum experiment was to discover within the existing framework of society 'adequate means of redress for those who are suffering the most', in order to extract from it 'maximum order, well-being, security and justice'. There was no question of destroying the capitalist system, 'which still has plenty of life left in it.'[12] Even if they had wanted to, they were prohibited by the Popular Front programme, for 'we are a Popular Front government, and not a Socialist government; our aim is not to transform the social system, but to carry out the Popular Front programme.'

To those who told him 'you are attempting to save bourgeois society,' Léon Blum replied:

> The ruin of bourgeois society has in fact already been achieved; a society is doomed when it is riven by insoluble internal contradictions. It is doomed when the needs of the productive forces have become incompatible with the existing legal property relationships; it is doomed when it has begun to negate the simple and eternal demands of human intelligence and morality.

What methods would Blum use to draw the maximum well-being from a ruined society? For him the Popular Front was no different from the other electoral alliances which were common during the life of the French Third Republic:

> An alliance between Radicals and Socialists has often existed in various forms. It has been called support, cartel, republican discipline . . . we will attempt to prove that it can be durable and effective . . .[13] The Popular Front government will take office in a completely normal way [since] we have agreed to accept the norm, the constitutional tradition.

The Socialist Party and the mass strikes

Léon Blum expected his government to last a long time; he reckoned on the support of a large and probably stable majority in the Chamber, stretching from the Radicals to the Communists. He believed that the masses would behave themselves. Certainly he was aware of their anxious impatience, but he expected that the material benefits which he was about to provide would calm their desires for change, given the 'tangible, imaginative, significant and substantial' results of his first governmental measures. From then on,

> the masses will give us plenty of time to work with, and we shall draw towards us all the doubters, all the people anxiously waiting or searching without knowing exactly what for, those who in other countries once formed the shock troops, and now form the armies of the victorious dictators.

As it turned out the workers did not fulfil Blum's confident expectations and confronted him on 4 June with a situation both unforeseen and unwelcome. There was only one course of action open to him: negotiate and mediate to blunt the sharpness of the struggle, while the Socialist Party activists were given the job of 'making sure that the strike-wave did not escape from the union leaders' control.'

Léon Blum gave a lengthy explanation at his Riom trial of his government's attitude to the occupation strikes. He described his two main priorities in June '36: firstly, re-establish order, and reimpose recognition of the rights of property, which had incontestably been violated; secondly, avoid violence and bloodshed.

> A government is not always faced with only one task at a time. Governments, like individuals, are sometimes faced with conflicting, even, incompatible duties, and they are obliged to try to establish an order of priority between equally compelling tasks, such as the need to defend the right of property, and at the same time the need to keep the peace . . . The duty which took priority over all others at that time was the duty to maintain public order, to keep the peace between citizens . . .
>
> The immense head of steam building up amongst huge numbers of workers, evoked by Mr Sarraut in his speech to the Senate in which he quoted the words of the employers themselves [proves that] any effort to have the workers forcibly removed from the factories would have led to violent clashes or bloody warfare . . . My clear, imperative duty was to save France from civil war . . . And in any case, my mind was already made up; I had no intention of using force. I would never have sent in the riot police, and the army after them . . . If I had not been able to bring about a return to public order by means of persuasion and mediation between workers and employers, I would have resigned from office, and perhaps even given up political life.

And Blum made clear:

A few months later the situation changed . . . we were able to enforce the law without running the same risks. The priority among conflicting duties changed from that moment on. We had no hesitation in enforcing respect for the law of property. If [in June] I had had to deal with only 10,000 strikers, the situation would have been very much easier.

The conclusion to be drawn from these observations made in 1942 seems to be that for Léon Blum, in this conflict between the aspirations of the working class and bourgeois property rights, his government's policy was to be dictated by the balance of class forces. In June, the clearing of the factories by force would have led to bloody confrontation with no certainty of success at the end of it, and this was apparently the only motive which held Blum and Salengro back from a policy of repression.

Such an interpretation seems to us to be mistaken. The circumstances in which Blum made these declarations must be borne in wind. Before the Vichy judges, he had to accept the terms of the debate as being 'dereliction of the duties entrusted to him,' and there can be no doubt that the views he expressed at the trial did not correspond to his intentions as head of the government. Nevertheless, there is a certain logic to this ambiguity. Léon Blum had agreed to try out his governmental 'experiment' within the traditional framework of capitalism and bourgeois democracy. The first problem he had to solve was the choice between his proclaimed fidelity to the working class and his position as manager of the economic interests of the bourgeoisie. Having never envisaged a possible socialist solution to this dilemma, he was obliged to call on all the resources of his subtle intellect in order to steer his way out of a difficult situation. He negotiated, he pacified, he tolerated the occupations, but at the same time Salengro was taking 'security measures'.

Faced with the dilemma presented by the workers — either lead a capitalist government which represses all breaches of the law, or lead the working class in its assault on the structures of the capitalist system — the Socialist Party chose an intermediate solution, 'the reformist solution, which attempts to resolve the contradiction.'[14] It was an impossible task. In the Senate on 7 July, Salengro disowned the factory occupations, and was forced to promise that he would not tolerate them any longer. This declaration provoked so much indignation that he was later obliged to retract it,[15] but the government did indeed eventually contrive to isolate the remaining occupations and proceed to forcible evacuations.

The same contradiction was at work in relations between government and parliament. Léon Blum told the Socialist Party's national council on 10 May:

I do not want to use the language of intimidation, but no one should forget that we are not just a few isolated individuals. No one should forget that we speak for vast numbers . . . to whom there would be no need to appeal a second time for help if their will was flouted.

And Salengro gave a warning on 19 July at Lille:

to those whose manoeuvrings are aimed at overthrowing the Popular Front government . . . The day the government fell, the debate would be carried on in the streets.

But this somewhat reckless bravado produced such consternation 'in political circles' that Salengro had to retract his remarks, which had been reproduced in full by all the journalists who had heard them . . . except the correspondent of **le Populaire**, the Socialist Party's own paper. A few months later, when the government was defeated in the conservative Senate, Léon Blum meekly went along to the Elysée palace to tender his resignation.

One final example of the fundamental contradictions which the Socialist Party seemed to delight in. 'We hear a lot about the flight of capital, and the amount of gold which is crossing the frontier,' wrote Paul Faure shortly after the elections . . .

It is a contemptible business, but it may prove to be a dangerous game for those who play it. Sabotage of the national interest, and its toleration by the government, whether through weakness or complicity, is a thing of the past. The people have spoken. The verdict is binding on us all, even the mightiest in the land.[16]

A little while later, Blum and Auriol poured forth reassuring declarations designed to show that the capitalists' fears were without foundation, and that there would be no tampering with the freedom of the currency exchanges.

The Socialist Party *Gauche Révolutionnaire*

The Socialist Party divided into three main tendencies at its June Congress. There was a majority tendency around Blum and Paul Faure; there was Zyromski's pro-Communist group, and there was the *Gauche Révolutionnaire*, the 'revolutionary left', whose main strength was in the Paris region, and whose best-known leader was Marceau Pivert.

Pivert and the leftists criticised Léon Blum as early as 10 May for not having insisted on taking office straight after the elections:

The leading bodies of the party are lagging behind the masses, whose initiative and activity are the supreme guarantees of our victory. We must . . . in three days root out the fascist sympathisers among the top civil servants; in three weeks rescue all the victims of the crisis from the stranglehold which is squeezing the life out of them; in three months, bring about such an upturn in economic activity, such an increase in the workers' standard of living that the immense majority of people will be won over to socialism.[17]

A little later Pivert was to write:

Everything is possible. Yes, everything is possible for those who dare to act, thanks to the atmosphere of victory, confidence and discipline which is spreading over the country. Let's mobilise the party; let's get others to follow us; let's decide; let's act; let's take up the challenge. And nothing will be able to stand in our way . . . The Radicals won't dare to try . . . [for] they have no taste for political suicide, and that would certainly be the outcome of their resistance to the masses' growing pressure for change . . . And it is not true that our brothers in the Communist Party can or wish to hold back the hour of social revolution in France for the sake of diplomatic considerations, important though these are . . . The masses are much more advanced than is realised . . . they want more than a cup of hot sweet tea brought on tip-toe to their bedside . . . Everything is possible, now, at top speed; such an opportunity will surely not come again soon.[18]

But the *Pivertistes* were a small minority in the party, and their own position was not free of contradictions. In spite of their declarations of principle, their practice was effectively to support Léon Blum.[19] At the party congress they rallied to the compromise motion which was carried unanimously. After the formation of the government Marceau Pivert even accepted an official post in the press department of the prime minister's office, and thus found himself obliged to support government policy.

Socialist Party members in the strikes

The part played by Socialist Party members in the June strikes has attracted relatively little attention from other commentators. However, particularly in the Paris region, where the Pivert supporters had their greatest influence, the Socialist Party members, a large number of whom were long-standing trade union members, were actively involved in the strikes of white-collar sections such as those in commerce, the big stores and the insurance companies. They proceeded more prudently, more diplomatically, but no less courageously than the Communists, in an area where the members were untested and had no traditions of struggle, and where those who turned out to be the most dynamic and the best organisers had to learn as they went along.

The party membership grew extremely rapidly,[20] and Paul Faure announced in November that the number of members had doubled since May '36 and that the Federations of the *Seine* and the *Nord* together had the same number of members as the party as a whole had had after the split of 1920.

The new members came primarily from the petty bourgeoisie, so the party decided to create the so-called *amicales socialistes*, as units of organisation in the factories to try to match the influence of the Communist Party's factory cells.

The Socialist Party put its trust in Léon Blum and his attempted experiment within the framework of the capitalist and parliamentary system. In this way the party hoped to find a way towards democratic socialism, for, according to Blum, even if the Popular Front government failed in its task, the masses would understand that this did not prove that socialism was impossible. On the contrary, it would be the proof that socialism was the only possible solution, as the capitalist system would have shown its inability to relieve the people's distress and satisfy their needs.

The whole orientation of French social democracy and reformism was on trial, and by its ambiguity and fundamental weakness it inevitably botched the 'opportunity which will surely not come again soon'.

The Trotskyists

We shall give less attention here to the practical intervention of the Trotskyist activists in the strikes than to their theoretical positions, expressed mainly in Léon Trotsky's articles[21] and in **La Lutte Ouvrière**, weekly paper of the Internationalist Workers' Party (POI).[22] The main thrust of Trotsky's analysis in the months before the elections was directed at the 'Popular Front' slogan itself, which he regarded as an ambiguous formulation masking class antagonism, and likely to disarm the workers' movement.

For Trotsky, the crucial factor in the situation was the dislocation of the French economy, which faced only two alternatives — fascism, or the overthrow of the capitalist system. In 1934 the people had forced fascism to retreat, and brought home to the bourgeoisie the need for prudence and temporisation. The Communist Party, abandoning its leftist phraseology and its dreams of taking over the streets, had turned sharply to the right. Faced with the threat from Nazi Germany, the Kremlin's diplomacy had turned towards France, but had forgotten, said Trotsky, that 'from 1918 to 1923 Soviet foreign policy often found itself obliged to manoeuvre and make deals, but no section of the International ever considered the idea that it could make an alliance with its own bourgeoisie.'

Stalin thought that a policy of 'status quo' in international relations should be accompanied by a policy of 'status quo' within France itself. Hence the alliance with the Radicals and the Popular Front, a 'safety valve to deal with action from below'. The Communist Party presented this agreement as an alliance 'between working class and middle classes', which was a caricature of Marxism.[23]

> To pretend that Herriot-Daladier are likely to make war on the two hundred families is to deceive the people. It is not a question of a struggle between the 'nation' and a few feudalists, but the class struggle between proletariat and bourgeoisie.

And Trotsky concluded:

> The fight against the two hundred families, fascism and war is either simply a trick, or else it is a fight to destroy the capitalist system. The French workers' task in the coming period is to face up to the problem of the conquest of power.

The workers' revolutionary mood was confirmed for Trotsky by the elections, when they voted massively for the Communist Party and ditched the neo-Socialists and the Radicals who were only saved from a worse fate by the workers' parties. Both the Socialists and Communists were preparing for a Radical-led government, but the workers' votes insisted on Léon Blum. From now on the fate of France was to be decided not in parliament, but in the strike-bound factories, to which Trotsky, the leader of the future Fourth International, looked for the emergence of *soviets*.[24] He wrote on 9 June:

> The French Revolution has begun. These are not craft strikes that have taken place. These are not just strikes. This is *a strike*. This is the open rallying of the oppressed against the oppressors.[25]

Certainly the first wave might die down, life return to an appearance of normal. But it was nonetheless true that the whole class had moved into action and that the struggle must finish either with the greatest of victories, or with a terrible crushing defeat. The uncertainty of the outcome lay in the lack of a revolutionary leadership while the class enemy disposed of a veritable general staff which was now giving most of the ground, but would soon return to the attack, through parliament, the Senate and the civil service. The working class had to forge a new leadership in the midst of the struggle. 'Soviets everywhere? Agreed! But it is time to pass from words to deeds.'

When the strike wave was over, Trotsky drew the lessons from the movement, showing that the reforms wrenched from the enemy by the workers' struggles could not be tolerated by French capitalism, given the ramshackle state of the economy, and that the much-wooed middle class would finish up as the victims of the experiment. If there were no new workers' offensive, this time carried right through to the end by a new revolutionary leadership, which would transform the half-defeat of June into a stage on the road to victory, then the defeat would last for many years, for already 'finance capital, with its auxiliary political organs, is cold-bloodedly preparing for revenge.'[26]

On the basis of this analysis, what slogans did the French Trotskyists put forward, which were to bring down the government's thunder on their heads? **La Lutte Ouvrière** of 12 June[27] headlined across its whole front page: 'In the factories and the streets, power to the workers!' and listed the movement's next targets:

> Move from strike committees to permanent factory committees . . .
> Form armed workers' militias . . . Join the factory committees together,
> and organise a Congress of factory committees to lead the struggle . . .
> Form committees of unemployed, soldiers, and peasants, alongside the
> factory committees.

Despite their slogans, the weakness of the Trotskyists' influence in June 1936 made a pure fantasy of those accounts which saw the POI members as the fomenters of the strikes, or as the *agents provocateurs* who were trying to turn purely economic strikes into political ones. Like all of the workers' parties, however, they saw their numbers and their relative influence growing in the months which followed.

The anarchists

At first sight, the political positions of the French libertarians, who within the trade union movement were to be found both in the *Confédération Générale du Travail Syndicaliste Révolutionnaire* and in the CGT, seemed similar to those of the Trotskyists. They were marked by the same distrust of the Popular Front, the same hostility towards a political movement which tied the working class to a section of bourgeois ideology — radicalism, and the same appeal for independent working-class action.

'The Popular Front victory is not defeat for the bourgeoisie,' noted **le Libertaire** on 1 May, 'prepare for direct and revolutionary workers' action!' On 5 June: 'Strike for bread! . . . the Engineers show the way.' On the 12th: 'The working class will have the last word. Direct action triumphs over parliamentary impotence.'

But the theoretical foundations of anarchism are different from those of Leninism, to which the Trotskyists adhered. For the anarchists, the fight against the bourgeois state is accompanied by a fight against those political aspects of the workers' struggle which tend to set up organs of dual power and to destroy the bourgeois state, replacing it with a socialist one. So the anarchists stressed that the June victories were brought about by those actions of the workers which showed the most distrust of elements of the state apparatus,[28] and congratulated the workers on avoiding overt politicisation of the strikes. In the anarchists' eyes, the great merit of the strikes was their tendency to remain within the domain of pure class demands untainted by political nuances.

In arriving at this position the anarchists were influenced equally by their basic principles, and by their hostile suspicion of the Stalinist Communists, whom they mistrusted, and whose growing influence over the working class they feared.

A reading of le Libertaire, their weekly paper, demonstrates the anarchists' lack of influence in the factories. There are few, if any, reports of workers' actions involving members of the anarchist federation and the paper's investigation into the origins of the factory occupations was never finished.

The CGT and the strikes

Did the CGT plan the strikes?

The CGT had made a ringing appeal to the workers on 1 May 1936: 'Workers, shoulder to shoulder in invincible unity, FORWARD!' However, during the course of May there was nothing in the CGT *bureau confédéral*'s demeanour which indicated that they were preparing a large-scale working-class offensive to fight for their slogans, nothing to indicate that they were mobilising their troops and arming their members for a campaign of industry-by-industry strikes.

The meeting of the *comité confédéral national* on 18 May was wholly and exclusively devoted to a discussion of Léon Blum's offer of a share in the government. The very academic debates, and the unanimous resolution which brought the monthly meeting to a close, contained no hint of an appeal for direct action. On the contrary, the Socialist Party leader was informed of the confederation's sympathy and support, and assured that while they preferred not to take any posts in the government, the CGT leaders were in favour of maximum participation in the government's technical and economic committees.

The report to the committee by CGT general secretary Jouhaux did not hint at any rapid fulfillment of the workers' demands for the 40-hour week, collective agreements, and so on, other than by the good offices of Blum the law-maker and — before the new laws came into effect — by government pressure on firms willing to do a deal with the state. The only speaker to allude to the possibility of independent action by the workers' organisations was Dumoulin, secretary of the *Union Départementale du Nord*, and his contribution was couched in very careful and moderate terms:

I am absolutely certain that we shall collaborate closely with the new government. But we should not act like a unit of the fire brigade. We are being asked to counsel patience. All right! It would be wrong of us to stand out against the general effort in this direction. But we should not turn ourselves into handers-out of tranquillisers. We have to gauge exactly how far to go in the struggle against poverty. We mustn't go too far, but we mustn't abdicate either.[29]

Did the federations themselves welcome the upsurge which the Confederation had done nothing at all to prepare them for? Hardly, as can be shown by an example from the building industry. On 29 May the committee of the Paris region building workers' federation met to plan for 'a big demonstration in favour of collective agreements by the Parisian building workers on 30 June.' One week later the federation had to issue a hasty order for a general strike in order to regain control of the spreading wave of stoppages.

The CGT during the strikes

In every phase of the strikes the CGT expressed its solidarity with the strikers. It followed the movement in order to try and give the impression that it was in control, and, as Lefrance has noted, 'the union movement exerted a powerful influence in the direction of restoring order,' by limiting and channelling the strikes.

In limiting the strikes, the CGT unions firstly exerted their moderating influence on the industries involved in essential services, which they wanted to isolate from the strike epidemic at all costs.[30] They first concentrated their attention on the public utilities, which, at least in Paris, were never interrupted. It is not without interest to note that the CGT had its greatest roots, and consequently its greatest influence, in this sector. The Confederation next turned to workers concerned with the preparation and distribution of foodstuffs, 'since the workers obviously understand the need to retain the full support of public opinion'.

Secondly they discouraged strike action: since the Matignon agreement was a victory for all workers, there should in no case be a recourse to strike action before the presentation of a list of demands, and discussion of these with the employer. A strike should only be decided on in the event of an employer's consistent refusal to discuss the workers' demands.

Thirdly there was the appeal to the authorities: in any case of a breach of a signed agreement by the employer, the workers should make an appeal through their union, at local, regional or national level, to the government for enforcement of the terms of the agreement. The unions were concerned, obviously, to avert fresh stoppages by workers who had previously ended their dispute.

And fourthly there were limitations on the forms which strike action should take: in July the CGT leaders fell into line with the slogans of the workers' parties, and condemned the use of the occupation tactic.

The CGT also set out to channel the strike movement away from political demands. 'The anarchic movement spread without knowing what demands to register,' writes Lefranc. 'The trade unions gave it a programme, of which the first effect was to bring a measure of discipline to the vast army.' This comment goes to the heart of the matter. The strikes did indeed break out spontaneously, often in firms where there were no union members. The strikers then turned to the unions for help in drawing up their lists of demands;[31] the result was that the unions unified the demands, but limited them at the same time.

However, once the demands were established, the workers wanted them met in total, and rejected the compromises recommended by the officials. This was at the root of the several successive instances of officials being disowned by mass meetings of strikers.

In order to channel the movement the union leaders sometimes resorted to calling an official general strike — as happened in the building industry, the mines, and cafés, hotels and restaurants — which allowed them to centralise the strikes and limit their duration and their objectives.

When strikes carried on in spite of agreements sponsored by the unions — the workers proving in this way their readiness to fight for more — the federations' every effort was bent towards the problem of getting the strikers to accept a return to work. In no case were further demands raised. In particular, the slogan of workers' control which figured in the CGT programme was never given prominence, even though the power, scope and character of the mass movement demanded exactly that.

Finally, in insisting on a return to work, the unions sometimes brought pressure to bear in fairly dubious ways which amounted to a betrayal of the workers' clearly and decisively-expressed wishes. When the engineers or builders demanded that their settlements should include payment for the days on strike, the union leaders signed without obtaining anything at all on this point from the employers.

Limiting strikes and the channelling of the movement, became in the CGT's vocabulary, maintenance of order and discipline, neutralisation of *provocateurs*, and defence of the Popular Front programme. The CGT indeed regarded itself as bound by the Popular Front pact, and endorsed its methods and tactics.

The CGT and the Popular Front

The CGT was doubly tied to the Popular Front. First of all because of the direct or indirect affiliation of its leading members to one or other of the workers' parties, whose policies they therefore followed. These policies consisted of stressing the unity of the working-class forces, and damming the strike wave. This explains the joint support of the two wings of the CGT for the lines of action which we have just analysed. Former CGT and former CGTU members, while disputing amongst themselves for the positions of influence in all the different unions, and at the different levels of the confederation, were unanimous when it came to voting for the important resolutions which would decide their strategy.

Secondly, the CGT was of course bound organically to the Popular Front as a constituent member, and its own programme had been put in cold storage. It was the government's programme which commanded the confederation's loyalty, and marked the limits of possible action, as was shown for example by the CGT's acquiescence in what we have called the 'second Matignon agreement'.

The CGT leaders justified their policies in the same terms as the workers' parties. They took every opportunity to stress that the government was giving unreserved support to the workers in their negotiations with the employers, and warned that there must be no reckless action which might put the government in difficulties.

They were also at pains to destroy the workers' lingering illusions in the outcome of the struggle. They should not believe that the final combat was at hand; this was only one of a number of class actions which marked out the movement's history. There had been many others in the past, and there would be more, aimed at new conquests . . . but later. For the moment, aspirations must be limited to what was underwritten by Matignon. The workers first had to show that they were capable of playing a decisive role in the nation's affairs, by showing their sense of responsibility, avoiding disorder and adventurism, and by honouring the signature inscribed by their leaders on their behalf.

The growth of the CGT

During the strikes, the CGT expanded enormously. Membership rose from one million before the strikes to 2,500,000 on 15 June,[32] and this explosive growth did not slow down until the figure of five million was reached in 1937. For the first time in French history there was mass trade unionism.

Until 1936, trade unionism in France had always been a minority current, a state of affairs welcomed by those who believed above all in the effectiveness of small groups of revolutionary activists, and accepted by others as an inevitable consequence of the structure of the French workers' movement. The unexpected encounter in 1936 between millions of workers and organised trade unionism had important consequences, allied to not a few difficulties. The first consequence was the overturning of the balance of forces within the CGT itself, in favour of the manual workers' federations which soon vastly outnumbered those of the civil servants and public service workers. This was the root cause of the decline of the reformists' strength, and the growing influence of the Communists.

Relations between the rank and file and the union leaders began to change in ways which the CGT attempted to take account of by mounting an extensive educational programme. This was to be the domain of the *Centre Confédéral d'Education Ouvrière*, whose efforts to provide the new members with training in trade union affairs were designed to limit the losses already expected by Jouhaux at a time when the CGT's membership was barely half of what it would be six months later.

The Confederation of Christian Workers

Here we ought to give a rapid analysis of the position of the *Confédération Française des Travailleurs Chrétiens* (CFTC) in the events of May–June 1936, though their role in the strikes was of course a minor one. The confederation endorsed the workers' demands as defined by the CGT, and to this end they were able to rely on several declarations emanating from the highest ecclesiastical authorities at the beginning of June.

On the 5th, Cardinal Verdier issued an 'Appeal to all Catholics' which, after an examination of conscience admitting Christians' share of the responsibility for the 'deficiencies of our social system', encouraged the faithful to 'lose no time in contributing courageously to the construction of the new order which everyone desires'. Monsignor Saliège and Monsignor Chollet in turn declared that 'Christianity is no friend of capitalism', and that 'the present social system cannot survive . . . based on the supremacy of money, devoid of all Christian spirit, tained with injustice and egoism, it is in chaos.'

The church authorities invited Catholics to join the CFTC,[33] and warned them against the attentions of the Communists.

During the strikes the CFTC's main preoccupation was to try to break out of the isolation in which the CGT tried to confine it. On 8 June the Catholic confederation wrote to Léon Blum asking to be included in the Matignon agreement. They had no role in the negotiations in the engineering industry, nor in construction, mines or the department stores. They were present, on the other hand, at the discussions affecting banking and insurance, and they signed numerous collective agreements.

But the CFTC's agreement on the demands raised did not extend to agreement on ways of winning them. The confederation opposed the occupations as being against its established principles of class collaboration.[34] CFTC members nonetheless took part in them and were met very often by extremely conciliatory attitudes on the part of the Communists.[35]

Like the CGT, the CFTC experienced rapid expansion in its membership, and its paper, **Syndicalisme**, which until then had been a monthly, began weekly publication.[36]

The channelling of the movement by the unions and the workers' parties

Various commentators have attempted an explanation of the origins of the May–June strikes. Some have seen in them the proof of a Communist 'plot',[37] conceived with the aim of taking power, or at the very least of discrediting the Socialist leaders by forcing them into conflict with the working class. Others talked of provocation by the employers, and yet others of secret machinations by the Blum government. But most, including the most serious, recognise that the fundamental cause of the strike wave must be sought in the conditions endured by the workers themselves. Driven to the point of striking by their miserable standards of living, all they needed was confidence in their own strength, which was provided by the new-found unity in their ranks, and by their electoral victory. As René Belin wrote:

People humiliated, exhausted by want, and beginning to raise their heads, that is the deepest and simplest explanation of the strikes. A concrete fact — hunger; a favourable climate — victory at the polls; faith rediscovered — union unity; a hypnotic example — Paris engineering. That is all there is to the mystery.[38]

Léon Blum added:

In the engineering industry, one of the causes of the strikes was the employers' prolonged refusal to meet the unions . . . It was natural, indeed obvious that the election results would give the workers hope that their demands would be more favourably received. What is more, anyone who has any experience of working-class life knows that it is impossible to separate completely the masses' political behaviour from their direct action.[39]

But the same writers, imagining that their explanations cannot account for all aspects of the strikes, seemed to find it necessary to bring in the occult powers of *provocateurs*, whom they blamed for the swamping of the union machines and for the revolutionary tendencies which we have described. Some persisted in discerning the hand of the Communist Party,[40] while others, more numerous, denounced Trotskyist or anarchist agitators.

The analysis we have made of the political attitudes of the various organisations, and their relative strengths at the beginning of the strikes should be enough to discount these fantastic suggestions, whose origins can only be their authors' shared fear of the truth. From the beginning of time the employing class, when faced by a workers' revolt, have always denounced ringleaders and agitators so as not to have to look upon the realities of the workers' conditions. In the same way the imperialist bourgeoisie faced with colonial rebellion looks no further than the actions of a few fanatics, or interference by a foreign power. It came as no surprise to find Mr de Kerillis[40] demanding that Trotskyists and Communists be brought to trial, thinking in this way to quell the workers' agitation. But when Blum and Thorez spoke in the same tones in 1936, this was something new. It had an obvious significance: all the workers' leaders desired to hold back a movement which was threatening to overwhelm them.

★ ★ ★

The actions of individual political or union militants had a decisive effect in sparking off the first strikes in the Paris region. But the important thing was that they immediately got the ear of the masses. It is very revealing to compare the repeated failures of the CGT-U in its attempts to start strikes, at a time when the Communist Party was daily talking recklessly about taking to the streets and setting up *soviets*, with the sweeeping success of the strikes for which no organisation claimed responsibility, and which were supported by the workers' newspapers only after they had begun.

Why this success? Because the working class had raised their self-confidence, because they were confident of their power as a result of the victorious struggle against the fascists, the reunification of the trade union movement and their election victory. This victory at the polls had two consequences for the workers. It proved the power of the alliance between their two parties, and it promised relative neutrality from the transitional government as well as positive sympathy from the government which would succeed it.

The final factor accounting for the immediate spread of the strikes was that for the masses the long years of want had made any possibility of delay in the redress of their grievances intolerable.

The movement now began to develop its own dynamic. Confidence grew with the reporting of early successes; demands met led immediately to the birth of new hopes, the discovery of new needs, the drawing up of new and more far-reaching demands. As Simone Weil wrote:

> As soon as the pressure began to slacken the suferings, humiliations, rancour and bitterness silently accumulated year after year immediately gathered a force sufficient to burst all bounds . . . Why did the workers not wait for the formation of the new government? . . . first of all, because they were not strong enough to wait. [Above all] because this wave of strikes was about something much more than this or that particular demand, however important . . . It was about daring at last to stand up straight, after bowing down so long, after accepting every insult and every indignity in silence for months and years. About getting off their knees. Speaking up for themselves. About feeling like human beings for a few days at least . . .[42]

This desire to feel like men meant, when it came to discussing the lists of demands, not giving in, sticking it out till the end, rejecting all compromise. It also meant trying to avoid having to return to the condition of 'human machines, isolated, suffering individuals with no means of escape.'[43] It meant, inside the factories, trying to hang on to that heady feeling of enjoyment of one's own spontaneous self-discipline, which came from working not for the boss, but for oneself, and for everyone.

That is why, when the agreements came to be signed, all the workers felt that what had been achieved was derisory when compared with their towering hopes. To the political activists, who understood the import and the revolutionary potential of such a mass mobilisation of workers, they were a betrayal.

The Downturn

These desires for change, this willingness to fight on for decisive victories, were accompanied by limitless illusions and collided with the efforts by the government the Communist Party and the unions to apply the brake.

Again in the words of Simone Weil, although 'the workers were not willing to wait for the formation of the new government . . . we should not draw the hasty conclusion that the working class distrusted the parties or the state machine.' On the contrary, they wrongly believed that the Popular Front which they had voted into power, which supported them every day in negotiations with the employer, would provide the decisive change which they were looking for.

These illusions were vitally important when the government,

the Communist Party and the CGT threw all their weight and all their prestige into the attempt to stop the strikes. We have shown how the movement in Paris subsided from 12 June onwards, after the hasty signature of the decisive collective agreements in engineering, construction and other industries. The workers thought they had won a very great victory and the Socialist and Communist papers maintained absolute silence about the last lingering resistance to a general return to work. When they did refer to it, it was in order to heap abuse, lumping anarchists, Trotskyists and fascists together, and accusing them of leading the workers into adventurism. A few isolated cases of resistance apart, the workers heeded the advice of their unions and their parties. There was no other organisation capable of showing them a way out of the impasse, destroying their illusions, and giving a form to their vague aspirations by means of concrete slogans.

So in June 1936, the French working class itself, as well as the Popular Front leaders, observed the limits which the latter had put upon their experiment.

The employers would need no more than two years to complete their revenge. But the workers had nevertheless exacted important social reforms, and some of these would never again be seriously challenged.

10
THE GAINS OF JUNE

THE WORKERS gained in two ways: directly from the employers through strike action, and through government legislation. Of course, if government and parliament had not been so pressured by the mass movement it is unlikely that the social reforms would have been passed and put into practice as quickly and fully as they were.

The collective agreements

Collective agreements were not completely unknown in practice or in French social law before 1936.[1] But their relative unimportance before June 1936 is shown by the following small table.

1919: 557 agreements made
1920: 345 agreements made
1925: 126 agreements made
1930: 72 agreements made
1933: 20 agreements made
1934: 24 agreements made
1935: 28 agreements made

According to a study done by the national economic council in 1934,[2] the conditions of barely 4 per cent of French workers were covered by collective agreements.

The first article of the Matignon agreement dealt with collective contracts, and its provisions were formalised and expanded by the law of 24 June 1936, of which the main elements were as follows. The contracts were to be negotiated with the most representative staff or union organisations in the industry, at the request of one of them. They were bound to include provisions for the right to belong to a union, for the functions of workers' delegates, for minimum wages for each grade of worker, for the length of holidays, the regulation of apprenticeships, procedures for conciliation and arbitration[3] and revisions of the contract itself. Contracts freely concluded between the different parties could be extended to the whole of the trade or the region by ministerial order.

In 1936, the Ministry of Labour recorded 1,123 contracts, and in 1937, 3,064. This shows how widely this new method of regulating working conditions was applied in practice. All commentators have described how the collective agreements wrought profound changes in the relationship between the employers and the working class. They deprived the bosses of one of their most cherished rights: 'The right to discuss working conditions face to face with each member of his staff.'[4] In general they had the effect of 'protecting the workers from the arbitrary power of the employers and ending their condition of abject dependence,' by substituting 'the collective strength of the class for the weakness of the isolated worker'[5] in negotiations.

Some saw in this the beginning of the end of capitalism, for example J-P Maxence:

> It was not the vacillating Blum government which carried out the structural reforms hoped for by the large numbers of gullible people who voted it into power. By mustering the power of strike action, the strength of the unions, the coercion of the occupations, that is, by methods which had nothing to do with the law, the industrial proletariat has imposed a profound structural reform which will sound the death-knell of liberalism. These collective contracts on working conditions do not derive naturally from the capitalist system, they are radically, doggedly, victoriously opposed to it.[6]

This attitude seems to us mistaken for two essential reasons.

Firstly, it was true that the collective agreements broke down the individual worker's isolation, which the employers had always tried to play upon, and they had an effect in stabilising wages and working conditions. But this stabilisation could be an obstacle to the improvement of conditions because the contract involved legal ties and obligations which would hinder independent working-class action.

Secondly, the collective agreements could act as a brake on the class struggle. Though they could be irritating to employers who wanted to cut wages, they tended at the same time to confine working-class action in a legal framework. This tendency was reinforced later by the legislation on compulsory arbitration.

But in the end each agreement could only be a reflection of the balance of class forces, and history had already shown this before

1936. In 1919–20, under the impact of a wave of strikes, a number of collective agreements were signed at the unions' demand. But the employers themselves were not averse to agreements which would impose a stable framework on working conditions continually subject to challenge by class action. As soon as circumstances changed, the employers opposed contracts which had for them become obstacles to wage 'adjustments', which, in short, prevented them from making the workers pay for the crisis. The employers' hostility is shown in the statistics by the small number of agreements signed in the 1920s, the weakened and divided workers' movement being unable even to defend the agreements already in force.

The situation evolved in the same way from 1936 to 1939, as is equally evident in the statistics.

1936: 1,123 agreements
1937: 3,064 agreements
1938:   972 agreements
1939:   461 agreements

Wages

We shall have several occasions to regret the sad lack of statistics which record the wages and purchasing power of workers in France before the Second World War. As we are unable to give any percentages for the overall increase in monthly or hourly wages which the workers enjoyed as a result of the 1936 strikes, we will have to limit ourselves to a few individual cases.

ONE: The Matignon agreement fixed the highest and lowest limits and the overall average for increases. The limits were 15 per cent and 7 per cent, with an average of 12 per cent in each firm. But the workers' action imposed a very wide interpretation of the Matignon provisions for the adjustment of abnormally low wages. At the same time, industry-wide or company agreements obliged the employers to pay increases on average very much higher than 12 per cent.

Thery notes that 'for many industries the original increases varied from 15 per cent to 20 per cent, and were sometimes as much as 25 per cent.'[7] In engineering[8] the average hourly wages in the Paris region were raised by 22 per cent:

Francs per hour for:	Tradesmen	Semi-skilled	Unskilled	Average
1936 1st quarter	6.35	5.05	4.09	5.62
1936 2nd quarter	7.43	6.60	5.55	6.84
Percentage rise	17%	30.1%	35.68%	21.7%

The increase was less in the coal mines, since it did not exceed 12.14 per cent for faceworkers and 16.47 per cent for surface workers, making an average of 13.51 per cent.

TWO: The collective agreements laid down scales of minimum rates for each trade. Their effect was therefore to standardise conditions in all factories covered by the agreement. At the same time they narrowed the gap between manual rates for men and those for women, reduced the overall differential between the highest and the lowest paid, and more often than not they abolished piece rates. Simone Weil underlined the psychological importance of these gains:

> I would like to draw attention to a question which particularly affects conditions in the prison-like machine-shops . . . That is, the consequences of the new wage-rates for the everyday life of the shop-floor. It would be deplorable . . . to maintain the old differentials between the different grades. Their abolition would be a tremendous relief, a giant step towards improving the relations between different grades. If one feels alone in a factory — and one does feel terribly alone — it is in large part because of the role played by these small differentials, big in relation to the paucity of the wages, in preventing the emergence of a feeling of comradeship between worker and worker.[9]

This reduction in the hierarchy of wage rates was undoubtedly a source of strength for the strike movement, helping to unify and reinforce the workers' struggles.

THREE: The sliding scale of wages to compensate for inflation, on the other hand, was a demand seldom raised or granted in June '36. Out of 700 collective agreements examined by Thomas,[10] only 114 contained clauses relative to a sliding scale, all using quite different methods to achieve their result.

The working week

The first article of the law of 21 June 1936 on the 40-hour week laid down that

> in all industrial, commercial, handicraft and professional establishments, and in their annexes of whatever kind, whether religious or lay, even if involved in vocational training or charitable work, including public hospitals and lunatic asylums, the number of hours worked by manual or white-collar workers of either sex and of any age shall not be more than 40 per week.

No reduction in salary was to follow from the reduction in hours of work, whose progressive application to each trade was to be regulated by ministerial decrees. The first such decree was dated 27 October 1936, and dealt with the engineering industry; more than 60 such decrees were published up to the end of 1937.

The 40-hour week was the measure which met with the strongest opposition in parliament, and its adoption without obstacles or delays was due above all to the persuasive power of the strikes.

Workers' delegates

The institution of the system of representation by workers' delegates resulted partly from the Matignon agreement, and partly from the law on collective agreements, which, as we have said already, made it compulsory for the new contracts to include 'the procedure for selecting workers' delegates in workplaces employing more than ten people.' In practice, all the collective agreements later signed reproduced the rules agreed at Matignon and filled out by the engineering industry agreement.

The delegates' role was to 'bring to management's attention individual grievances which cannot be settled at lower level, relating to application of wage-rates, the Code of Labour, and other regulations and laws governing working conditions, health and safety.'

The CGT considered that shop delegates should be controlled and supported by the union. Jouhaux told the *comité confédéral national* on 16 June:

> The experience last time[11] caused us plenty of problems. This is not the first time that shop delegates have been set up, especially in engineering. We know what the consequences of such a system were, because the unions were not involved from the beginning, and were unable to control the delegates' activities. Therefore, if we want a system of workers' delegates that will produce the results which the workers are hoping for, it is essential that the delegates should be elected and will fulfil their functions by and under the control of the trade unions. That does not mean that we want to interfere with the operation of universal suffrage . . . but the delegates should be nominated by the unions . . . certainly, they will have to be responsible to the whole workforce of the factory, but they will also have to have responsibilities towards the union.

This insistence on the role of the unions had a double motive: firstly to secure more independence for the delegate — his or her union designation would help to neutralise the pressure exerted by the employer; secondly to co-ordinate and harmonise the activities of all delegates within one workplace, and to link these activities with those of the local union section, which would be possible if each of the delegates lived 'in a union atmosphere . . . bounded by union preoccupations.'[12]

This attitude could have been more fruitful if the CGT had linked the setting up of a system of workers' delegates with the demand for workers' control, and had fought for an extension of their powers. But, given the delegates' limited scope for action as defined by the collective agreements, when the pressure coming from below was on the wane they found that their area of responsibility was reduced little by little until their role was no more than that of intermediary between management and their workmates.[13]

Paid holidays

The introduction of two weeks paid annual leave for all workers was one of the most popular of all the gains of June. During the summer of 1936, for the first time ever, hundreds of thousands of workers were able to leave their factory, their office, or even their town, and enjoy a period of rest and recuperation which had previously been the privilege of the bourgeois and middle classes.

Along with the reduction in the length of the working week, the paid holidays were the source of an immense boom in working-class tourism, which has been sustained since 1936 — except during the war years, and periods of sharp reduction in real wages.

The Popular Front legislation

The social reforms which we have just described formed part of the overall strategy of the Popular Front government which went under the name of 'the theory of increased purchasing power'.[14] The first thing to be said about this doctrine is that it was conceived as a way of levering capitalism out of its crisis, through an increase in wages and public expenditure. With an increasing volume of consumption calling forth increased production, the end result should be budgetary equilibrium due to higher tax returns caused by the improvement in economic activity. Blum explained:

> We want to give back the zest for work to those who are in danger of losing it. We want to tap the resources of our natural wealth, and that is what we mean when we use expressions like 'increase in total consumable incomes' that is, wages. We want to bring back a sense of security, and to promote more well-being, in so far as these things are possible, given the social system within which we are working. We are well aware that a nation cannot manage without proper and healthy finances, but, you know, we expect precisely a return to a real and stable budgetary equilibrium to result from an increase in national wealth, an increase in the total consumable income of the nation.[15]

To put these ideas into practice, parliament passed the law of 18 August 1936, setting up a programme of big public works aimed at reducing unemployment, and the law of 11 July 1936, providing for financial assistance to firms who were in difficulties as a result of the application of the social reforms.

Other parts of the government's programme passed at the same time were the raising of the school-leaving age,[16] the measures dealing with civil servants' pay, changes to the statutes of the Bank of France, nationalisation of war industries, and an amnesty for political offences.

A measure of benefit to the peasants was the law of 15 August 1936 setting up the Cereals Office, whose aim was to revalue wheat prices by clamping down on speculation. It was planned to fix a legally-enforceable price once a year.[17] The basis of the new organisation would be producer co-operatives which would buy grain and stockpile it. They would then sell according to a staggered programme worked out by the central council of the Cereals Office, which was also to have a monopoly of all imports and exports. The Senate, however, refused to agree to a monopoly of the entire home market for the Cereals Office and its co-operatives.

Two other points in the Popular Front's social and economic programme did not become law — the creation of a national system of unemployment benefit, and old-age pensions for workers.

Leisure activities for the workers, and popular culture

Léon Blum told his judges at Riom:

> I did not often come out of my ministerial office during the life of my government, but each time I did emerge to traverse the great suburban districts of Paris I found the streets full of old bangers, motorbikes and tandems bearing working-class couples whose variegated pullovers revealed that their ideas about the uses of leisure included the revival of a simple and natural affectation in dress. I had the feeling that, despite everything, I had given them a respite, a break in the clouds, which hovered over their hard and humble lives. We had not only dragged them out of the bars, not only given them the chance of a proper family life, but we had also opened up a future, given them hope.

Within the government, Léon Blum created the post of under-secretary of state for sport and leisure, with responsibility for encouraging and helping workers to gain more access to culture, sport, and tourism. The job went to Léo Lagrange, whose name has ever after been linked in France with the expansion of workers' excursions, camping, youth hostelling, and non-commercial sport. Lagrange introduced 'workers' holiday' tickets in conjunction with the railway companies, helped the Lay Centre for Youth Hostels to develop its network of hostels, and assisted the 'workers' sports and gymnastic federation' to expand its activities in proportion to the growth in its membership.[18]

The years 1936 and 1937 saw an influx of thousands of young

people into the Youth Hostel movement, most of them, it is true, ill-prepared for a collective way of life. The movement was swamped by a membership far out of proportion to its structure, and it lacked the necessary organisation to push through a programme of education and training for the new members, who all too often were content to use the hostels as a source of cheap tourist accommodation without acquiring the desired sense of solidarity and communal living. The early hostellers, strongly influenced ideologically by Jean Giono, did not sufficiently link their own problems with the general problems of the workers' movement, and allowed the development of all kinds of individualist and particularist tendencies which later led to the isolation of youth hostelling as a movement.

1936 was also the year which saw a tremendous boom in camping, previously popular only amongst rather select groups of nature-lovers, who were regarded by the rest of the population with astonishment and amusement.

We should also mention here the formation of intellectual groupings around the Popular Front,[19] the literary and aesthetic discussions on the theme of 'culture and the people', the efforts of the *Théâtre du Peuple*, supported by the CGT in Paris, the radio broadcasting group 'May 1936', and the production of the film 'The Marseillaise'.

These achievements were slight, it is true, when compared to the degree of popular enthusiasm. In the use of their leisure opportunities the workers showed the same maturity and the same high level of consciousness as in the conduct of their strikes. They had an interest in culture and a thirst for knowledge which could have had a considerable impact on all forms of artistic expression if the movement, here also a victim of its own failings, had not finally been led to defeat.

The Second Stage

Could the revolutionary offensive of June, with the conquests which we have here briefly described, be the prelude to a second onslaught from the workers which would this time clearly raise the question of power? The Socialist and Communist leaders had given their answer already. There was no question of socialism or communism, but rather an experimental Popular Front within the framework of the capitalist system. They believed that a balance between the existing social forces was possible; they thought that defence of the June victories was possible with the economic structure of France unchanged, dominated by the law of profit, and ruled by the traditional institutions of bourgeois democracy.

The second stage was indeed about to begin. Yet it was to be marked not by a resumed workers' offensive, but rather by a reconquest of the ground they had gained: by the capitalists' revenge. The inertia of the workers' organisations would allow the bourgeoisie to regroup their forces; price rises would wipe out the wage increases; financial problems would rock the Popular Front governments until they were finished off by the conservative Senate. Playing the game to the end, the workers' leaders would oppose any fight-back, while international preoccupations provided the pretext for any number of capitulations. The ranks of the workers would be ravaged by uncertainty and weariness. The hour of defeat was near.

11
THE BOURGEOIS COUNTER-OFFENSIVE

THE EMPLOYING CLASS were given a severe shock by the size of the strike-wave, which exposed the extent to which they were ill-informed and poorly organised. Their disarray did not last long. Important changes in the structure of the employers' organisations were under way from the beginning of August 1936. The *Confédération Générale de la Production Française* became the *Confédération Générale du Patronat Français*,[1] but more was involved than a simple name-change.

The old-style CGPF was criticised for not representing all branches of commerce and industry, and it was decided to bring the small and medium-sized firms into the new confederation. Co-ordination of the various federations and the authority of the centre was reinforced, with Mr Duchemin, castigated for his signature of the Matignon agreement, being forced to give way as president to Mr Gignoux. Under the new leadership, the department charged with studying employee affairs was strengthened, and a 'social forethought and action committee' was created in September 1936, with the tasks of influencing public opinion, and collecting and centralising information of use in resisting the workers' demands.[2]

All these preparations amounted to the institution of an employers' co-ordinating centre for resistance and counter-attack. The CGT congress recorded in 1938:

> From the summer of 1936 the employers began to organise resistance. It grew from month to month. The assistance which they soon received from the Senate encouraged them to continue on this path.

The Senate against factory occupations

From 7 July 1936 the Senate announced the beginning of a political counter-offensive, and the Socialist leaders rapidly found it awkward to satisfy workers and Senators at the same time, that is to prolong their ambiguous 'experiment' in Popular Front government by combining mass action with the defence of their record in parliament. On 7 July the Socialist Minister of the Interior, Roger Salengro, had to answer complaints concerning the maintenance of law and order, and the whole debate was rapidly focussed on the factory occupations.

The Senate sought to obtain the government's formal condemnation of the occupations, and the assurance that they would no longer be tolerated. The minister tried to throw off his pursuers; his replies were peppered with interruptions; the Senators returned obstinately to the charge. One last time, Mr Bienvenu-Martin called on Salengro to reply, in an exchange which is worth reproducing.

> *Mr Bienvenu-Martin*: This serious debate must not end with equivocation. (Applause.) As I had the occasion to say a moment ago, we believe that one of the most serious breaches of public order is the occupation of certain factories.
>
> *Several Senators*: And farms!
>
> *Mr Bienvenu-Martin*: And farms of course. I ask the Minister of the Interior if he shares our opinion. If so the result must be that any further occupations of factories would not be tolerated. (More applause from the same benches.)
>
> *Mr Salengro, Minister of the Interior*: I thought I had given the clearest of possible answers to Mr Bienvenu-Martin's question. (Exclamations and protests.) The answer which he wants is as follows. The government is determined to maintain public order. We intend to put a stop to any activities, arising from whatever quarter, which disturb the peace.
>
> If tomorrow there were occupations of shops, offices . . .
>
> *Several Senators*: Factories!
>
> *Salengro*: Factories.
>
> *Several Senators*: And farms!
>
> *Salengro*: Perhaps the Senate will accept that I am trying to put an end to any ambiguity. If tomorrow there were any attempts to occupy shops, offices, sites, factories or farms, the government would take all appropriate steps to bring them to an end. (Lively applause on the left and in the centre.)

The debate was closed. The Senate immediately and unanimously adopted a motion which 'noted the government's declaration', and did not even formally raise the question of 'confidence'.

But the second act was only just beginning. The workers gave vent to a highly understandable tremor of indignation. Delegations from the CGT and the *Union des Syndicats de Paris* went to see the minister, and at the close of their meeting the press published the following astounding communiqué:

> Mr Salengro told the Senate that he would take the appropriate steps to end the occupations, by which he meant: first, persuasion by the representatives of the trade union movement, and then by the government authorities; if this was not enough, there would be more vigorous intervention from the unions and from the authorities; if the desired result was still not obtained, then these two would mount a joint effort to persuade the workers to leave, and only if all these attempts at persuasion should fail would the government use different means. That is, they would send in the Gendarmes, having previously disarmed them.

The Senate had scored a point. So much so that the *Délégation des Gauches*[3] issued the following communiqué on 10 July:

> Regarding Roger Salengro's declarations to the Senate, we express our complete confidence in the Minister of the Interior, and appeal to the working class not to oblige the government to resort to force after exhausting all efforts at conciliation.

Likewise Maurice Thorez and Socialist Party secretary Paul Faure were moved to ask the workers 'not to get carried away by ill-considered actions' (Thorez), or 'ill-considered gestures' (Faure).

The Senate took advantage of this first success by continuing to harass successive Popular Front governments, and, helped by the government's financial problems, as we shall see, eventually forced their resignation. Although the campaign which now got under way was originally directed against the existing occupations, the spiralling cost of living, which reduced the value of the recently won wage increases, soon pushed the workers into new strike action.

Inflation

The wage increases had hardly come into effect when prices began to soar. The weak, insufficient, even imaginary nature of French official statistics can never be stressed enough. But such as they are, they do not fail to show the sudden and rapid rise in prices. The *Statistique Générale de la France* weighted index of the wholesale prices of 126 goods showed a rise of 21.5 per cent between May and November 1936, while industrial prices rose 35 per cent in the same period.

It should be stated straight away that these rises could not be explained by the wage increases alone. The rise in prices was considerably in excess of the rise in wages, and of course the price of labour is not the only element which goes to make up overall costs. Nor should any credit be given to the argument that the application of the 40-hour week had greatly increased the costs in each firm. The new legislation on the permissible number of working hours had not yet into effect and the weekly average hours worked had even gone up from 45½ in May to 46½ in November.

The increases went on throughout the whole Popular Front period and the statistical index of wholesale prices (for 126 goods) records the following stages (1933 = 100):

April 1936	371
January 1937	538
April 1937	552
July 1937	582
October 1937	628
January 1938	636
April 1938	643

— which adds up to an increase of the order of 73.3 per cent in two years.

Retail prices followed a similar course. A general table gives the following figures:

Retail prices in Paris (SGF weighted index)

	29 foodstuffs (*July 1914 = 100*)	17 items of clothing and household linen (*1930 = 100*)	10 household goods (*1930 = 100*)
April 1936	449	57.6	70.6
April 1937	580	93.7	96.7
April 1938	690	100	114.9

These show that retail prices in Paris rose by 29 per cent for foodstuffs between April 1936 and April 1937, by 62 per cent for clothes, and by 37 per cent for household goods. Between April 1936 and April 1938, the date of the fall of Blum's second government, which can be considered as the last of the Popular Front governments, the increases were 53.6 per cent for foodstuffs, 73.3 per cent and 62.7 per cent for clothing and household goods respectively. The rise in the cost of living was not noticeably smaller in the provinces.

By how much did wages rise in compensation? In his book **La Politique du Pouvoir d'Achat Devant les Faits,**[4] Mr Piettre estimated the overall rise as between 27 per cent and 44 per cent. Let us accept these figures for the moment. In his calculation of the increase in the price of labour, Mr Piettre included the cost to the employers of the effect of the 40-hour week and paid holidays, which he estimated as 20 per cent and 4 per cent respectively. Mr Piettre further took account of decreases in productivity. Such decreases did undeniably take place — they were the result of the workers' growing capacity to resist speed-ups. But they have been distinctly exaggerated by the employers for their own purposes. 'It seems clear to us,' reported the research body the *Statistique Générale de la France*, 'that if a sharp and widespread drop in hourly productivity had occurred, then production could not have been continued at the levels observed.'[5] However, Mr Piettre arrived at an overall increase in costs to the employers of between 64 per cent and 107 per cent.

Two remarks spring immediately to mind. In the first place it should be remembered that there is always a time-lag between price increases and wage rises, a time-lag which is a source of super-profit for the employers. Secondly, was it not the case that the Popular Front government had always had as its aim a change in the distribution of the national income in favour of the workers and against the capitalists, by drawing the workers' wage increases from company profits?

Yet even if we do not dwell on these observations, but accept Mr Piettre's figures, a very simple comparison shows that the increase in the employers' costs was very little more than the increase in wholesale prices. There is one very obvious conclusion — the price rises were not justified by the wage rises, but were quite clearly speculative in nature.

What share do wages actually have in the determination of costs? A study carried out in 1931 concluded that wage costs are on average 17 per cent or 18 per cent of the total. If we add the cost of salaries for higher grade staff (on average 4.4 per cent for all industries) and the rise in prices of raw materials which itself results from previous wage rises, we arrive at an overall figure of the order of 30 per cent. This is the generally accepted figure, confirmed by studies carried out in other countries. So if we return to the figures given by Mr Piettre for overall cost increases arising out of the events of June '36, then we must conclude that the wholesale price increases should not have been more than between 20 and 32 per cent.

The Blum government was worried by inflation on such a scale. On the one hand it put a question-mark over one of the essential points of the experiment: to give a boost to the economy by increasing real purchasing power. And on the other it was liable to cause social conflict which would seriously threaten the climate of confidence which the government was attempting to create. Two quite different remedies were decided on.

Firstly, the law of 19 August 1936 provided for special loans to industrial and commercial enterprises which were in temporary difficulties because of the wage rises. These loans were made available at a rate of interest corresponding to the Bank of France current discount rate, to an amount equalling 12 per cent of the wages bill. 3,500 million francs was put aside for this purpose. Six months later only 1,200 million had been loaned by the Bank of France through the intermediary of the commercial banks.

Secondly, the law of 19 August also set up a 'national committee for monitoring prices' within the Ministry of Economic Affairs, along with bodies which would operate at departmental level. The national committee's role was essentially one of information. It had the job of working out what should be the 'normal' price, both wholesale and retail, of certain essential products. The documentation thus elaborated was transmitted to the committees for each geographical *département* through their chairmen, the prefects. These committees had duties both of information and of enforcement. They could demand explanations from retailers who were putting goods on sale at exorbitant prices, and administer a warning. Punitive measures were available in the event of repeated infractions.

This represssive legislation was of negligible effect. **Le Temps** of 25 February 1937 could report triumphantly: 'Thousands of inquiries have been completed, a very small number of unjustifiable increases have been discovered, and only a few dozen penalties have been imposed.' By that date, it transpired, 800 warnings had been given, and only 30 transgressors had been convicted. The government therefore organised new bodies at local level which consisted of a member of the Court of Appeal, to act as chairman, a member of the *Cour des Comptes*, and a member of the Council of State.[6]

'. . . We need quick and stringent action,' declared Dormoy, the new Minister of the Interior,[7] but this was not and could not be more than a pious wish. There were deep-seated reasons why such a system could not work. The composition of the committees themselves, most of whose members were indifferent or opposed to the minister's experiment, and where the consumers were of course hardly represented; their essentially bureaucratic working methods, continually hampered by ponderous administrative and judicial procedures; finally, the lack of hard facts to go on. The committees had neither the will not the means to pursue their inquiries as far as the only meaningful direct source of information — the manufacturers' account books. Such measures would have been in evident contradiction with the oft-repeated intention to abide by the rules of the capitalist system, which forbade scrutiny or constraint.

Financial problems

The problems encountered by the government in its efforts to curb prices reappeared in similar terms in the field of financial policy, in relation both to the governmental budget, and the national currency.

The years of crisis were the years of big budgetary deficits. In 1933, 13 billion francs; in 1934, 14 billions; in 1935, 12 billions. By June it looked as if the 1936 deficit would be similar to tht of 1935. The Popular Front's policies could only make it worse in the short term — the government looked to a long-term economic revival to balance its books. But the treasury had to be supplied with funds from one day to the next, and there were promises of new expenditure which had to be met. It was therefore necessary to resort to credit, or, as some people call it, 'savings'. Everyone knew what was meant by the terms 'credit' and 'savings'. The bulk of the state's borrowing was normally from the banks, but the banks would only lend if the government of the day enjoyed their confidence. Should this not be the case, not only would they refuse to lend the state the billions it needed, but their newspapers and their lackeys would set about discouraging small savers from investing in government stocks.

Was it really possible for a Popular Front government, even with all its protestations of moderation, to avoid coming up against what Herriot had called the 'wall of money'?

It was not only a question of the bankers' attitudes, of course, for the economy was steadily accumulating fresh difficulties. The basis of capitalism being the maximisation of profits, capital was on the look-out for investment opportunities in countries where the rate of profit was higher and more secure than in France, no matter what might be the consequences for the national currency. The export of French capital had of course been going on since well before the 1936 elections and the subsequent strikes. In January 1936, the general council of the Bank of France recorded that the year 1935 had seen 'massive exports of gold . . . downward pressure on the franc . . . frantic speculation against the franc, . . . [and a] considerable export of capital encouraged by the recovery of share-prices in the USA.'[8]

Could a Popular Front government really hope to win the capitalists' confidence, and repatriation of their escaping millions? It was to just this hopeless task, the creation of a 'climate of confidence', that the Front's leaders applied themselves. We shall trace their efforts through four successive phases — devaluation, the pause or breathing-space, the fall of the first Blum government, and the rapid elimination of the second. The record is that of their eventual failure, and the parallel elimination of their 'experiment'.

Devaluation

All the Popular Front ministers, and especially Vincent Auriol, Minister of Finance, had constantly reiterated their opposition to a devaluation of the franc. But at the end of September 1936, the Cabinet suddenly produced a bill for a 'realignment' of its value in relation to other currencies. Passed into law on 1 October, it changed the regulations which had been in force since 25 June 1928, abolishing the definition of the national currency established by Poincaré (that is, one franc = 65.5 milligrammes of gold of 900/1,000 purity). The new weight was to be between 43 and 49 milligrammes.

The law established an 'Exchange Stabilisation Fund', which was intended to bring some order into relations between the franc and other currencies. It also contained a series of measures designed to stamp out speculation, measures which were to prove so ineffectual that the government rapidly abandoned them. Finally, the new law included provisions of a social nature. We shall examine later the treatment which parliament reserved for them. The monetary reform was accompanied by an agreement known as the 'Tripartite Convention' between the treasuries of Great Britain, France and the USA, which the French government made a big fuss of, but whose real usefulness has been rightly disputed.

What were the causes of the devaluation? Numerous authors have appeared baffled by this question. Mr Mossé goes so far as to conclude that the determining factor was the pressure exerted by certain advisers in the Ministry of Finance, who were involved in speculation.[9] This cannot of course be excluded. But the economic and financial difficulties facing Léon Blum and his ministers amply explain their decision. Vincent Auriol declared before both houses of parliament that the crisis and deflationary policies of previous governments were responsible for the devaluation. At bottom, this is certainly true. But if the Minister of Finance was able to tell the lower house on 25 July that 'the danger of devaluation has been averted', yet was forced to resort to it two months later, then more immediate causes must have been at work.

Vincent Auriol himself indicated what they were when he defined the purpose of the devaluation as not only the expansion of French exports, but also an attempt to 'stop the haemorrhage of gold and re-establish confidence', adding:

> Our internal policies were just coming to fruition when external events forced us to run up heavy debts for the sake of national defence. This was just the moment chosen by some elements to exaggerate the seriousness of industrial conflicts born of a long period of poverty and distress, in order to spread sinister rumours, and incite people to desert their duty to the nation.

The annual statement of the General Council of the bank of France for January 1937 revealed claims on gold continuing apace. 4,818 million francs left the country in April 1936; 3,724 million in May; 3,023 million in June; after an interruption in July and August the figure climbed sharply, back to 4,400 million in September. 'The drain on the gold reserves,' reported the Bank, 'has been due, as it was in the preceding year, to massive exports of capital.'

Budgetary problems? These were incontestable, although the finance minister told parliament that there were none. On 19 June he estimated that total expenditure from this date until the end of 1937 would reach some 17 billion francs.[10]

To cope with this situation the government arranged for themselves an extra loan facility of ten billion francs with the *Institut d'Emission*, and simultaneously announced the issue of ten billion francs worth of new government stock. When this issue proved slow to take off, another operation more favourable to investors was launched on 11 July. Although open for two and a half months, the issue attracted only 4.5 billion francs. The government was thus obliged to turn for assistance to the Bank of France. In the Chamber of Deputies, Vincent Auriol declared that only 1,800 million francs out of a ten billion franc facility had been used. This figure was inaccurate. In reality, when the point of devaluation was reached 4.5 billion francs had been called on, including, significantly, 2,430 million in the last few days.

This situation could not be prolonged indefinitely. Devaluation was the chosen remedy because it fitted, in the ministers' minds, the attempt to create a 'climate of confidence'. Mr Mossé points out that a particularly appropriate step at this juncture would have been to control the rate of exchange of the franc against other currencies, a measure in keeping with the spirit of the Popular Front programme, moreover, which had envisaged 'controls on the export of capital'. But financial circles were resolutely opposed to this idea. So much so, that Mr Frédéric Jenny, the economics correspondent of **le Temps** and an opponent of devaluation, nevertheless found it preferable to exchange control. Each time any of the Popular Front governments hinted that they were considering exchange control measures they ran into vigorous opposition in the Senate.[11] Mr Mossé hit the nail on the head when he asked:

> Shouldn't we remember that freedom of movement of capital is the same as freedom for the capitalists, and as soon as the government turns its back on energetic measures against those who control big blocks of capital, it risks handing itself over to them bound hand and foot? If you give the capitalists the freedom to do as they please, you may soon have to go to them cap in hand, and then perhaps it will be their turn to impose conditions.[12]

The devaluation bill had a mixed reception in the lower house. The right saw it as an excellent opportunity to attack the Popular Front. The coalition parties, apart from the Socialists, who exhibited a kind of compulsory optimism, did not show much enthusiasm. The Radical Party was worried about the consequences for the middle classes. The Communists were convinced that devaluation 'equals a rise in the cost of living.' They proposed instead a wealth tax on all fortunes of more than a million francs, and made it clear that they were voting for the law 'only so as not to damage the unity of the Popular Front.' They declared their support for a sliding-scale of wages and salaries.

This brings us to devaluation's consequences for the workers. Léon Blum demonstrated the government's attitude when he attacked the factory occupations during a speech in the Chamber on 28 September, and stipulated that compulsory arbitration would be the method used to compensate the workers for inflation, instead of the originally planned sliding-scale.

The breathing space

The pause — the breathing space. The expression was to be repeated many times. Perhaps the first time it was heard in an official context was in Léon Blum's speech on the radio on 13 February 1937, aimed at the civil servants. His audience was not happy. The inter-union group of public employees, civil servants and Paris regional railway workers had just declared on behalf of its members that 'our patience is not unlimited'. Blum began by recognising that

> the rise in the cost of living over the past eight months has imposed on the average public employee's family a burden greater than all the benefits we have been able to offer them . . . [to adjust their salaries] would be not only in accordance with natural justice, but would be to put our principles into practice.

However, the state servants had to understand that there were 'orders of priority'. The government had never believed in the idea of a balanced budget, but it could not let the deficit go on growing 'out of all proportion'. There were difficulties in obtaining credit. The sums which had been exported or hoarded were equal to three times the treasury's annual revenue needs. Conclusion: 'That is why we need a small breathing space.'

What was the source of Blum's anxiety? The gold reserve in the Bank of France had fallen by some seven billion francs between November 1936 and February 1937. On 17 December a new 'National Defence' loan issue was launched. Its terms were especially favourable for people willing to subscribe gold (or who had certificates testifying their desposit of gold in the Bank of France under a scheme which was part of the October Nationalisation Act) and for holders of Auriol stock. But even so it raised only enough — 2.5 billions — to pay the interest on stocks falling due in the January-March and July-September periods, and resulted in no net inflow into the treasury.

Despite a nine-month credit of £40,000,000 sterling from a group of English banks, the government had to ask for a loan from the Bank of France. Seven of the ten billion francs previously authorised had been taken up in five months. The stabilisation fund was no longer adequate to support the franc on the foreign exchanges — its coffers were empty. In this situation the 'breathing space' was nothing but a capitulation to French finance capital and the City of London.

On 21 February, Blum addressed the workers of Saint-Nazaire and Nantes, taking the opportunity to explain himself — why a breathing space? First of all because an immense legislative programme had been completed in eight months. Secondly, because inflation was still raging, and its source could be traced only to the 'inadequacy of production in relation to consumption,' as well as to 'a rather greedy desire for profits' which was 'a consequence of the crisis, for every economic crisis has certain demoralising effects.' For Léon Blum

> There can be no doubt . . . that wage increases play only a very moderate part in raising overall costs. Nevertheless, general and continuous wage-rises would in turn eventually lead to higher costs, and perhaps to higher selling prices, and that is precisely the vicious circle, as Jouhaux calls it, which our enemies, the enemies of our policies, those who are counting on the failure of our experiment, would like to see us get caught up in.

Hence 'the need for what I have called a breathing space, the need to halt the race between wages and prices.' Hence the need to act on both wages and prices. On prices, the steps taken will 'make use of the powers we already have, powers which in the event of deception or resistance, will become powers of coercion.' Blum had in mind the laws against 'unjustified price increases' whose futility we have already described, as well as certain changes in customs regulations.

The government was not 'kow-towing to capital' . . . but on 5 March 1937, in a solemn communiqué, it undertook to refrain from any kind of control on the exchange of the franc with other currencies, announced the re-establishment of a free market in gold,[13] the setting up of a committee to manage the Exchange Stabilisation Fund,[14] the postponement of all new government expenditure, and the issue of a new national defence loan.

'This is more than a breathing space — it is a conversion,' wrote **le Temps**.[15] It was also a capitulation to British capitalism; the degree to which the successive Popular Front governments were in hock to the City of London cannot be overstressed.[16]

Léon Blum in particular had anticipated a certain amount of assistance from British financial circles. His abandonment of the idea of exchange controls was not due only to the opposition of French financiers and the Senate, but also to the hostility of the City. Likewise, the attitude he adopted in the Spanish tragedy[17] was formed as much by his anxiety at finding himself in the opposite camp to the City, as by the fear of inevitable international complications, for during the entire civil war, the City was positively sympathetic to Franco. Blum was of course repaid with scorn. The January 1937 credit, which we are particularly concerned with here, and which was initially to have been £50 million, had to be reduced to £40 million when two of the 'big five' British banks withdrew.

The fall of the first Blum government

In announcing the 'breathing space', the first Popular Front government had made important concessions. But the men of finance nevertheless did not forgive Léon Blum for remaining attached to his social policy, and failing to use coercive measures against the remaining workers' struggles. His fate was sealed.[18] The first signs of the impending manoeuvre were violent attacks on the 40-hour week and the government in the Senate on 11 June 1937. The financial situation was critical. 'On 28 June the situation was particularly dramatic,' Georges Bonnet would declare shortly afterwards.[19]

First, the drain of gold. This had begun on 8 June, and in less than three weeks had reached a value of some eight billion francs, 7,860 million to be exact. Secondly, treasury balances amounted to 474 million francs on 15 June, and on the 29th, the day after I took over, only 20 million were left, although 1,700 million was required on 1 July, simply to pay the state employees and meet all the expenditure provided for the budget.

The conspiracy has been denounced by André Ferrat:

From March 1937, declaring a 'breathing space', the Blum government agreed to place finances under overall control of Finance Inspectors,[20] C Rist, P Baudouin, J Rueff, who were straightforward agents of the big banks. At the beginning of June, after a meeting attended among others by Moreau and Laval, the banks sold 400 million francs worth of government stock in a single operation, creating panic. In agreement with Mr Rueff, the director of the *Mouvement Général des Fonds*, the banks withdrew 1.8 billion francs from the Exchequer between 15 and 18 June. The government, betrayed by its high officials and left without sufficient resources to make its end of month payments, had no option but to resign.[21]

To be more exact the Senate twice forced votes which put the government in a minority, and thus forced its resignation. The ministers, evoking the necessity of 'breaking the offensive which has been cleverly prepared over several weeks and now viciously launched against the value of savings, money and credit,' demanded plenary powers over financial policy. The lower house, after specifically excluding exchange controls and 'forced conversions', granted the powers sought in two sessions on 18 and 19 June, by 346 votes to 248.

But the Senate did not follow their example. After to-ing and fro-ing between the two houses, and despite various efforts at conciliation, the government was defeated in the upper house at midnight on 20 June.

On 29 June a government was formed by Camille Chautemps, the Radical who had been Blum's deputy, with the participation of Socialist ministers. The Ministry of Finance was entrusted to Georges Bonnet, a Radical who had consistently opposed the Popular Front. On the 30th, the Chamber of Deputies, by 374 votes to 206, and the Senate, by 167 to 82, granted the government plenary powers over finance. The banks lent the necessary money. Their object was achieved.

The end of the Blum experiment

The Blum government was removed from power with no effective protest from the workers' movement. The official organisations attempted to damp down the workers' resentment, rather than call on them to demonstrate their dissatisfaction.

The aim of the new ruling-class offensive just beginning was to finish with the Popular Front's social policy, and its tolerance of the workers' economic struggles. To this end it was necessary to break up the Popular Front's parliamentary majority, and, as a first step, to kick out the Communists. Although the Socialist Party resisted this tactic, the Senate began to receive more and more open support for their purposes from the Radical leaders in the Chamber of Deputies. The three stages of the offensive were: first, in June 1937, the Radical-led Chautemps government with Socialist participation; second, in January 1938, a second Chautemps government, this time without Socialist ministers; third, in April 1938, the formation of Daladier's government with no Socialists, but with participation by the right.

In between these, in March-April 1938, a new Popular Front government headed by Léon Blum lasted no more than a few days.

On 13 January 1938, Camille Chautemps, speaking in the Chamber, blamed the workers' struggles for the government's financial difficulties, made threatening noises against the working class, and gave the Communists their 'freedom'. The Socialist group of deputies immediately distanced themselves from the prime minister, declaring that the government 'would no longer claim to be of the Popular Front'. The Socialist ministers withdrew; Chautemps resigned, and immediately began a period of provisional government, while he attempted to form a new administration.

At the beginning of March he made a fresh attempt to apply the old formula minus the Communists; the Socialists again refused to take part, and there was a renewed period of governmental crisis.

All hope of an eventual redemption of the Popular Front pledges was finally abandoned with the defeat of Blum's second government. Just after Chautemps' departure, Hitler's armies entered Austria, and the *Anschluss*[22] became a reality. Blum, charged with forming a new administration, saw in this another chance to organise a government of national unity. The speech[23] he made to this effect, to a collection of right-wing deputies, gave an insight into the way the Socialist leader was thinking, along with the other groups which made up the Popular Front.

> I must admit that it had never crossed my mind that refusal to participate would come from the opposition groups who have always claimed to be the defenders of the nation, a refusal which of course makes a government of national unity impossible . . . The national committee of the [Socialist] Party spent no more than half an hour in discussing this, and accepted the idea enthusiastically. The Radical Party is in agreement; the Communist Party have just held a meeting of their central committee which resulted in a vote for unconditional participation.

What were the rightists' objections? The presence of the Communists? But in the event of war they would certainly have to appeal to the party's worker-members.

> When I was the head of a Popular Front government I think I can say that I maintained the government's independence, and my personal independence, against certain demands, and even against certain pressures. Why should I not do so again, and would I not be in a better position to do so as the head of a government including all the republican parties?

Fear of structural reforms?

> In a Popular Front government we could not carry out such reforms without the consent of all the parties which make up the Front. And you are afraid that a national unity cabinet might attempt such reforms?

Financial policy?

> The only thing that need worry you is the choice of the Minister of Finance. If it were someone you could trust, what other problems could there be?

Only a few of the deputies and a single rightist Senator came out in favour of accepting Blum's offer. There was no deal.

On 13 March 1938, a new Popular Front government took office.[24] Blum added the role of Finance Minister to his own responsibilities as leader of the government. **Le Temps** reported on 15 March:

Sensational news! The Communists are not included. Better still, they themselves have chosen not to press their claims. Though indispensable in a broad national government, their presence in a Popular Front government is undesirable.

The government's platform stressed the need for a period of stability and re-armament. The elaboration of a 'Modern Labour Code' would be continued, while the organisation and extension of family allowances, along with pensions for retired workers, also formed part of the new programme. Léon Blum made repeated appeals to the opposition — if they supported the motion of confidence, he would resign immediately to make way for a national government. The vote was 369 in favour, 196 against, with 36 abstentions, which were divided equally between right and left.[25]

Once again the government was immediately up to its neck in financial problems. It fended off the most urgent of them by asking for, and getting, on 25 March, ratification of an agreement with the Bank of France which raised the ceiling on loans by a further five billion francs. Various financial schemes were drawn up. They were intended to amount to an overall plan to get the country back on its feet. Published on 4 April, the explanatory text stressed the difficulties of obtaining long-term credits 'when capital everywhere is nervous about investing, when its jitters and tendencies to leave Europe are reinforced by *coups de théâtre* and surprise developments in foreign affairs.' The short-term market manifested

a complete dearth of funds . . . Although 38.9 billion francs have been launched into circulation since 1 January 1935, as a result of loans to the state . . . the majority of the francs thus newly created have not been slow to return to the Bank of France, to be turned into gold, either in order to pay for an excess of imports over exports, or to facilitate the export of capital.

The banks were in on the operation:

Capital has even been drained through credit institutions and the banks themselves, where very large franc accounts have been converted into foreign exchange accounts.

The new measures envisaged included an increase in general income tax, a wealth tax on all fortunes of more than 150,000F, and the abolition of bearer bonds in an effort to stamp out tax evasion. Superprofits accruing to firms working on defence contracts were to be taxed, while at the same time there would be tax-relief for small businessmen and industrialists, as a result of the broadening of the definition of artisanship. Various other measures were judged necessary: more centralised control by the Bank of France over currency movements; before releasing quantities of new notes, the *Institut d'Emission* would demand, and be the judge of, an explanation of why the issue was required. In practice, this was exchange control. In the broader economic field, there would be price-monitoring and import controls. In defence industries — a lengthening of the working week.

The government asked for plenary powers until 1 July. The Chamber granted them by 311 votes to 250, with 43 abstentions. 7 April saw the Senate Finance Committee reject the financial measures by 25 votes to 6 without even bothering to listen to the ministers involved. The committee's spokesman, Mr Gardey, in reporting to the full Senate session, attacked the

Inequality of sacrifices: on the one hand, sacrifices demanded of the property owners which are necessary, it is true . . . but severe; . . . on the other hand, extremely excessive timidity when it comes to the organisation of working conditions.

By a majority of 214 to 47, the Senate refused to give the articles a reading. The government was overthrown. The debate had lasted less than two hours.[26]

Le Temps reported on 4 April:

In its first two sessions of the week, the Stock Exchange was very depressed because of continuing uncertainty over the nature of the new financial measures to be brought forward by the government. but since Wednesday this mood has been replaced by greater optimism, which is obviously based on hopes for the imminent arrival in power of the sort of government of national salvation which the Exchange has desired for a long time.

On 10 April the Radical Daladier brought several right-wing parliamentarians into his new government. On the 12th he got plenary powers from the Senate, for, as Mr Gardey declared: 'Exchange controls by decree now no longer arise. There will be no taxes either on investment income, or on capital.'

Daladier immediately declared his government's orientation: 'Not many words from me are needed for the French people to understand that the time has come to serve their country with hard work, and respect for the law.' The fervent wish of the Stock Exchange had been granted.

The weaknesses of the Popular Front governments

We have traced the unfolding of the actual steps which led the Popular Front governments down to defeat. But it must be said that the financial difficulties, concessions to the 'money-men', to the 'feudalists' as Mr Caillaux[27] called them, were the direct consequence of Léon Blum's undertaking to work within the framework of traditional institutions. The Popular Front governments were also flawed in some other quite different areas, all of them highly significant: the lack of any attempt to reform the civil service, and of any effective measures in the fields of credit, insurance and war industries, and not least, the tolerance of continued activity by the fascist groups.

'A breath of republicanism' in the civil service

It is above all on the civil service that the whole behaviour of the state depends, wrote Lucien Romier of **le Figaro** in 1925. The Popular Front, taking up this idea, inscribed in its programme the purging of the civil service, into which would be infused 'a breath of Republicanism'.

André Ferrat, in the book already mentioned,[28] examines all the different cogs in the state machine: army, police, judiciary, Council of State, diplomatic corps, financial administration. Everywhere he notes the existence of solidly entrenched and hierarchical castes, all bounded by the same way of thinking, of similar social origin, and the products of the same schools. With rare exceptions, all the top civil servants came from wealthy backgrounds, and went through the *Ecole des Sciences Politiques*. Connections with the big bourgeoisie were maintained since the top civil servants attended their *salons*.

Different parts of the machinery, in different ways, all acted against the Popular Front governments. The inquiry into the CSAR plot brought out the close connections between this secret paramilitary organisation and the officer corps, particularly the *deuxième bureau*, the intelligence section of the army general staff. In fact the plot itself was only discovered when a policeman who had been dismissed from his post as a result of the Stavisky scandal of 1934, voluntarily provided the Minister of the Interior with the necessary information in order to satisfy some personal grudge. As soon as it was made possible by a change of government, the police halted the successful inquiry and the affair was hushed up.

The judiciary, for its part, imposed a derisory fine on Colonel de la Roque when he was found guilty of reconstituting the banned *Croix de Feu*, even though the law stipulated a prison term and the liquidation of the organisation's assets.[29] The Council of State was only too anxious to appease the desires of those who wanted to destroy the law on the 40-hour week. Numerous decisions of the Council, on the pretext of application or amendment of the law, diluted it to the point of abolition.

We have already described the activities of the financial officials — they had worked hard to prepare a suitable gift with which to welcome the new government in June '36.

André Ferrat assessed the strength of the 'breath of republicanism':

> There were no new dispositions affecting the prefects. As for the police, nothing remarkable, unless one counts the early retirement of the head of the municipal police — his replacement hardly amounting to an improvement — and sideways moves such as that of the director of the sûreté to an important post at the Quai d'Orsay.[30] In the colonies, there was a re-allocation of governorships caused by the promotion of the governor of French West Africa to the same post in Indo-China, where he proved to be no less reactionary than his predecessor. In the same fashion Peyrouton became an ambassador and was replaced as resident-general in Morocco by General Noguès, who followed the same policies.

For all practical purposes, there were no changes at all in the financial departments. In the judiciary there was promotion for the 'most reactionary' judges.

> . . . The overall record was more or less zero. In the past, some bourgeois ministers had occasionally gone much further in the pursuit of their policies. The top levels were practically untouched.

Indeed there was actually 'a considerable swing towards reaction in the state machine', marked in particular by an extension of the role of the Council of State, increasing influence for the Financial Inspectorate, and the strengthening of police powers and numbers.

The Popular Front and the banks

What attitude did the Blum government adopt in the face of the banks' incessant attacks?

The reform of the Bank of France was prepared by a ministerial committee nominated by Vincent Auriol. A Dauphin-Meunier describes in his book, **The Bank of France**,[31] how the committee was reduced to operating clandestinely by the attitude of the high officials, and even some of the lower-grade staff in the Ministry of Finance. 'For example, the documents drawn up were typed out personally by ourselves and the representatives of the prime minister's office.' At the end of its work the committee voted unanimously in favour of nationalisation. But this idea was dropped at the request of the prime minister, who feared losing the vote in parliament. Partly this was due to the attitude of Caillaux, the Senate Finance Committee chairman, who, while favouring reform in principle, had declared his hostility to the threat of statism. And Caillaux was supported by the Communists, whose spokesman Berlioz told the Chamber on 16 July that 'there is no question of expropriation here. There is no intention of creating an issuing bank in the Marxist sense.' So a new text was prepared. Accepted by the Chamber, slightly modified by the Senate, it became law on 25 July 1936.

The new law abolished the regents of the Bank of France, and replaced them by a 20-member general council. Two were to be elected by a general assembly of shareholders; nine were to represent the 'collective interests of the nation', including particularly the public banking sector; nine others were supposed to represent borrowers and the bank's employees,[32] while the private banks were to have no place on the council.

Furthermore, the composition of the general assembly was to be altered: from now on, all the shareholders should theoretically be able to attend.

Finally, the governor and deputy governors were no longer bound by the previous obligation to possess a certain number of shares in the bank (100 and 50 respectively). But they were also forbidden, during their tenure of office, to take any part in, or to work for or advise any private business interests. They were further forbidden to accept any post in private business during the three years following their leaving the bank's employ.

The Popular Front programme set as its object, we remember, 'to protect credit and savings from domination by dynastic economic interests,' to 'turn the *Banque de France*, today a private bank, into the *Banque de* **la** *France*.' Let us look at the results.

Barely a thousand shareholders (out of 40,000) attended meetings, and when they did, it was to express violent hostility against the governor and the government. The prohibition against governor and deputy-governors accepting posts in private business was designed to prevent their subordination to private interests. In the past there had been the example of Mr Moreau, who vacated the governor's job to become chairman of the *Banque de Paris et des Pays-Bas*, and of five or six other big firms; of Mr Moret, who became a director of the *Crédit Lyonnais* and the insurance company *La France*; of Mr Charles Rist, who joined the *Banque de Paris*, the *Banque de Suez*, and the *Banque de Syrie* . . . It is easy to appreciate the governor's and deputy-governors' concern to make their personal plans for the future during their terms of office. However, scarcely a year had passed before a decree of 31 July 1937 abolished the prohibition set up by the law of 1936. Straight away Mr Guirand, first deputy-governor of the Bank of France, became chairman of the BNCI bank.

Meanwhile, though expelled through one door, the private bankers soon returned through another. In September 1937, the governor, Fournier, simply called a meeting in his office of the representatives of the big banks, in order to inform them of his intention to call them together from time to time to discuss the questions of the day. Meanwhile it was an open secret that certain top civil servants who were *ex officio* members or nominated by the government to membership of the general council, also had intimate links with private interests. So much was this the case that Pierre Ganivet, an official of the CGT's bank and Stock Exchange section, was of the opinion that 'When you look down the list of council members, the sight of certain names almost makes you wish you had the old council back again.'

In the public banking system, a few new laws and decrees defined the status of bodies such as the *Crédit maritime, Caisse de crédit aux départements et communes* and *Banques Populaires*. But there was no overall re-organisation. In fact this would have been impossible without reform of the *Caisse des Dépôts*, and the *Crédit National*. Vincent Auriol's only initiative, however, was to appoint to the chairmanship of the *Crédit National* Mr Baumgartner, a member of the Financial Inspectorate, a teacher at the *Ecole des Sciences Politiques*, and brother-in-law of Mercier, a magnate in the electrical generating industry.

There was not the trace of a reform in the key private banking sector; not the slightest attempt to imopse controls. 'Or, more exactly,' wrote Pierre Ganivet, 'it was they [the Popular Front ministers] who were subject to controls, to control by the private banks.'

> There has not been and there could not be any control of the banks, because in the circumstances of the time, the public finance department and the treasury could not get along without their help. Even the nomination of the director-general of the *Mouvement des Fonds* required their prior approval. If the treasury's activities escaped parliamentary control, they certainly did not escape that of the banks.[33]

Nationalisation

True to the spirit of its authors, the Popular Front programme did not envisage extensive nationalisation. Only nationalisation of war industries was mooted, and this was conceived in the context of 'defence of the peace' and not as a weapon in the fight against the economic system. Some firms were in fact taken over. 'Cosmetic statification,' wrote J-P Maxence.[34] Statification of deficits, we might add.

The law of 11 August 1936 went no further than nationalising a few firms in the manufacturing sector, leaving iron and steel under the control of the *Comité des Forges*. And the new law was activated with great restraint. Edward Daladier, Minister of Defence in Blum's government, said at his Riom trial:[35]

> Given the terms of the nationalisation law, which was passed by a huge majority, I could have exercised my powers over a considerable number of firms, but I did not do so. I deliberately limited the application of the law to ten or so. The entire nationalisation programme carried out by the Ministry of War involved only ten enterprises . . . and during the same period I increased the number of private firms working for national defence from 7,000 to 11,000.

The le Creusot combine was the cornerstone of the war industries. 'I had a meeting with Mr Schneider,' continued the former Minister of Defence, 'and suggested a joint operation between his firm and the state. This was in 1936. I was never able to overcome, I won't say his objections, but his resistance.'

In the end a technical committee came down in favour of nationalisation of the artillery sector only. The bosses received large amounts of compensation. They quite simply reinvested the sums in new factories with modernised and improved equipment, for, as Daladier further remarked at Riom, 'apart from the Brandt concern, all the factories we took over were using extremely obsolete methods.'

Another typical feature of the episode was that the former owners became the new heads of the nationalised concerns. Thus the bosses of the six aircraft companies (Potez, Marcel Bloch, Dewoitine and so on) all belonged to the Chamber of Aeronautical Industries, whose chairman, Mr de l'Escaille, was managing director of SNCA, the nationalised aircraft manufacturing enterprise. The CGT technicians' federation complained at the beginning of 1937 that they had to deal with something more like 'a super-organisation of employers' cartels' than with a genuine nationalised industry.

It was the same story with the new organisation of French railways, established by an agreement between the state and the private companies on 31 August 1937. The old companies retained a dominant influence in the new administrative council of the SNCF through their direct representatives (12 out of 33) and the inevitable close links between the top civil servants and capitalist interests.

The struggle against fascism and the leagues

The government's political deficiencies were also demonstrated by the course of the continuing fight against the fascist groups. The latter were still a considerable danger to the workers. Of course there was no threat to democratic rights or the existence of the workers' organisations, but the leagues engaged in continual harassment of worker activists, and their combined strength acted as a counter-weight to the workers' struggles.

Blum's government, making use of a law of 10 January 1936 against 'fighting units and private militias', pronounced the dissolution of the *Croix de Feu* by a decree of 23 June 1936. On the very same day its leader Colonel de la Roque founded the French Social Party (PSF), which two years later was declared to be 'the reconstitution of a banned organisation', by the judicial authorities, but which nevertheless continued its activities, oriented like those of the *Croix de Feu* towards the forcible seizure of power. The 'defence squads' were replaced by 'flying propaganda units'; provincial rallies continued, including a typical manoeuvre in the Dordogne which involved more than 1,400 motor-cars. **Le Populaire** of 21 December 1936 revealed a PSF plan for the 'occupation, cleaning out and organisation of certain key-strongholds'. Fights with worker militants went on unabated. The PSF tried to prevent a Communist rally in the *Parc des Princes* in Paris by a forcible occupation of the stadium, but the attempt was unsuccessful.

The threat represented by the PSF was soon reinforced by that of the *Parti Populaire Français*, founded by the ex-Communist Doriot. The PPF was smaller in size than the PSF but its leaders and members were considerably more aggressive towards the left parties and organisations.

The fascists supplemented their political activities by an attempt to infiltrate the workers' ranks through industrial-type organisations known as 'professional unions'. The *Confédération des Syndicats Professionels Français* (SPF) denied that it was an off-shoot of the PSF. A sign displayed near the entrance to its offices read: 'No politics here; if you wear a party badge you are requested to remove it'[36] — a sensible precaution if the aim was to hide links which were only too visible. Many people noticed the similarity between the initials PSF and SPF, the second seeming to be an anagram of the first. But more convincing still was the symmetry of their programmes.

The SPF, like the PSF, declared itself for *la profession organisée*. The capitalists should enjoy all the rights conferred on them by their spirit of enterprise, on condition that they provide work. The state should arbitrate between consumers and producers on the one hand, and in industrial relations on the other. The SPF movement was in favour of restrictions on the right to strike. It elaborated a scheme of arbitration which included a procedure lasting up to 36 days, and a ban on occupations and political strikes. It denounced the CGT as a Marxist political organisation.

In lining up against the employers, whose abolition they [the Marxists] seek, they are really lining up against the firm whose fate is bound up with that of the workers. This reveals the ineptitude of a tactic of which the declared aim is contradicted by the interests it is supposed to be defending . . . [A solution] can only be achieved when employers and employees learn to recognise the extent of their respective rights so that they are better able to understand the nature and importance of their reciprocal obligations.[37]

The programme included an appeal to the employers to renounce 'arbitrariness' and 'out-dated egoism'.

The first *syndicats professionels français* were formed in 1936. In January 1937 a national council set up a confederal bureau and the first national congress was held on 23–25 July. Its composition, like that of the CGT and CFTC, was based on a dual geographical and industrial structure. It was impossible to make an accurate assessment of the membership. Its leaders, although they claimed the status of a representative organisation, steadfastly refused to reveal the numbers paying subscriptions. But they claimed that at the elections to fill some workers' delegates positions in January 1938 they had roughly the same number of members elected as the CGT.

Parallel with these forms of action, and doubtless because of their relative failure, several groups of fascists turned towards the hatching of conspiracies. We have already seen how the CSAR plot was uncovered. It was described in more detail in a communiqué from Marx Dormoy, Socialist Minister of the Interior, on 24 November 1937.

We are talking about a secret paramilitary organisation which mirrors exactly the organisation of the army. It has a general staff with four departments, and a medical corps. The organisation of its membership into divisions, brigades, regiments, batallions, and so on, shows the conspiracy's undeniable orientation towards civil war.

L'Action Française, which had not forgiven the principal conspirators for deserting its ranks, tried to ridicule them; they were baptised '*cagoulards*', and as such they are known to history.[38]

The '*cagoule*' had a legal wing. This was the UCAD, the *Union des Comités d'action défensive*, led by General Dusseigneur, whose assistant was Mr Pozzo di Borgo.[39] UCAD had officially registered its constitution at the end of November 1936; its declared aim was to fight against the imagined threat of a Communist *putsch*. But various clandestine organisations operated behind UCAD. The biggest was the CSAR, *Comité Secret d'action Révolutionnaire*, a mixture of petit-bourgeois fascist elements, declassed adventurers, and members of the ruling class. An unusual number of employees of the Michelin company, especially engineers and managers, were involved in the conspiracy. Its moving spirit was Eugène Deloncle, manager of the River and Sea-going Mortgage Agency, a member of the central committee of French shipowners, and a director of the Penhoët dockyards. At his side were Mr Moreau de la Meuse, a director of the Ardennes textile company; Mr Parent, a director of the *Union des Mines*, vice-chairman of the *Mines de Phosphate de Constantine* in Algeria, and director of *Consommateurs de Pétrole*; Mr Pierre Proust, vice-chairman of the technical committee of the Corn Exchange at the Paris *Bourse de Commerce*, and various others of the same breed.

The inquiry into the CSAR plot led to the discovery of a dozen cleverly-disguised arms depots, hundreds of rifles and sub-machine guns, thousands of grenades, two hundred thousand rounds of ammunition, hundreds of pounds of explosives, underground prisons with torture-chambers, a list of hostages to be taken amongst the leaders of the left-wing parties, a plan of Léon Blum's apartment . . . Also revealed were the assassinations already carried out by the 'cagoule'. The victims included a certain arms dealer named Juif, who had given cause for complaint, Dimitri Navachine, a well-known economist of Russian origin, Mlle Toureaux, the former mistress of a certain Gabriel Jeantet, one of the conspirators, and accused of indiscipline, and the Italian anti-fascist activists, the Roselli brothers, murdered in June 1937 with assistance from Mussolini's secret service.

The CSAR could also turn its hand to acts of provocation. The outrages of 11 September 1937 which cost the lives of two policemen bore witness to this. On that day there were almost simultaneous explosions in the buildings occupied by the *Confédération Général du Patronnat Français*, at 4 *rue* de Presbourg, and by the Engineering Employers' Federation, at 45 *rue* Boissière . . . As the authors of the attacks had hoped, the right-wing press made sure to blame the Communists and the CGT.

Pursuit of the affair through judicial channels was so slow that it was still not finished in June 1940.

The German occupation would offer new opportunities for action in the fascist ranks to the former *cagoulards*; one of their first victims was to be Marx Dormoy, whom they assassinated in Lyons in 1942.[40]

12
THE WORKERS' RESISTANCE AND DEFEAT

THE WORKERS' resistance to the bosses' counter-offensive, and to their economic and political weapons, was expressed first of all through the trade unions. Following their policy of social peace, the unions appealed to the government to defend the gains of June '36 which one after another were being challenged. Thereafter the workers' resistance was manifested in a number of strikes. But the workers' camps, sapped by political divisions, finally went down to defeat. 30 November 1938 marks the end of the Popular Front and the wave of class struggle.

The rising cost of living

We have already noted the speed and scale of the price rises under Popular Front governments. We shall now examine the effects of this inflation on the purchasing power of the working class. The researches of the *Statistique Générale de la France* were carried out in October each year. The figures for October 1938, compared to 1935, in all provincial towns, show a rise in men's average earnings of 6 per cent, and a rise in women's average earnings of 41 per cent. Over the same period, in the Paris region, the average hourly wages in 21 men's occupations showed an increase of 69 per cent. More detailed studies of certain occupations show that increases varied in this period from 20 per cent for those in domestic service to 80 per cent for miners.

The Paris engineering industry will serve as an example of the stages in which these increases were won. From employers' sources, the average increase for all Paris engineering workers, following the strikes of May and June 1936 was 22 per cent. During the second half of 1936, wages were unchanged, despite a rise in the cost of living of about 25 per cent. A rise of 8.5 per cent was obtained on 18 January

1937, and a further rise of 4 per cent from 15 March. By this date, the overall increase on those wage levels fixed by collective agreements was 12.84 per cent.

There was no further change until the end of October 1937. Now at this date the rise in the cost of living since June 1936 had reached 50 per cent. At the end of 1937 there were two arbitration awards (called the Brin awards, after their author); they gave 6 per cent from 30 October 1937, and 3 per cent from 24 December 1937. There had been, incidentally, a one-hour warning strike between the two dates! So the position was that in the spring of 1938 there had been an overall increase of 22.6 per cent on wage levels fixed in the collective agreements, and 50 per cent over the levels of April 1936.

How can we calculate the effect on purchasing power? Here we have a considerable problem. There are no overall figures available. The facts given are often contradictory. The errors committed are not always accidental, as the figures from which calculations are made are usually provided by the employers' side. Sauvy and Depoid have studied the evolution of purchasing power in this period with considerable competence and objectivity.[1] They have also come up against the difficulties we have just mentioned. Their overall results are as follows:

Workers' purchasing power
(final quarter of 1928 = 100)

4th quarter 1935	131.5
4th quarter 1936	140.5
4th quarter 1937	145.5
4th quarter 1938	148

This would give an increase in relation to October 1935 of 10.6 per cent by October 1937, and 12.5 per cent by October 1938. These results almost certainly overestimate the reality. A proof of this is provided in the same set of tables from Sauvy and Depoid, which gives the following figures for the Paris engineering industry.

4th quarter 1935	126.5
4th quarter 1936	150.5
4th quarter 1937	144.5
1938	138.5

Here we have a percentage increase of 9.4 per cent, a figure which was surely higher than the average of improvements recorded, for, as the authors themselves remark, Paris engineering 'by reason of its importance and the activities of the unions in this sector, has always been the first to benefit from increases in pay since 1936.'

We should note also that the same authors calculate that the increase in purchasing power was much more noticeable for labourers and semi-skilled workers than that for tradesmen.

When we turn to the civil service it is possible to be more definite because of the greater uniformity of wage-rates. The study by Sauvy and Depoid shows that amongst civil servants purchasing power actually fell by between 5 per cent and 13 per cent according to the different grades.

The overall results of the policies of the Popular Front governments and the unions in this period can be summed up as follows:

ONE: The wage increases won at the height of the struggle were more or less wiped out by the increase in the cost of living.

TWO: The results differ according to occupation; industries with a very large number of workers and high level of union organisation such as engineering and mining were better able to resist than those where the level of union organisation was low and the workers were spread out in many different workplaces (such as domestic service, agriculture, and many female occupations).

THREE: The civil servants were undeniably victims of the experiment.

FOUR: Wage-differentials, reduced in May-June '36, were not substantially altered thereafter.

The 'modifications' to the 40-hour week

A second full-scale offensive was launched against another of the conquests of '36 — the 40-hour week enshrined in law. The common refrain to be heard from the employers, their press, and the politicians who had voted for the law in July 1936 against their deeper inclinations, was that 'the forty-hour week (the week with two Sundays) is an obstacle to recovery.' It is fair to add that this found a resonance among certain worker-militants, both political and trade union, especially when the development of the international situation led to increasing efforts at re-armament.

Shortly after the passing of the first orders bringing the 40-hours law into effect, the employers demanded the working of days in lieu of the Christmas and New Year holidays. They justified this by referring to the terms of the law on the length of the working week itself, but they were of course in violation of the principle of acceptance of existing benefits. The government, however, supported their demands, and some powerful union leaderships recommended that their members work the days demanded, which were at first supposed to be in compensation only for the two at Christmas and New Year. In fact this working of days in lieu was eventually extended to all public bank holidays and even to local holidays. In this way the employers obtained an average of 80 hours-a-year overtime at flat rates.

With this first blow already struck, the next three phases in the attack on the 40-hour week can be followed through the relevant legislative texts.

The first phase was the imposition of extra hours worked in industries where there was a fall-off in activity at certain times of the year. Here we can quote from the general decree of 31 December 1937: 'concerning hours to be worked in lieu of working hours lost as a result of a reduction in economic activity which has not come within the definition of periodic or seasonal fluctuation, in industries or businesses subject to the law of 40 hours per week.'

The second phase was the authorisation of overtime in key sectors of the economy. An order of 29 July 1937 authorised the working of overtime in the iron-ore mines. Another order, dated 21 December 1937, permitted the lengthening of hours in the coal mines.

Meanwhile the famous Committee of Inquiry into Production, set up by government order on 24 August, had got down to work. The initiative for this came from the CGT leadership, who wanted to prove the slanderous nature of the bosses' claims about decreases in productivity. The CGPF employers' federation agreed to take part in the inquiry after receiving assurances that questions of structural reform would not be raised. The inquiry's terms of reference were to improve production and reduce costs. The measures proposed would be enacted by decree. As it turned out, the only decrees to emerge were on 'different modes of application of the 40-hour week.' The committee finished its labours about 15 December. Its recommendations were for the 'moderation' of earlier decrees, and further exemptions for defence industries.

The wide-ranging 'moderations' were issued by 21 December. The first was a special exemption for industries subject to the 40-hour law, but suffering from a shortage of skilled labour; the second, a similar exemption for industries whose output was essential to the activity of a large part of the economy.

The third phase was to argue that the defence of the nation justifies all exemptions. This phase came after the end of the Popular Front governments strictly defined, but the ground for it had been prepared by them. It began, as soon as Daladier took over as prime minister in April 1938, with the publication of an ever-increasing number of texts granting exemptions to the 40-hour law. And it continued, by means of decrees in November and December 1938, with the introduction of penalties for refusing to do overtime. It reached its height with the order of 21 April 1939 which abolished enhancements to basic rate for all hours worked between 40 and 45.

The appeal to the state

The response to the employers' offensive from the major workers' organisations, particularly the CGT, can be summarised as the appeal to the state.

Léon Jouhaux explained: 'Our attitude to the state cannot be the same as previously. The problem is no longer posed in the same way when you have a democratic state.'[2] We have already given our view of the result of this confusion between the nature of the state and the state machine on one hand, and the presence of Socialist Party ministers in the government on the other. But the unions' main concern was social peace. They wanted it firstly so as not to embarrass the Popular Front government, and afterwards so as not to interfere with rearmament. This was the cause of their repeated appeals to the government and parliament.

Two types of measure, inseparable from one another, were adopted: suspension of the collective agreements, and legislation on conciliation and arbitration. The chronology was as follows:

Law of 31 December 1936 on conciliation and compulsory arbitration.

Law of 18 July 1937 on prolongation of the collective agreements.

Law of 11 January 1938 on prolongation of the collective agreements and compulsory arbitration.

Law of 4 March 1938 and subsequent decrees on the procedures involved in conciliation and arbitration.

The law of 24 June 1936 on collective agreements had laid down that each of these contracts must have as part of its provisions the definition of procedures for resolving differences concerning its application, and the procedure to be followed in the event of demands for revision or modification. Thus the 1936 agreement in engineering laid down that there must be a delay of one clear week before resort to strike action or lock-out. It is difficult to imagine a more rudimentary version of a grievance procedure; this state of affairs is explained by the Communist Party's then opposition to all conciliation and arbitration procedures.

In October 1936, after the devaluation of the franc, the CGT leadership began to demand the sliding scale of wages and a conciliation procedure which would go as far as compulsory arbitration. The Devaluation Act itself had provided the framework for the establishment of such a system. There were contacts between the CGPF and the CGT with a view to getting an agreement on the subject. The talks had almost reached their end when a strike broke out among engineering workers in the Sambre basin, north of Paris, on 27 November 1936, the same day that the Minister of Labour had been informed of the two sides' willingness to go to arbitration. The workers' action seemed to demonstrate their hostility to this. The employers' representatives immediately broke off the talks with the CGT.

The CGT then appealed to the government, who drew up a bill; this in due course became the Act of 31 December 1936. It took a week of debates before the Senate produced an acceptable text. It was an effort made all the more necessary by the fact that the working class had once again clearly demonstrated its hostility to the principle of arbitration. At a big meeting in the Japy gymnasium manual and white-collar workers in the food industry refused to ratify the agreement made under the auspices of the Minister of the Interior and the head of the prime minister's office, and comprehensively disowned their own representatives.

The law of 31 December 1936 was valid only for a certain period: until the end of the present sitting of Parliament. On the other hand its scope was very wide-ranging: 'All collective disputes in industrial or commercial enterprises must be submitted to conciliation and arbitration procedures before any strike or lock-out.' The employers made a show of opposition to the law, but this was entirely due to the political complexion of the government in power.

Thereafter wage disputes were very often resolved by arbitration. The arbitrators allowed claims made on the basis of a rise in the cost of living, but usually they awarded only a partial compensation. They did not make use of a sliding scale as such.

At the CGT's *comité confédéral* on 14 April 1937, Léon Jouhaux declared his 'satisfaction with the results of arbitration':

> If we compare the results of arbitration with the results obtained from other methods, we are bound to say that the outcome of arbitration is very often better than what we would have obtained by the previous methods. But it seems as if there is a state of mind which opposes every arbitration award unless it gives us 100 per cent of what we had asked for. We said when we were involved in discussions about the law; arbitration cannot give complete satisfaction to the workers' demands. People should understand this.

René Belin explained the close connection between the breathing space and compulsory arbitration:

> Conciliation and arbitration as accepted by the CGT are not fundamental parts of our trade unionism, any more than they were before. They have been imposed by the needs of the breathing space . . . and we have accepted them for a limited period only. Mr Duchemin indeed took the

opportunity of reminding me . . . that I myself declared on 7 June 1936 that the CGT would not seek abitration. That is because at the time of the talks he was referring to we were far from thinking of a breathing space. We were in the thick of a battle, and its outcome was still in doubt.[3]

It was this same idea of a breathing space which dominated the question of renewal of the collective agreements. Being of a year's duration, their renewal was due for the most part in June and July of 1937. The government, concerned to avoid unrest during the International Exhibition in Paris, suggested the extension of the agreements. The CGPF accepted, on condition that the government effectively prohibit workplace occupations and that the employers retain their right of hiring and firing. The CGT accepted as well, but demanded that the life of the law on arbitration be extended likewise and asked for the introduction of a law to regulate hiring and firing. Belin wrote:

> We were still dominated by the idea of the breathing space, at least in part when we asked that the law be used to regularise the delicate problem of hiring and firing, a point on which various unions and federations had already prepared for battle.

The law of 18 July 1937 extended for six months both the life of the collective agreements and the government's powers in the field of conciliation and arbitration. The extension of the collective agreements was done in such a way as to allow modifications in the clauses concerning wages. Any such amendments to wages were to be negotiated within the conciliation procedure, with its aim of avoiding strikes.

The law of 11 January 1938 extended the collective agreements and the powers of compulsory arbitration for a further six months. But meanwhile there had been talks between the government, the CGPF and the CGT. Noting the CGT's respect for the 'growth of national production and the rule of law,' Mr Chautemps, the prime minister, declared that it was necessary to work out certain measures for 'inclusion in a new general agreement which would constitute, like the Matignon agreements of June 1936, the voluntary Charter of French Labour.' This was the origin of the famous idea of a 'Modern Labour Code'.

The outcome, on 27 January 1938, was the presentation of six bills dealing with hiring and firing, deployment of labour, collective agreements, conciliation and arbitration, the legal status of strikes, and the status of workers' delegates. The only one of these which ever became law, on 4 March 1938, was the one on compulsory arbitration. The government's scheme did not mention the sliding scale, but it provided for the arbitration scheme to come into play in the event of a significant variation in the cost of living, causing disagreement over the revision of wage-scales laid down in a collective agreement. The Communist deputies suggested an automatic wage increase in the event of price rises equal to, or more than, 5 per cent. This was rejected. In its place the government produced an amendment from Jules Moch which provided for consideration of an individual firm's financial situation. The Communists in turn proposed an amendment allowing the unions a measure of financial control in the firm. Partially accepted in the Chamber, this was thrown out by the Senate.

Another feature of the legislation as passed was that revisions to wages and family allowances could only be made every six months, unless the rise in the index in question reached 10 per cent, in which case revisions could take place as soon as the rise became known. Finally, the Act included the creation of a Higher Arbitration Court.

All the Popular Front parties voted for the measure. Ambroise Croizat, speaking in the Chamber on 17 February 1938, explained the Communist vote in these terms:

> The working class wants order. For the workers, a strike is a weapon of last resort imposed by the employers' intransigence. The working class will be only too glad if we give them something to use instead of a strike.

He was echoed by G Monmousseau;

> In the present situation, compulsory arbitration cannot hope to resolve problems which proceed from the existence of classes themselves. At the very most it can reduce the violence of this confrontation and pull in the direction of the peaceful solution of conflicts, by everywhere applying the same standards of justice which alone can create a favourable climate for economic progress and social peace.[4]

Restrictive interpretation of the new law brought forth protests from the Catholic union federation CFTC,[5] while the CGT continued its campaign for the sliding scale. And the law was indeed interpreted restrictively; the arbitrators had no power to demand from the employers the access to their accounts which was needed for an assessment of their objections to wage increases; the employers were free to give their own figures, and the arbitrators had no powers of investigation. The higher arbitration court decided that only a wage or part of a wage which was equal to the minimum needed for survival should be open to adjustment, and they furthermore defined different minimums for different occupations.

It is now time to look at the overall effect of the arbitration laws on wage levels. Mr B Lavergne has calculated that, in general, arbitrations of one sort and another led to increases in pay of only about a half or two-thirds of the rise in the cost of living.[6] Mr Gaetan Pirou has shown clearly how in the early stages, when it came to applying the system:

> The employers groups had much better organised litigation departments than the workers' federations. Furthermore the employers had the assistance of people who were not themselves businessmen, (usually lawyers, skilled in picking their way through the labyrinthine intricacies of the regulations) while the trade unions, with one or two exceptions, presented their cases through one of their own workers.

The lawyers' arguments were based on law; those of the workers on equity. Mr Pirou also emphasised 'the exaggerated slowness of the procedure'. Furthermore, and in our opinion this is the fundamental point,

> this whole experiment [was conducted] within an economic framework which was still capitalist — it did not form part of an integrated scheme within an ordered or planned economic system. The firms affected by arbitration awards were still subject to the law of competition in the market. Because of this there was, if not actually a contradiction, a problem of adaptation between the new situation and the economic environment in which it was expected to work, and that sometimes posed agonising problems for the arbitrator conscious of his responsibilities.

The appeal to the state involved other more general questions which have been spotlighted by Lefranc:

> Little by little, trade-unionism retreated from high-level negotiations and approached a kind of adaptation, at first unadmitted, but later more explicit. Union activity took on new forms; centralism triumphed over federalism; the nation was accepted as a fact of life, and the unions' place in the management of the state claimed as a right, sometimes as a duty.[7]

CGT representatives had been sitting on the National Economic Council and in the International Labour Organisation since 1918; Jouhaux had several times been a member of the French delegation at the League of Nations. During the 1930s the union leaders were appointed increasingly frequently to consultative positions such as membership of public and semi-public bodies, and they also took part directly in the work of the bodies charged with amplifying and administering the various laws which had their application in the trade union field.

This participation was a form of commitment of the trade union movement. It had the effect of sanctioning some of the more debateable measures of the Popular Front governments. Was not the presence of Jouhaux and Luche on the general council of the Bank of France a guarantee that the central bank had been really reformed? Likewise, did not the CGT representation on the boards of the nationalised aviation concern and the railways seem to give the seal of authenticity to these forms of public ownership? More serious still, the unions were in this way implicated in the management of the bourgeoisie's affairs, and made to bear a part of the responsibility of this management. The wordy reservations made during the passing of motions at the Congress of Toulouse, the unity congress of March 1936, were forgotten even by those who had so carefully drafted them.

Workers' struggles

The policy of counter-attack embarked on by the bourgeoisie and the feebleness with which it was met by the Popular Front governments led to profound unease in the ranks of the workers. This explains their continuing militancy. But the unions' use of the conciliation procedure limited the scope of the workers' struggles, and the differences which gradually emerged inside the movement gave the struggles of the period from the end of 1936 until November 1938 certain characteristics which we must analyse.

We have seen the significant growth in union membership. The CGT distributed 4½ million cards in 1936, 5 million in 1937, and its growth was particularly marked in areas where there were big concentrations of workers. The *Union Syndicale de la Région Parisienne* grew from 200,000 members in 1936 to 1,250,000 in April 1938. The membership in the department of *Nord* went from 80,000 in February 1936 to 300,000 in 1937; in *Bouches-du-Rhône* the growth was from 28,000 at the beginning of 1936 to 140,000 in 1938. In engineering, the membership of the *Fédération des Métaux* went from 50,000 on 1 March 1936 to 775,000 on 1 March 1937; the chemical workers' federation grew from 4,000 to 190,000 . . .

This expansion of the unions was accompanied by a similar reinforcement of the ranks of the workers' parties: the Socialist Party grew by 120,000 members from December 1935 to December 1936; while on 30 September 1937 the Communist Party announced it had 340,000 members, including 115,000 in the Paris region.

But a growth in membership did not necessarily mean a corresponding strengthening of the organisations' control of the class, especially for the trade unions. 'The newcomers to trade union organisation', according to Lefranc, 'were inexperienced and impatient'. They were often quick to show their dissatisfaction with union policy, and even to break discipline.

From 1937 on, 'wild-cat' strikes broke out everywhere, led from the ranks by union members who had often not bothered to consult with the federal and confederal bodies.[8]

This had a bearing on the character of the workers' struggles. J-P Maxence described the differences between the strikes of 1936 and those of 1937–8 in these terms:

They had not the same atmosphere, as they had not the same origins. Unanimity was lost. Confidence undermined. Gone was that bantering good humour which had given them courage to brave the rigours of the law. In six months the workers' drive had been blunted, weakened, broken . . .[9]

One more thing which sums up this phase of the struggle was the increasing incidence, as the employers' offensive gathered pace and strength, of defensive strikes, compared to offensive, of defeats for the workers compared to victories.

Statistics show that the strike movement in 1937–8 was bigger than it had been at any time since 1920. We shall try to draw out some of the typical features by following the course of some of the biggest and most important strikes.

The Martyrs of Clichy, and the strike of 18 March 1937[10]

The semi-fascist French Social Party was due to hold a meeting at Clichy on 16 March. The Socialist-controlled local council, the Communist deputy and the local Popular Front called for a counter-demonstration. The march assembled, 10,000-strong, at the town hall. The Popular Front representatives then took the head of the procession and led it away from the place where the fascist meeting was to be held.

But one section of the demonstration broke away and made for the meeting-place. They ran up against the forces of law and order, and a full-scale battle followed which lasted for several hours. The police opened fire. The prefect of police and the Minister of the Interior (greeted by cries of 'Dormoy, resign!') were unable to restore order. André Blumel, chief of Léon Blum's private office, was wounded, and five workers were killed. The demonstration was 'an error, that is, something more serious than a mistake,' Léon Blum would tell the Chamber on the 23rd. The government were convinced that the PSF was a reconstitution of the *Croix de Feu*, but only the judicial authorities, informed by the government, were competent to judge. Until that happened the government regarded it as their duty to defend freedom of speech.

But these legalistic scruples were little appreciated in the workers' ranks; to them the government's behaviour semed like a double game which had ended in tragedy. Indignation was stronger than amazement. On the 17th there were numerous walkouts on the International Exhibition sites, and tremendous agitation in the factories. The CGT called a general strike, limited to the morning of the 18th, to protest against the fascists' shadowy activities. H. Raynaud, a Communist leader of the CGT, wrote on the 18th:

> During the course of yesterday strikes broke out here and there spontaneously, in an anarchic fashion. They grew and were generalised in a way which could have provided considerable opportunities for all kinds of provocation. Some of these strikes were only stopped on the Wednesday when the workers were told that the *Union Syndicale* was planning a general strike for the Thursday. So this general strike has been a strike in defence of law and order.[11]

It was in fact a considerable success and certain factories (Alsthom, Hispano, Amiot, Hotchkiss, Lavalette, among others) even stayed out for the whole day.

The aim of the 18 March strike, therefore, was to channel the workers' anger, and turn it away from those at whom it should have been directed — the state, the police, the government and its policy of tolerance towards the fascists.

December 1937 — the Goodrich strike

The strike which broke out at the Goodrich plants on 15 December 1937 was the result, in part, of difficulties in the implementation of various arbitration awards relating to the so-called Bedeaux rationalisation plan, and, in part, of the sacking of a worker apparently wrongly accused of having planted a bugging device in his boss's office. The site was occupied. On 23 December, at day-break, the *Garde Mobile*, the auxiliary riot police, took up positions around its perimeter. The government had decided to have the occupiers physically ejected. However, while defence was organised on the inside, the factory's sirens blasted a warning to workers living or working nearby. The news spread from factory to factory, and from factory to factory the walkouts followed one another. Some of the workers occupied their plants, the rest made for Goodrich, until thousands of workers surrounded the threatened workplace. The *Garde Mobile* was withdrawn, and the arbitration procedure set in motion.

First of all, at the management's suggestion, which was accepted by the union leaders, the factory was 'neutralised', that is evacuated by the workers, but with no possibility of any kind of work being restarted. Meanwhile the prime minister, Camille Chautemps, worked out an arbitration verdict which was published on 6 January after consultation with the CGT's *bureau confédéral*. The decision went almost entirely against the workers. Worse still, the arbitration made no reference to the Goodrich management's decision to sack 52 workers for going on strike. The mainly Communist leaders of the Goodrich union organisation and the federation of chemical trade workers recommended acceptance of the award, and disclaimed any responsibility in the event of the strike continuing.

The strike committee met in order to decide its position. It was composed of 35 workers and technicians, mainly young, who had gained their experience in the battles of '36. Five argued for acceptance of the decision on grounds of wider policy; eleven were absolutely opposed; and nineteen abstained, in order not to embarrass the union officials. There was a turbulent mass meeting of two thousand strikers. Cries of 'Traitors!', 'Sell-outs!' rose from all sides. It took three meetings in succession before the strikers, feeling abandoned by their union, voted by a slender majority, with 40 per cent abstaining, for a return to work. Hundreds of union cards were torn up.

The Paris Engineering Strike, 24 March – 19 April 1938

This strike brought to light, among other things, the workers' dissatisfaction with their leaders' policy of social pacifism, differences between the Socialists and the Communists, and attempts by the Communists to use the strike for ulterior purposes. Pressure for a strike built up around the discussions leading to renewal of the collective agreement. Grievances accumulated over several months, and the bosses' resistance to demands which the workers wanted to include in the collective agreement led to confrontation.

The workers' readiness for a fight coincided with the union leaders' wishes, for they wanted a means of exerting pressure on the employers, but the leaders in question were Communists, and they had something more in mind — they wanted to oppose the government's drift to the right and to raise the question of direct CGT participation in the administration. But their desire for social peace, as well as fear of losing control of the strike, ensured that they opposed the unleashing of a generalised offensive. So they set about fragmenting the strike movement, giving it political slogans and denouncing provocateurs — that is anyone who was in favour of generalisation.

On 24 March the Citroën plant at Javel struck on the orders of the CGT's *commission exécutive*. The other Citroën plants at Clichy, Levallois and St Ouen followed suit. But each had different demands, the purpose being to pretend that these were entirely spontaneous actions. Offers of mediation by the government (Blum) were turned down by the employers, while the strike spread between 24 and 26

March to SNCASO, *l'Air Liquide*, Gnôme-et-Rhône, SKF and Lockheed, bringing the total of workers involved to more than 30,000.

Already on the 25th the Paris region of the engineering union made it clear, 'there is no question of a call for a general strike.' On the 28th, the Boulogne-Billancourt section issued a leaflet denouncing the 'Trotskyist beast' which was seeking to drag the engineers into a 'wild adventure' by calling for a general strike. At a factory gate meeting outside Renault, local Communist deputy Alfred Costes repeated the same themes. On 27 March it was the turn of the *amicales socialistes*, the Socialist Party factory sections, to be attacked — by the engineering union and the Communist Party at the same time. They were accused of being the fomentors of the strikes, and of 'putting round petitions calling for a general strike against the Senate.'[12] The *amicales socialistes* denied this, and reaffirmed their readiness to fight the Senate. But in the same edition of **Le Populaire** appeared an article by Desphillipon recommending 'socialists and socialist sympathisers to abandon a struggle for which no one is willing to claim responsibility,' a movement 'which can only create difficulties for the second Blum government'.[13] Nevertheless the movement grew little by little.

Between 30 March and 1 April workers at SKF at Ivry and Bois-Colombes, Gnôme-et-Rhône at Gennevilliers, and Rateau at La Corneuve were drawn in in their turn. Another offer of mediation by Blum on 1 April was again turned down by the bosses. On 6 April there were more than 40,000 on strike; on the 8th, more than 60,000, with 40 factories occupied. Meanwhile, on the 7th, the second Blum government had been brought down by the Senate and a period of governmental crisis ensued.

On the 9th, the engineering union leaders asked the local factory leaderships to make approaches to their managements.

> The workers will decide their attitude according to the results obtained. The central council is recommending the greatest possible spirit of conciliation on our side, and if the employers do not wish to discuss with us, then they will bear the entire responsibility for any ensuing conflicts which may take on a general character.

On 11 and 12 April, Renault, Latil, Bloch, *le Matériel Téléphonique*, Somma and other factories all came out. There were now nearly 100,000 out, which grew to 160,000 on the 13th, with 170 factories occupied.

Now the arbitration procedure got under way. It operated at two levels. In the aircraft factories, the verdict awarded an increase of 0.78F per hour, but virtually established a 45-hour week. The union expressed its satisfaction, and considered that the engineers 'will now, just as they promised, get down to work in a much happier frame of mind, with all the conscientiousness and enthusiasm which the present needs of national defence require.' The workers were far from being so enthusiastic. At Lioré-Olivier 70 per cent of a mass meeting refused to go back on the basis of the award. At Gnôme-et-Rhône (Kellerman) 600 workers voted against acceptance. And there was serious opposition at Bloch.

In the non-aircraft sector the government decided on the 13th to impose arbitration, 'reminding everyone that when the arbitration procedure is brought into operation there is a legal obligation on all parties to return to work.' The factories were to be cleared immediately, and work was to re-start on the 19th. It was agreed that there were to be no penalties for having been on strike. On the 19th, the Giraud arbitration award turned down the claim for a substantial wage increase, and recommended, for factories engaged in defence work, the application of the award already made; for other firms — nothing more than a 0.35F to 0.40F per hour incrase. 'The skies are clearing,' wrote **L'usine**, publication of the *Comité des Forges* on 23 April:

> People are beginning to see the way ahead, and to return to common sense. There is a rebirth of confidence . . . The first condition for this is obviously order and respect for the law on all sides. In this respect, the outcome of the dispute in the Paris engineering industry is a positive achievement which will be of lasting worth. The increase in the length of the working week in the defence industries can only have a beneficial effect on economic activity . . . Now, let's put our backs into it, and get down to work.

In a pamphlet[14] written about the March–April strike the CGT-affiliated technicians' and white-collar union for Paris engineering drew out the following lessons, lessons which go beyond the bounds of this particular strike and seem to us to have a validity for the whole period:

> The experience of the Popular Front in power confirmed that no government could carry out policies within the existing system which did not fit in with the vital interests of the industrial and financial oligarchies, which did not indeed safeguard those interests.
>
> At a certain stage in the development of the crisis, the defence of these vital interests merges with the employers' everyday resistance of the workers' demands, a resistance employing all the means at the employers' disposal, and relying on all the means which the state can bring into play against the workers.
>
> In such conditions, which are present in this period, a movement for the usual trade union demands can only be successful if it takes the form of direct collective action involving at least all the workers in a single industry, if not the entire working class of the country.
>
> For this to happen, permanent, active intervention by the unions'

leading committee is essential both to unify the claims put forward, and to co-ordinate the front-line struggle. Failing this, there are only simultaneous sectional strikes, even when a large number of workplaces are affected. Then the result is that local considerations, running contrary to any kind of joint effort, have a seriously distorting effect on the internal development of strikes which become isolated, subject to enormous pressures steadily built up and concentrated by the employers. The workers' feeling of belonging to a powerful trade union which extends beyond their firm dwindles rapidly as it becomes more and more difficult to see a way forward for strikes rendered impotent by dissipation of their forces.

A further point, which is especially applicable in the present circumstances, is the lack of preparation for big strikes, which can be an important reason for their defeat. For when the struggle breaks out the mass of workers do not know what the organisation wants, or how it wants it done, as no preparatory agitation has done the job of focussing their aspirations on certain concrete objectives. Likewise, no steps have been taken to secure certain strategic advantages for the workers, nor to build support among sections of the middle classes.

That is why, on this last point, the March–April strikes had the effect of widening the gap that can exist between these social groups and the workers' movement.

So the engineers' strike was defeated. This defeat accentuated the movement's retreat. During the year 1938, the number of victorious strikes in relation to the total was very small, barely more than 20 per cent — roughly the same as in 1935.

The proportion of defensive strikes, forced to respond to some act by the employers or the government, was continuously on the increase. From July onwards, a new category of strike appeared in the records of the Ministry of Labour — strike in protest against the lengthening of the working week. Also evident was the reappearance and growth of employers' coalitions and lock-outs. Strikes became longer and harder.

Differences in the workers' camp

The main workers' organisations had acted together to finish off the May–June 1936 strike wave. We have noted their agreement, in general, on a policy of social peace. Nevertheless differences began to emerge, which the development of the international situation tended to aggravate.

The first serious disagreements were on the question of what to do about Spain. The Popular Front in that country too had won a notable victory on 16 February 1936. And the Spanish Popular Front had tried to implement the same fatally flawed policies as their French colleagues. They were met by the same fierce resistance from the big bourgeoisie and the aristocracy. But, because of particular historical conditions, the situation in Spain proved much more explosive, and reaction resorted to open warfare.

On 18 July the fascist-military revolt led by General Franco began. On the 25th the French government announced its neutrality and its desire not to get involved in the conflict. On 1 August they appealed to all governments to adopt the same position, and immediately forbade the export of war material. It was not until 24 August that the German and Italian governments responded to this appeal; beforehand they had supplied the rebel forces with abundant quantities of men and arms, and would continue to do so.

For the next 30 months what has been called 'the hypocrisy of non-intervention' took shape. On 13 August the politbureau of the French Communist Party stated that Hitler and Mussolini were 'systematically following a plan for the encirclement of France,' and 'we must not retreat further in the face of Hitler's blackmail . . . we protest most indignantly [against the] de facto blockade' of Spain. On 25 August, Jacques Duclos used the pages of the Cahiers du Bolchévisme, the French Communist Party journal, to appeal for protest motions and resolutions to be voted everywhere. Some raised the question of workers' action. Thus the Paris engineers struck for one hour on 7 September, partly in defence of their collective agreement, but also 'in support of the freedom fighters'.

The Communists' campaign unquestionably evoked a response from the bulk of the working class. Activists from many different tendencies — Socialist, Communist, Trotskyist and anarchist, went to fight and to die in Spain. Collections for the Spanish fighters were taken up everywhere. For months on end the cry 'Guns and planes for Spain!' echoed in political meetings.

The Socialist leaders were fearful of the attitude both of their Radical coalition partners, and of international complications. The first appeal from the Communist Party, a letter to the Socialists' commission administrative permanente on 9 September, went unanswered. The second, on 30 September, was met by a more or less point-blank refutation: on behalf of the Socialist Party Paul Faure wrote that it seemed to his party

> that any international action to be undertaken should have the aim of putting the working class on their guard, rather than pressurising our Popular Front government into steps which could endanger peace.

This point of view was of course not shared by the whole of the Socialist Party; its left wing was passionately in favour of sending aid to fighting Spain. The CGT took an identical position. So the Spanish issue was to remain a bone of contention between the two big workers' parties.

The Popular Front government's general political evolution provided another source of reservations by the Communist Party. They have often been accused of playing a double game. Although the party's parliamentary group constantly supported the government, the speeches and actions of their leaders, and perhaps even more so those of their middle-level members in mass meetings of workers, often sounded a different note. At one and the same time the Communist Party was trying to apply a policy of social pacifism, and to reflect the aspirations of its working-class base, dissatisfied with their living and working conditions. Hence the Party's reservations over the 'breathing space'.

Another aspect of the contradictions inherent in their policy was that they called for economic and social policies which met constant opposition from the Senate, but they opposed any campaign directed against this same Senate. This illustrated *the* basic contradiction of the Popular Front — the alliance between the workers' parties on the one hand, and the Radical party on the other.

This was the background against which the Communists mounted a campaign for unity between the two workers' parties. On 8 November 1936 they addressed the Socialist Party's national council, repeating their proposal for fusion into a single united workers' party. In a special report on this question presented to the Communist Party's ninth Congress at Arles in December 1937, Jacques Duclos exalted the strength which such a pooling of resources would mean:

> Just think of the power represented by a single party which could claim the allegiance of the 450,000 Communists, adults and youth, and the 300,000 Socialists and Young Socialists, fraternally united . . . Just think of the power of such a party, with a parliamentary group of 250 members, with a newspaper like l'Humanité, which has a print order of 430,000 copies, with another paper like le Populaire which prints 200,000 copies, not to mention the provincial press.
>
> Just think as well of the force of attraction which a single party could exercise over multitudes of workers who stay out of the movement because it is still split in two . . .

In his general policy report Maurice Thorez had also dealt with the question and admitted that 'difficulties arose some time ago'; difficulties concerning the programme, and over methods as well:

> We have agreed bit by bit to the ever-increasing list of demands from the Socialist Party's *commission administrative permanente*. We accepted the conditions laid down by their Marseilles Congress as necessary and sufficient for unity — one, democracy at every level of the organisation; two, sovereignty of national and international congresses; three, independence from the government, of whatever shade.

But the Socialist Party was not interested in unity for the moment. According to Thorez, the *commission* had now demanded that

Communist groups be instructed to stop making unity proposals to the Socialist sections . . . then, having spurned discussions at rank-and-file level, the *commission* used the pretext of an article by our great comrade Dimitrov to break off talks at the top.[15]

The Socialists' hesitations were reinforced by problems which the former '*confédérés*'[16] were having inside the CGT. The explosion of May–June '36 brought into the Confederation very many members who had been formed by the struggle, and who became the backbone of working-class organisation. These were more attracted by the dynamism of the Communist Party members, and their undeniable desire for revolutionary change, despite current Communist Party policy, than by the ideology and practice of traditional reformism. The former CGT-U members in the united unions formed a solid and coherent block. They had a weekly newspaper, **la Vie Ouvrière**, with a print order of 100,000; they were not slow to gain a majority in the most important unions — engineering, construction, railways, textiles, leather trades and certain important *unions départementales* such as those of Paris and the *Bouches du Rhône*. Lefranc, himself a former *confédéré*, writes:

By means of agitation for day-to-day improvements, in which they were always ready to take the lead, the younger, more disciplined, more dynamic former CGT-U members often won a majority against the former *confédérés*. They didn't always use this to eliminate the latter from the leading positions; in many *unions départementales* the old, former *confédéré* secretary retained the post of general secretary, but found at his elbow a young former CGT-U assistant secretary or education officer who travelled back and forth across the department establishing his presence.[17]

This situation led to the appearance in October 1936 of a new weekly paper, **Syndicats**, produced by a few of the old CGT leaders grouped around René Belin, now an assistant secretary of the reunified CGT, and Raymond Froideval, secretary of the Seine locksmiths. **Syndicats** denounced the 'colonisation' of the CGT by the Communists. As differences grew the number of examples quoted became more numerous, and the tone became more violent. As the situation developed the founders of **Syndicats** found that they could not restrict themselves to a simple defence of the idea of trade-union independence. Belin in particular went as far as to say that 'trade unionism cannot ignore its obligation to respect the vital forces of the nation.' For him trade unionism could not be both reformist and revolutionary at the same time; in fact the choice in favour of the first of the two alternatives had been made in June '36. This outlook tended to interpret trade-union independence as independence from parties, that is, from one party, and not from the establishment.[18] But not all the former *confédérés* were involved with **Syndicats**; quite a number of officials grouped around other former *confédéré* members of the *bureau confédéral*, refusing to follow the paper in its systematic struggle against the former CGT-U members.

These differences of emphasis among the old CGT members were aggravated by the developing international situation. Indeed, from March 1938, the date of the *Anschluss*, the overriding question for everyone became the accelerating drive towards war. On 13 March the Communist Party declared that after Austria would come the turn of Czechoslovakia, and on the 19th Thorez spoke at the *Mutualité*, a meeting hall in the Paris latin quarter, announcing that 'it is the duty of France to take the initiative in rallying the free nations in defence of peace.'

However, on 10 April Daladier formed a government in which the Foreign Secretary was Mr Georges Bonnet, whose pro-German sympathies were well-known. In the circumstances the Communist International's appeal to its sections 'to exert pressure on the bourgeois-democratic governments to persuade them to make a firm stand against the aggressors' was particularly appropriate in France.

The Communist Party fulfilled their task by a nation-wide campaign. **L'Humanité** published the text of a speech which Duclos was to have made at the **Vélodrome d'Hiver** stadium at a meeting which was banned by Daladier. The speech contained the main themes of the campaign: end non-intervention in Spain; 'honour the terms of the treaty binding France to Czechoslovakia,' in other words, declare war on Germany in the event of German aggression against the Czech republic; 'unite all democratic countries against fascist oppression'; and at the same time act against the big capitalists, 'who are sabotaging production and national defence', and defend the social reforms. But the Communist Party also intended to exert pressure on the government by means of guerrilla strike action. This was how they understood the March–April strike by the Paris engineers. It was also behind the Communists' unsuccessful efforts in August and September to start a general strike among miners in the Nord. A further example, among others, was the decision by workers in the aircraft industry on 1 October 'not to work, today, Saturday, because of the weakness towards fascism demonstrated at Munich.'[19]

The Communists' attitude of course exacerbated differences both within the Popular Front (at the 14 July 1938 demonstration there were no speeches as it had not been possible to reach agreement) and among workers generally. The 'resistance against aggressors' tendency predominated in the CGT, supported by Jouhaux, and in the Socialist Party, supported by Léon Blum. But their desire for resistance was allied to a search for deals which could reduce the prospect of war, even if only for a short time. This is how the Munich agreement of 29 September 1938 — rightly denounced by the Communist Party as an attempt by the 'four' to come to terms at the expense of the Soviet Union — came to be approved with one vote against by the Socialists' parliamentary group, and also, although with infinitely more reservations, by the *commission administrative* and the *comité confédéral national* of the CGT. Most of the supporters of **Syndicats** took a resolutely pacifist attitude. The paper opened its columns to the 'Trade Union Group for action against War' (CSAG). On 26 September the national primary school teachers' union, together with the postal workers, organised a vast petition against war. Part of the campaign was to win support from influential politicians, including ministers in office.

Clashes became more embittered. One was either 'pro' or 'anti' the Munich agreement. But, as Lefranc has noted, from now until August 1939 the number of those willing to defend the agreement was in continual decline in comparison with the anti-Munich faction.

Other, smaller, completely minority currents in the working class expressed themselves on the fringes of these two big groupings, refusing to be drawn into either camp. These were the Socialist Party's *Gauche Révolutionnaire* tendency,[20] the Trotskyists and some trade union groups. They denounced what they called the phoneyness of the democracies' war against fascism. For them, the coming war was a war of two imperialist camps in which the workers had no part; the fight against the war was the same as the fight for the revolutionary overthrow of the capitalist system.

The Congress of Nantes

The 25th Congress of the CGT assembled at Nantes from the 14–17 November 1938. Three central questions were debated — peace, trade union independence, and the attitude to be adopted towards Daladier as prime minister.

The congress was divided into three main tendencies: the former CGT-U delegates, who were supporting the so-called 'skins and leather' resolution (named after its sponsoring union); the **Syndicats** faction; and the group around Jouhaux and his friends. A few additional delegates called themselves *'Cercles Syndicalistes lutte de classes'*.[21] These last were represented by Serret, a primary school teacher from Ardèche who was the second delegate to speak. He bitterly noted that only 0.75 per cent of the CGT's budget had been spent in support of strikes, while hundreds of thousands of francs had been subscribed to the national defence loan. We believe first of all, he said, that the CGT must act in the spirit of revolutionary trade unionism, class struggle trade unionism. On the question of independence,

> it is absolutely essential to guard against two dangers which threaten the unions. We do not accept the CGT's collusion with bourgeois governments and their institutions; we condemn arbitration committees and courts; we do not want the CGT to take part in the National Economic Council, which is a bourgeois body, nor in the International Labour Organization, which is a tool of international capitalism. But neither do we want the CGT to be colonised by the Stalinists.

On the question of war or peace, Serret continued,

> whatever you may say, our position, along with that of the entire working class of this country, is that we do not want war; we do not want it at any price, even if it is passed off as the democracies' struggle against fascism. We do not accept the policy which the CGT has been pursuing; we think infringements of the 40-hour week for the sake of national defence are unacceptable; we are disgusted at the idea that strikes are broken because they might harm defence interests . . . The 'firmness' policy requires armaments. You know that armaments weigh almost exclusively, if not 100 per cent exclusively, on the backs of the workers. An armaments policy is incompatible with a social policy beneficial to the working class.

The supporters of the **Syndicats** group denounced violations of trade union independence by Communist Party members. Froideval denounced the fact that many federations were led by people who were also Communist deputies or central committee members. He gave examples of former *confédérés* who had been removed from their posts by factional manoeuvres. Delmas described how attempts were made to force the hand of the *bureau confédéral* in the same way. Dumoulin even demanded the CGT's withdrawal from the Popular Front; the CGT 'cannot be itself unless it has its own programme — its own programme of demands, and its own constructive proposals.'

The former CGT-U members fought back vigorously. Parsal accused the **Syndicats** leaders of having 'organised a banquet to which Marcel Deat, Montagnon, Jean Piot and Emile Roche were invited,' all enemies of the Popular Front and of the working class. Nedelic demanded, amid great applause:

> We would really like to know if there is any truth in what has apparently become an open secret, namely that during the September crisis the ante-rooms of Mr George Bonnet's Foreign Affairs Ministry were the

subject of frequent visits from certain trade union leaders who talk about independence but go to government offices to receive their orders.

Jouhaux appealed for both sides to make concessions:

When it was needed in the past you felt able to make political concessions which were essential for the defence of our freedoms against the threat of fascism. Today we are facing an even greater danger — one which threatens us from the inside. We are asking you, for the sake of the CGT, to consider what sacrifices you can make to help us unify our movement once and for all.

When the **Syndicats** group broached the question of the coming war, it was to emphasise the pacifist mood amongst French workers. The Munich agreement had at least granted a breathing space; it was a point from which the conditions for genuine agreements could be developed. They insisted on the obvious contradictions in a policy which at the same time sought expanded arms production, and the defence of the gains of June. In reply, the former CGT-U men objected that Munich would only accelerate the drive to war. Everything must be subordinated to the defeat of fascism. Semart declared:

There is no question, as some would have it, of a holy alliance with the 200 families, and still less of an alliance with arms dealers. What we have to do, in the difficult conditions of a bourgeois democratic state, inside the capitalist system — we have no choice about where and when we have to defend our freedom — what we have to do is forge the unity of the working class on the platform of defending peace. I am not interested in the 200 families, or their nephews and nieces. I know what plans we have got for them when we have dealt with the fascists.

Once again, Jouhaux pleaded for compromise.

A compositing committee was formed, which managed to work out a compromise between the positions of the former CGT-U group, who probably were in a majority at the Congress, and of Jouhaux and his friends. The **Syndicats** group, and the *Cercles lutte de classes* refused to endorse the ensuing text. The voting was as follows:

Motion	On peace	On union independence
Vivier-Merle (composite motions)	16,784	16,582
Delmas (**Syndicats**)	6,419	7,221
Serret	118	121

A large number of telegrams were sent to the congress demanding protests and action against Daladier's government-by-decree. All the speakers in turn denounced the new decrees, and suggested the action which the CGT should take. A unanimous resolution blasted the government. As far as the action to be taken was concerned, the resolution left this rather open, by giving

> a mandate to the *bureau confédéral* and the *commission administrative* to organise resistance to the decrees, which infringe the rights and interests of the workers, in consultation with the unions affected. This congress also gives them a mandate to prepare without delay whatever action may be necessary, including collective withdrawal of labour, should this be required, to defend the social reforms recently enacted.

30 November 1938

The Radical Party devoted its Marseilles Congress to a violent attack on the Communists. The executive bureau adopted a motion declaring that 'the Communist parliamentary group has deliberately withdrawn from a political arrangement to which it still claims adherence.' But the Socialists' national council, meeting on 5–6 April 1938, refused to exclude the Communist Party from the Popular Front. On the 10th, the Radical Party assistant secretary read a statement to the Popular Front national committee which announced his party's withdrawal from this body. The Radical Party no longer wished to sit down at the same table with the Communists.

This was the signature on the Popular Front's death certificate. It remained only to consummate the defeat of the workers' movement. Paul Reynaud, Minister of Finance, declared on 12 November:

> We are living in a capitalist system. The capitalist system being what it is, if it is to function, its laws must be obeyed. These are the laws of profit, of individual risk, of a free market, of the incentive of competition . . . Do you think, in today's Europe, that France can at the same time maintain her way of life, spend 25 billion francs on arms, and rest for two days out of seven?

This speech was the prologue to a series of anti-working-class decrees. These included the re-establishment of the six-day week, the abolition of wage rate enhancement for the first 250 hours overtime, the abolition of the clauses in the collective agreements which forbade piecework, the imposition of penalties for refusing to work overtime in defence industries,[22] the 'staggering' of paid holidays, the imposition of restrictions on foreign workers, and the formation of an auxiliary police force of 1,500 gendarmes.

Indignant protests came from all sections of the working class. The workers' organisations reacted violently. The Communists unleashed an aggressive campaign, while the Socialist *commission administrative permanente* on 16 November invited 'all party sections, and all federations to use all possible means — meetings, rallies, posters, leaflets, press campaigns, and so on — to fight the decree-laws of the Daladier-Raynaud government.' On 20 November, the executive committee of the CFTC added their voice to the protests. At the same time the Radical group in the Chamber passed a vote of confidence in Daladier.

From the 21st, strikes broke out in the *Nord*, in the *Basse-Seine*, and in the Paris region. Factories were occupied, and then cleared by the police. Renault stopped work on the 23rd. The workers were confronted by a huge police mobilisation — 100 squadrons of the *Garde Mobile* (1,500 men) attacked the plant, where battle raged for between 20 and 24 hours. Amid clouds of tear-gas, hundreds of workers were injured, and 300 imprisoned. On the 25th, in **le Peuple** the Paris **Union Syndicale** and the engineers' union earnestly invited 'all workers in engineering establishments to wait for the word from the CGT and not to begin any premature action.'

The same day the CGT communiqué appeared. 'The CGT *commission administrative* and the secretaries of the national federations held an important meeting on Friday afternoon. All decisions were taken unanimously.' A 24-hour general strike had been decided for the 30th.

> Whatever may be the surrounding circumstances or events, work must begin again on the morning of Thursday 1 December . . . The CGT declares that the strike will take place without any occupation of any factory, office, or site. On Wednesday 30 November no demonstrations and no meetings will be held.

But already ministers and top civil servants had been in high-level conferences for several days. As soon as the *commission administrative* decision was made known, Daladier organised a conference involving the Paris Prefect of Police, the Prefect of the *département* of the Seine, the military commander of the Paris region, the head of the Minister of Defence's military office . . . for five days the government carried out requisitions, mobilised their men, threatened the civil servants and railwaymen, stiffened the employers' resistance, made full use of the radio . . .[23]

A workers' movement weakened by two years of capitulation could not resist such a mobilisation. The strike was widely observed in the mines, in engineering, construction and printing, but by ten o'clock on the morning of the 30th the government was able to announce that 'the railways are working normally'. On the Paris Metro the strike had to be reduced to eight hours, and to fourteen hours in the Post Office. There was no response from office workers, and a partial strike, rapidly petering out, among taxi-drivers. In some provincial centres there was a good turn-out; but the general lack of response from civil servants, railwaymen and public services had a dampening effect everywhere. The attempted strike was a disastrous defeat.

Dumoulin in **Syndicats** on 28 December drew what seems to use the essential lessons: the general strike was an attack on the government, and

> therefore necessarily took on the character of an insurrection . . . But an insurrection cannot declare in advance that it will act in accordance with the law. That, however, is just what the CGT did . . .

Severe repression followed in the wake of the defeat. Thorez drew the balance sheet;[24] 40,000 sacked in the aircraft industry; 32,000 locked out at Renault; tens of thousands in Levallois, Colombes, Argenteuil, Courbevoie, Clichy, St Ouen; 100,000 in Marseilles (where 100 engineering factories were closed); 100,000 in textiles, 80,000 miners in the Nord and Pas-de-Calais . . . In addition the positions of importance which the CGT leaders held in various public authorities were withdrawn from them (Bank of France, railways, *Caisse des Marchés, Caisse d'Amortissements*).

The working class was left dazed. The unions and parties saw their memberships sink rapidly. It was the bourgeoisie's turn to think 'now, everything is possible.' The outbreak of war in August 1939 was near, and, not far behind, June 1940 — when France would fall to Hitler's armies.

13
SOME CONCLUSIONS

FROM THE EVENTS of February 1934 until 30 November 1938 we have passed through one of the most dramatic periods of French working-class history. February 1934 had brought to power a reactionary government which was the result of a temporary balance between two antagonistic forces: capitalism, and its most extreme form, fascism, on the one hand, and the workers' movement on the other. After 30 November 1938 reaction was once again triumphant, but the second victory of the conservative social forces occurred *after* the workers' movement had been dislocated, divided, and temporarily defeated, after the destruction of a gigantic festival of the oppressed which had shaken French society to its foundations.

The extent of the social advances made in June 1936 should not be underestimated. The French working class had never before in its history won such a series of reforms some of which were to remain almost unassailable by reason of the circumstances in which they had been wrenched from the employers. It is impossible, however, not to wonder whether June 1936 was something more than an industrial struggle of particularly huge dimensions, and especially whether it might have had much greater immediate consequences.

We should not forget that June '36 happened at a time when the world working class was in retreat. After the stabilisation of the period of revolutionary crisis which followed the 1914–18 war, and which recorded only one victory, that of the Russian working class, after the crushing defeats in Italy (1922), Bulgaria (1924), Britain (1926), China (1927), Germany (1933) and Austria (1934), the French struggle seemed to be a rear-guard action. But could it not have been the starting point for a counter-attack, the beginning of a new upsurge in the working-class movement throughout the world?

The strike wave of May–June 1936 created the conditions for a revolutionary crisis in France. It was born out of a period of economic chaos and political confusion; it took the bourgeoisie by surprise, and won the support of the middle classes.. The preliminary conditions for the collapse of the economic and social system were fulfilled; if the workers' struggle had indeed achieved the destruction of the capitalist system, the course of history might have been decisively altered.

We obviously cannot say with any certainty that if the class struggle had developed into a full-scale battle for power it would have ended with the workers' victory and the construction of socialism. But there is one thing we can say — that such a struggle was not engaged because the leaders of the mass organisations took a deliberate decision that it should not be. Taken unawares by the fascist-inspired riots in 1934, forced to unite their organisations by the weight of popular pressure, surprised again by the outbreak of the strikes, the reformists, both Stalinist and trade-unionist varieties, had but one common objective: bring the workers' struggles to an end as soon as possible, defend the traditional social order, bring about a return to work. They justified this attitude by identifying two imperatives: unity with the petty-bourgeoisie, and the fight against fascism, both within and without. The value of their solutions to these two intimately-linked problems can be judged by the results.

Working class and middle classes

The workers' leaders based their action on a single premise: the struggle against fascism required an alliance between the petty-bourgeoisie and the working class. Since the middle classes were firmly attached to law and order and traditional parliamentary democracy, every time that the workers infringed one or the other of these, the middle classes would be impelled further and further towards the right, and finally towards fascism. This alliance would therefore have to take the form of a political deal between the workers' parties, and the parties to whom the petty-bourgeoisie habitually gave their votes. The programme which would serve as the basis of this alliance must not be such as to frighten the middle classes, so it would have to be the programme of the most right-wing of the parties involved, in other words that of the Radical Party itself. It would have to be put into practice, moreover, using traditional parliamentary methods, in stages, interrupted by breathing spaces.

What were the results of this policy?

It is true that democracy is more stable when the rural and urban petty-bourgeoisie play a more active part in the life of the nation. But industrial development had deprived the petty-bourgeoisie of much of their importance in the economy, and, as a result, in the social, political and cultural domains as well. At the same time deeper and more frequent economic recessions had impoverished the middle classes, provoking them to outbursts of rebellion which were all the more violent in that they relied on no doctrine of their own nor traditions of struggle. Desire for change began to outweigh respect for order; confidence in parliamentary democracy dwindled. It seems to us, therefore, that in order to win over the middle classes the workers' movement needed to appeal to their desire for change. To achieve a united front with them, the workers' organisations should have presented a real programme of reconstruction, and given an example of decisive action against the roots of the evil in the old society.

Jouhaux himself even said:

> If, at one time you had to water down your programme in order to get support from the middle classes, today that is no longer the case. Today's middle classes are much more likely to support a bold programme which gives some promise of relief for their distress, than to be attracted by sterile policies dreamed up from one day to the next, with no drive or imagination.[1]

The petty-bourgeoisie could begin to feel solidarity with the workers' struggles when the workers' movement developed a programme for the profound transformation of society which expressed the needs and hopes of all the oppressed.

But by signing a pact of unity with the Radical leaders, the workers' parties tended instead to give a new lease of life to the discredited and weakened Radical Party. And of course the agreement was made on the basis of the Radical programme. The logic of the situation was that, as soon as the strikes were over, the Radicals would demand a return to their traditional policies, and the possibility of their withdrawal of support would leave the Blum government paralysed and powerless.

The aim had been to weld the unity of workers' and middle classes. But the endless compromise had brought about inflation and devaluation, aggravating economic instability and affecting the middle classes worse than any other group. They lost confidence in the workers' leaders, who no longer seemed to have anything to offer them. Worse still, when the workers had to begin a new round of struggles to defend their living standards, their strikes and demands found no echo among the middle classes; in many cases they were met with hostility, based on the fear that strikes would only aggravate existing economic problems. The gap between the two groups opened up again, and the petty-bougeoisie remained passive and indifferent spectators of the defeat on 30 November 1938.

Democracy and fascism

The pacificatory and compromise policies pursued by the workers' parties were of equally little effect in the struggle against French fascism. Fascism, of course, is not the accidental phenomenon, the sociological monster, that some people have made it out to be. It is only one of the by-products of the capitalist system, a particularly authoritarian form of political rule by a bourgeoisie determined to defend its position. And effective struggle against fascism is therefore above all a struggle against capitalism.

The conclusion is inevitably the same if we consider the danger of fascisms from abroad. The whole Popular Front period was dominated by the threat of a new world war. The analysis of the international situation put forward by the workers' parties was one of fearful confusion. For them, on a world scale, there was a struggle between democracy and fascism. The peaceful democracies were threatened with being dragged into a war which was a product of fascism. The formula was certainly a convenient one — it avoided any need to examine the real issues.

Fascism and war were and always are closely linked; they are concomitant phenomena having the same origin: capitalist degeneration and crisis. They have the same role — to defend ruling-class profits. But it is a misuse of language to say that fascism bore the only responsibility for the threat of war. The causes extended well beyond fascism, for Mussolini's odious aggression against Abyssinia was not essentially any different from the colonial expeditions which are regarded as one of the historical 'glories' of the democracies, and the origins of the 1939 war do not fundamentally distinguish it from that of 1914–18.

By its failure to face up squarely to these problems the workers' movement got bogged down in vain and divisive quarrels; for lack of serious analysis of the origin of fascism and the threat of war, the workers' leaders forgot that their movement ought perhaps to work out its own independent policy. The workers' movement split into factions for and against the Munich agreement, each one of them coat-tailing a section of the bourgeoisie, and getting tangled up in their own contradictions. The anti-Munich wing claimed that it was possible at the same time to back the arms programme and expand the social reforms. They ignored the reality of the 'guns or butter' dilemma, while the pro-Munich, pacifist wing didn't hesitate to exploit it. Their weakness was to seek the resolution of international conflicts in dubious diplomatic compromises, forgetting that territorial transfers or the sharing-out of spheres of influence have only ever shifted the focal point for the conflagration from one place to another, without solving the basic problems.

'Pro' and 'anti' factions were in any case agreed on one point: nothing should be done which might weaken France in the face of potential Nazi aggression. Too vigorous a pursuit of the class struggle would damage the country's stability, and make France an easy prey for Germany.

A policy must be judged by its results. To love up to the City of London, from whom it expected financial miracles, the Popular Front abandoned the Spanish revolution. The miracles were not performed, Blum's government was forced out, and Franco crushed the Spanish people.

The workers' movement must not go beyond the limits of the Popular Front pact, it was argued, for there was too great a risk that a great social upheaval would divide and weaken France. The result is well known: the workers' movement was broken, the middle classes abandoned the workers in the hour of defeat; war came, the country suffered Nazi occupation, and many months passed before the working class could gather the strength and confidence to mount an effective fight against the occupier.

Equally serious problems surrounded the question of trade unionism and the state.

When French trade unionism, from its earliest beginnings, declared its independence from the workers' political organisations, it was for fear of being drawn into reformist parliamentary activities, and, directly or indirectly, into collaboration with the state.

But, as Lefranc noted, there was a creeping tendency towards a *'politique de présence'*; 'the workers' place in the management of the state was claimed as a right, sometimes as a duty.' At a time when the state's role in the social and economic fields was expanding from one day to the next, and when capitalist concentration had forged strong links between the top civil servants and the owners of the means of production, this tendency to incorporation of the unions had two consequences. On the one hand, in their economic struggles the unions had to face an adversary with close links with the authorities and which operated in a centralised fashion. Thus the reformists began to consider that one of their essential tasks was to free the state from the capitalists' grip (personified by the 200 families), by using their own presence in the apparatus as a counter-weight. It was this theoretical underpinning which justified the Socialist Party's transformation into a party of government from 1936 onwards.

On the other hand, the participation of the workers' leaders in para-governmental organisations obliged them to take a share in responsibility for the management of the system. And not only did more and more trade unionists accept positions in the state apparatus, but they also made repeated appeals to the government to arbitrate on points of dispute between workers and employers. They either asked for or simply accepted the arbitration regulations which compressed workers' action into one side of a legal case. They justified their action on the ground that the state had become democratic. This was a serious conflation of the ideas of state and government. Blum undoubtedly tried to lean towards the workers, but the presence of a socialist leader at the head of the government was not an antidote to the permanent operation of the administrative, judicial and coercive branches of the state apparatus, all of which were undisturbed, and continued to be run by the same men. But undertaking to respect the existing economic and political system, the Popular Front governments virtually denied themselves the right to change their servants. If they had changed them this would not have altered the situation very much, for the problem was above all one of institutions. In order to attack the institutions the workers' struggle would have had to go beyond economic demands and be 'directed towards smashing the present state and replacing it with new and truly democratic organs of power.'[2]

The fundamental issues on which we have briefly dwelt here are the key to a history of the Popular Front. All of them, of course, bring us back to June '36, to that decisive moment when, after their victory in the economic struggle, the working class remained alert and ready for more action. All the problems which the Popular Front was unable to resolve lead us back to the crucial days of June '36 when the revolutionary spirit of the class collided with their leaders' determined passivity.

The leaders emerged victorious; but though they must take responsibility for the events which were to follow, the working class alone bears the honour for the successes achieved. The conditions and the lessons of that success deserve to be remembered today.

The main lesson of 1936 is without any doubt the irresistible power which comes from united working-class action for common aims.

But June 1936 was not only an important date in the history of social progress; it was not only an aborted revolution; it was the moment when the French working class showed the full measure of their militancy, of their immense resources in imagination, audacity and organisation. They proved that they are the only force capable of sweeping away the rotten system which is threatening to bury us in its ruins.

NOTES ON SOURCES

From the preface to the 1972 edition by Marcel Gibelin

This book, first published in 1952, was, we believe, the first study to attempt to trace the development of this important period in the history of the French workers' movement.

Our principal sources were original documents, especiallly the press, leaflets, factory newspapers and the minutes of mass meetings. We have also drawn in large measure on the documents collected for the Riom trial, especially the testimony of Léon Blum before the Vichy magistrates. Some people might think it inappropriate to make use of the Socialist leader's declarations made at a time when he was fighting for his freedom and his life against his persecutors. But the courage shown by Blum in such adverse circumstances, the confusion he sowed in the ranks of his enemies, which they were spared only when Hitler ordered the suspension of a trial which had transformed them from accusers into accused, and not least the publication of Blum's complete testimony by the Socialist Party itself, justifies frequent quotation from the SFIO leader's defence, which we take to be the result of his mature reflection on the meaning of the events of 1936–7. We have also made use of G Lefranc's **Histoire du Mouvement Syndical**, and certain documents taken from *A Gauche de la Barricade*, the memoirs of Delmas, former secretary of the Union of Primary-School Teachers.

During the 1960s a number of works appeared dealing with the Popular Front. Some of these are the collection of eye-witness accounts collected by Georges Lefranc, **Juin '36: Archives**, the memoirs of Jules Moch, **Le Front Populaire: Frande Espérance**, as well as those of Daniel Guerin, **Front Populaire: Revolution Manquée**, which are especially interesting. There are also Lefranc's **Histoire du Front Populaire**, Jacques Fauvet's **L'Histoire du Parti Communiste Français**, and Antoine Prost's **Le CGT à l'Epoque du Front Populaire**. The Communist version is given by Jacques Chambaz in **Le Front Populaire pour le Pain, la Liberté, la Paix — Contribution à l'Histoire du PCF**. The review **Le Mouvement Social** has published a special edition on the Popular Front. The reader may find it useful to consult these works.
MARCEL GIBELIN

For English readers: a note by Peter Fysh

There is a dearth of material in English covering the period in France between the two world wars which is accessible, fairly readable, and gives anything like a fair hearing to the workers' movement.

The most readable, not to say anecdotal, history is William Shirer's **Decline of the Third Republic**. The author was an American foreign correspondent who divided his time between Vienna, Paris and Berlin during the 1930s. One drawback of his book is that he tends to spend more time on events to which he was personally a witness. Thus he devotes more pages to 6 February 1934 than to the whole of June 1936. The reader who knows little about France is likely to get a more balanced account from Alfred Cobban's **History of Modern France**, whose three paperback volumes are frequently re-issued by Penguin Books, though he still gives little on the Popular Front.

The outstanding academic historian of modern France writing in Britain today is Theodore Zeldin. His books contain a wealth of scholarly detail, but unfortunately pay little regard to conventional subject divisions and none at all to chronology. If you can find copies in a library, study the contents list carefully. On economic background there is Tom Kemp's **The French Economy between the Wars — a History of Decline**. Also acclaimed is R F Kuisel's **Capitalism and the State in Modern France**, of which a reasonably-priced paperback edition appeared in 1983.

PETER FYSH

NOTES

Chapter One: THE MASSES TAKE TO THE STREETS

*1. These were fascist or semi-fascist organisations. Background details of some organisations and leading individuals mentioned in the text are to be found in the Glossary that follows these notes.

*2. The attack was the climax of a series of demonstrations sparked off by the Stavisky Affair. This financial scandal involved prominent members of the Radical Party who were parliamentary deputies and government ministers. Millions of francs were embezzled. When the scandal broke early in January 1934, the body of the banker Stavisky was found in a remote hunting lodge in the Alps. He had apparently committed suicide, but there were allegations that the government had arranged his murder in order to shut him up. The affair rumbled on throughout January, with repeated right-wing and fascist demonstrations, the arrest of deputies, the resignation of ministers, and finally the fall of the Radical-led government. 6 February was the day on which the re-shuffled government, now headed by Daladier, another Radical, was to meet parliament for the customary vote of confidence.

*3. Chiappe, prefect of the Paris police, had been sacked by the new government on the grounds that he had been too soft on the earlier right-wing demonstrations.

*4. In common with most Marxist writers, Danos and Gibelin include in the term 'petty bourgeoisie' not only that layer of the lower middle classes which includes shopkeepers, small businessmen, and some professionals, but also some sections of the peasantry.

5. See Daniel Guérin, **Fascism and big business** (New York 1983).

6. P Frédérix, **Etat des Forces en France** (Gallimard 1935).

7. During the 1936 election campaign, the powerful cartel of insurance companies was to finance the Radical Party even though it was part of

the Popular Front which included the Communist Party. See Maxence, **Histoire de Dix Ans** (Gallimard 1939).

8. Under the headline 'Demonstrate!', the Communist Party paper **l'Humanité** published on 6 February an appeal to the Republican Ex-Servicemen's Association: 'All out to the *Rond Point des Champs Elysées* . . . against the fascist gangs, against the government, and against social-democracy.'

9. This parallelled the party's reduction in size to fewer than 40,000 members.

*10. Divisions of local government roughly equivalent to the English county.

*11. The structure of the French trade union movement in 1936 is briefly outlined in the glossary which follows these notes.

*12. Daladier as prime minister and Frot as minister of the interior were considered responsible for the deaths of demonstrators on 6 February.

13. Lefranc, **Histoire du Mouvement Ouvrier en France** (Edition Montaigne 1947).

14. **Le Populaire**, 25 February 1935.

15. The terms of the pact were:
1. OBJECTIVES: The Socialist and Communist parties agreed to work together
— against the fascist organisations, for their disarmament and dissolution
— for the defence of democratic rights
— for proportional representation and the dissolution of parliament
— against preparations for war
— against the decree laws
— against fascist terror in Germany and Austria
— for an amnesty for all imprisoned anti-fascists.
2. MEANS: The campaign was to be carried out by means of joint meetings and mass demonstrations or counter-demonstrations. Members of both organisations were to give each other aid and assistance where necessary. Defence of meetings and demonstrations was to be organised jointly. Joint demonstrations should not degenerate into sectarian debates. No criticism should be made of individuals or organisations loyally engaged in joint actions, although each party was to remain independent in its own propaganda and recruitment policies, 'avoiding insults or provocations' with regard to the other. A co-ordinating committee was to decide the overall planning and character of the joint demonstrations, and all conflicts were to be referred to it.

16. The committee, which the Communists dominated, is better known as the 'Amsterdam-Pleyel Committee'.

17. R Millet, **Bilan du Communisme** (Librairie technique et économique 1937).

*18. The proposed change of title was to reflect the bank's intended new role in the service of *the whole of* the French people.

*19. The CGT claimed 700,000 members in 1935. It should be noted, however, that of these scarcely more than 200,000 were blue and white-collar workers in private industry. The numerical importance of the public employees' union accentuated the CGT's reformist tendencies.

20. The CGT-U claimed between 200,000 and 250,000 members in 1935.

21. Under this form of unity, the CGT-U would make a better showing, especially among railway workers.

*22. Separate organisations of Communist Party members within the union.

23. Article by Gitton in l'Humanité, 6 June 1935.

24. In the previous parliament, the Socialist Party had had 97 deputies and the Communist Party 16.

Chapter Two: THE BEGINNINGS OF THE STRIKE MOVEMENT

1. Le Temps, 2 May 1936.

2. Hitler's re-militarisation of the Rhineland had taken place on 7 March 1936.

3. Le Temps, 6 May 1936.

*4. The Radical Albert Sarraut had taken over as prime minister in one of several government re-shuffles between 1934 and 1936.

5. We know now that Thorez, who favoured participation in the government, had been in a minority in the politbureau.

6. Letter of 12 May 1936 and article by Léon Blum, Le Populaire, 8 May 1936.

7. Press conference, 7 May 1936.

8. *Communiqué* of 9 May 1936.

9. Letter from the Communist Party to the Socialist Party, 15 May 1936.

10. Speech of 17 May 1936.

11. Le Populaire, 15 May 1936.

12. Le Temps, 5 May 1936.

13. On 21 May 1936.

*14. Delmas, A Gauche de la Barricade (1950). His reference is to the authoritarian Vichy government, headed by Pétain, which ruled by agreement with the Nazis after the occupation of France in 1940.

15. Le Temps, 5 May 1936.

16. Authors' emphasis.

17. On 14 and 23 May 1936.

*18. The site in Paris where many of those who had taken part in the uprising of the Paris Commune were executed in 1871.

9*19. Speech to the Socialist Party national committee on 5 May, reprinted in L'Exercice du Pouvoir (Gallimard 1938) page 45.

20. 'This social upheaval which had come and, as it were, struck my government in the face right from the beginning,' as Blum said later (Léon Blum devant la Cour de Riom (Editions de la Liberté 1945)).

21. For example Lefranc in his Histoire du Mouvement Ouvrier and Prouteau in his excellent thesis Les Occupations d'usine en France et en Italie (Paris 1938).

22. L'Humanité, 26 May 1936.

23. Le Temps, 28 May 1936.

24. Le Temps, 28 May 1936.

25. Le Populaire, 27 May 1936.

Chapter Three: THE MOVEMENT BEFORE 4 JUNE

1. **Le Temps**, 29 May 1936.
2. Marcel Cachin in **l'Humanité**, 30 May 1936.
3. **Le Temps**, 31 May 1936.
4. *Communiqué* from the Paris region employers' organisation for the metal-working industry, 28 May 1936.
5. Declaration by Mr Lehideux, the Renault manager.
6. **L'Humanité**, 29 May 1936. Doury was an official of the Paris region federation of the engineering union. He was also a member of the Communist Party.
7. Senate sitting of 7 June 1936.
*8. The name *Bourse du Travail* means literally 'labour exchange'. The *bourses* had grown up in reponse to the employers' need to control the hiring and firing of labour. In the course of time rank-and-file militants took over these organisations as local centres for their own struggle against the employers, and they became integrated into the union structure.
9. Authors' emphasis.
*10. The agreement signed at Gnôme-et-Rhône on the afternoon of 29 May stipulated a pay increase of between 1F and 1.25F per hour, a paid lunch-break of half an hour, the abolition of overtime, a 2F enhancement for hours worked at night, a week's paid holiday per year — rising to two weeks after a year's service, the recognition of shop delegates and the right to belong to a union, and payment for all the time spent on strike.
11. **Le Temps**, 31 May 1936.
12. There were 900 present, out of a total 1,200 members.
13. Letter to Blum from the Engineering Employers' Federation.
14. Declaration by Salengro, 4 June 1936.
15. *Communiqué* from the politbureau, 4 June 1936.
16. The correspondent of **le Temps** noted that 4 June was a better day for the stock exchange because 'it is generally thought that the new government will rapidly bring the strike episode to a close.'

Chapter Four: THE POPULAR FRONT TAKES OFFICE

1. See **l'Humanité**, 3 June 1936, in which an article by Gitton attacked the left Socialists' revolutionary phraseology. According to the author there was no question of a confrontation or of a revolutionary programme, but simply a concrete programme to put into practice 'in an orderly, calm and tranquil fashion. We regard as impossible any policy which would prejudice France's safety in the face of the Hitlerite menace.'
2. 'If we were to fail . . . I would be the first to say to you: it was a chimera; I would be the first to come and tell you how and why we failed, and what consequences should be drawn from that. (Léon Blum, congress speech, in **l'Exercice du Pouvoir**, page 55.)
3. **L'Exercice du Pouvoir**, page 63. See also speech to the national committee, page 46.

4. The text was repeated word for word in the Communist Party polit-bureau's resolution of 4 July, which 'fully approves the declaration adopted by the Socialist congress.'

5. See **Léon Blum devant la Cour de Riom**, page 79, and **La Réforme Gouvernmentale** (Grasset 1918, second edition 1936).

6. Its political composition was: 19 Socialists, 13 Radicals and three members of the *Union Socialiste et Républicaine*. Its social composition: eight journalists, six academics, one doctor, ten lawyers, three account-ants . . . Its parliamentary composition: four Senators, 27 deputies and four non-parliamentarians.

7. Delmas, page 85.

8. **Léon Blum devant la Cour de Riom**, page 93.

9. **Léon Blum devant la Cour de Riom**, page 94.

10. 'Those who guide the destinies of the workers' organisations must do their duty; they must put an end to the unjustified agitation without delay. For my part I have made my choice; between order and anarchy I will maintain order before and above all else.' (30 June 1936.)

11. *Communiqué* from the Ministry of Labour, 5 June 1936.

12. Declaration by Salengro, 6 June 1936.

13. See Delmas, pages 94–5.

14. On the 5th, a strike by the workers at *Messageries Hachette*, as well as the kiosk-holders, had paralysed newspaper distribution. On the 6th, with the exceptions of **le Peuple, le Populaire, l'Humanité** (and **Action Française**), the press decided not to publish. When the return to work took place, the appropriate unions and the Popular Front newspapers were on the point of an agreement which would allow their distribution during the strike.

15. The editorial in **l'Oeuvre**, a Radical paper, read on 4 June 1936: 'What is most striking, and, it must be said, most worrying about the present strikes is the way they have blossomed so spontaneously. The move-ment has begun. Who will stop it? The trade unions? One is better able to stop a movement which one has planned oneself than one which has started independently. It is clear that the re-unified CGT has not planned this.'

16. *Messageries Hachette, les Halles* and the hotel industry went back.

17. The two documents, addressed to Léon Blum, were published by **le Temps** on 6 and 7 June 1936.

18. A headline in **l'Humanité** on 7 June read: 'An immense movement in perfect order, in support of uncontested claims. Result of the week: more than 500 victories.'

19. To this end, **l'Humanité** published on 6 June the complete text of the intended contract.

20. Authors' emphasis.

21. Authors' emphasis.

22. Authors' emphasis.

23. **L'Humanité**, 7 June 1936.

24. 500,000 on strike, reported **l'Humanité** on 6 June under the headline 'Order is the guarantee of success'.

25. **L'Humanité**, 6 June 1936.

*26. The *Hôtel Matignon* was the prime minister's official residence.

Chapter Five: THE MATIGNON AGREEMENT

*1. Blum, Daladier and others were arrested by the French Vichy authorities after the occupation of France by the Germans in 1940 and put on trial on charges of 'failing in the duties entrusted to them'. The trial, which took place at a small town near Vichy called Riom, was the Vichy government's attempt to bolster its own standing in the eyes of the French people and ingratiate itself with the occupying Germans. Blum, now 70 years old, eloquently defended his government's record. Daladier no less effectively reminded the judges that he had banned the Communist Party following the Hitler-Stalin Pact in 1939, suppressed its newspapers, and thrown most of its leaders into jail. The trial was abandoned amidst much embarrassment in April 1942.

2. Delegate of the *Comité des Forges*, the employers' umbrella organisation for the iron and steel industry.

3. **Léon Blum devant la Cour de Riom**, pages 95–6.

4. See especially Manevy, **Histoire de la Presse 1914–39** (Correa 1945) page 291; Duchemin, **l'Organisation Syndicale Patronale en France** (Plon 1940), and Prouteau, page 126.

5. Duchemin, **l'Organisation Syndicale Patronale en France**.

6. Duchemin, **l'Organisation Syndicale Patronale en France**.

7. Delmas, page 99.

8. Delmas, page 100.

9. Duchemin, **l'Organisation Syndicale Patronale en France**.

10. Delmas, page 100.

11. **Léon Blum devant la Cour de Riom**, page 97; Duchemin, 'l'Accord Matignon' in **Revue de Paris**, 1 February 1937; Duchemin, **le Syndicalisme Patronal en France**; René Belin, **Syndicats**, May 1937; and B Frachon, speech at the CGT national committee, 14 June 1936, quoted in **le Peuple**, 15 June 1936.

12. **Léon Blum devant la Cour de Riom**, page 98.

13. **Léon Blum devant la Cour de Riom**, page 99.

14. **Le Peuple**, 17 June 1936.

15. **Léon Blum devant la Cour de Riom**, page 98.

16. The CGPF contested this interpretation in a *communiqué* published by **le Temps** on 14 June 1936: 'From certain statements in the press it could be deduced that the CGPF leadership have accepted . . . the principle of the 40-hour week. We would like to make it clear that the question of a 40-hour week has been mentioned only in passing. We did not hide our opinion that a 40-hour law would have even more serious consequences for the country's economy than the wage increases which have been arbitrated by the prime minister.'

17. **Le Temps**, 9 June 1936.

18. This sentence in Frachon's speech does not figure in the report carried by **l'Humanité**, but is reproduced word for word by **le Populaire** and **le**

Peuple of 17 June. We owe this information to Walter, **Histoire du Parti Communiste**, page 321.

19. Speech made on Monday 8 June at 8 pm and broadcast by the main government services.

20. This *communiqué* estimated the rise in real wages that had been obtained at 35 per cent, made up of 20 per cent due to the 40-hour week, 4 per cent due to the paid holidays, and 11 per cent due to the rise in money wages.

21. Duchemin, **l'Organisation Syndicale Patronale en France**.

Chapter Six: THE CRUCIAL DAYS: 7–12 JUNE

1. Delmas, page 103.
2. **Léon Blum devant la Cour de Riom**, page 101.
*3. **L'Humanité**, 9 June 1936, and **le Temps**, 10 June 1936. This *communiqué* was not published by either **le Peuple** or **le Populaire**.
4. **Le Peuple**, 10 June 1936.
5. **Le Peuple**, 12 June 1936.
6. **Le Peuple**, 12 June 1936.
7. **Le Peuple**, 9 June 1936.
8. **Le Peuple**, 12 June 1936.
9. **Le Peuple**, 12 June 1936.
10. **Le Peuple**, 10 June 1936, and **le Temps**, 11 June 1936.
11. **Le Temps**, 12 June 1936.
12. **Le Peuple**, 11 June 1936.
13. **Le Peuple**, 9 June 1936.
14. The enhancement was thus raised from 10 per cent to 22 per cent. See **le Temps**, 13 June 1936, and **la Voix des Mineurs**, July 1936.
15. **Le Peuple**, 11 June 1936.
16. **L'Enchaîné du Nord**, 5 June 1936.
17. **Le Peuple**, 10 June 1936.
18. For example the levy undertaken at Cambrai.
19. **Le Peuple**, 12 June 1936.
20. **Le Temps**, 12 June 1936.
21. **Le Temps**, 13 June 1936.
*22. Thorez, **Fils du Peuple** (1949 edition) page 112. The bourgeois revolution of 1848 won broad popular support but was brought to an end when thousands of Parisian artisans and unemployed, who had risen in revolt in June, were massacred in six days of street fighting. The Paris Commune, which Marx hailed as 'essentially a working-class government', controlled the capital for two months in 1871. Like their predecessors in 1848, the Communards were surrounded by an army predominantly composed of conscripted peasants, and massacred.
23. Here Thorez was replying to Marceau Pivert's article: 'Everything is possible.'
24. The full text of the report was published in **l'Humanité**, 13 June 1936, which vehemently reproached **le Populaire** for not having publicised the *communiqué* which was sent to it.
25. 'We in the Communist Party, conscious of our responsibilities, have

thus courageously taken up our position without shrinking from the need to attack the hysterical gesticulations of the Trotskyists and their friends, just as we led the Popular Front to victory by combatting the phrasemongering of those sections who condemned the alliance between the working class and the middle class.

'The central committee fully endorses the politbureau's condemnation of those who, without any notion of the responsibilities which weigh on the workers' organisations, declare that "everything is possible"; we must oppose this dangerous formula with the Communist declaration — everything is not possible. The party's central slogan is still "Everything for the Popular Front, everything by the Popular Front".'

26. Maurice Prax, **le Petit Parisien**, 13 June 1936.
27. Thorez, **Fils du Peuple**, page 112.

Chapter Seven: The WAVE RECEDES

1. **Le Peuple**, 13 June 1936.
2. **Le Temps**, 14 June 1936.
3. **Etudes**, 5 December 1936; Prouteau, page 170.
4. In the print industry the collective agreement in fact included a clause allowing for the sliding scale.
5. **Le Temps**, 17 June 1936.
6. **Le Temps**, 19 June 1936.
7. With the exception of the first two days, a scale of daily compensation of from 10F to 20F was envisaged, as in engineering.
8. 25 per cent for wages equal to or below 6,000F per month; 5 per cent for wages between 18,000F and 20,000F per month.
9. **Le Temps**, 24 June 1936.
10. We can also quote the appeal by Raymond Vidal, Socialist deputy-mayor of Marseilles: 'There is something I do not understand. At this moment we have a government which is doing the impossible for you. At an incredible speed, it is giving you benefits you have long sought. Don't you understand that indefinitely-maintained agitation could do the government considerable harm? (Quoted in Paul Lombard, **Quatorze Mois de Démence** (Paris 1937) page 70.)
11. A seamen's strike had already broken out at la Rochelle on the 16th, in solidarity with the dockers, who, having won an increase in their daily rate from 33F to 36F, stopped work and demanded 42F.
12. **Le Temps** of 12 June 1936 noted that the Rouen refinery workers, who were still out, 'declared themselves ready to wait for the nationalisation of this industry'.
13. Compare Blum's letter to Jouhaux immediately on taking office, page 98 above.
14. Senate debate, 7 July 1936. Extract from the circular to prefects, 4 July 1936: 'We intend that France should remain faithful to her tradition of giving political asylum. However, we cannot accept that foreigners . . . should take an active part in discussions of domestic politics, provoking troubles and disorder.

*15. The 'decree laws' were the French Third Republic's elegant way of breaking the deadlock in legislation that tended to result from the chronic government instability and the difficulty in getting votes through a parliament split so many different ways. The constitution gave the government the right to go before both houses of parliament and ask for 'plenary powers'. If granted, these allowed the government to issue laws by decree, on the authority of the cabinet alone.

      The granting of plenary powers sometimes had nothing to do with approval of a government's programme; powers might be granted in order to give parliamentarians something of a respite — if the government fell there would have to be yet another round of exhausting negotiations to form another.

      It was the use of plenary powers in 1935 to issue decrees that aimed to cut public employees' pay which led to mass strikes that summer, the precursors of June '36.

16. **Le Temps**, 16 June 1936, which stressed the anti-semitic slogans coming from the extreme right counter-demonstrators.

17. **Le Temps**, 21 June 1936.

Chapter Eight: THE OCCUPATION TACTIC AND ITS REPERCUSSIONS

1. Léon Blum in the Chamber of Deputies, 6 June 1936.
2. Léon Blum in the Chamber of Deputies, 6 June 1936: 'I have been asked if I consider these occupations to be legal . . . I do not consider that they are legal . . . They are not in conformity with the rules and principles of French civil law.' Maurice Thorez, report of 11 June: 'They are saying illegality. Eh! No! It's quite simple — it's just a new legality that is developing.'
3. English readers could consult Paolo Spriano, **The occupation of the factories** (London 1975).
4. Prouteau, page 81.
5. Occupations took place in France at Halluin in the Nord in 1920; in Poland there were several occupation-strikes in 1931–35, which were copied in Romania; in Spain there was an engineers' strike in Madrid in 1933; in Britain miners at Nine Mile Point pit occupied in 1935; and in the USA there was the Akron rubber workers' strike in Ohio in January 1936.
6. The events in December 1937 at Goodrich-Colombes give some idea of what might have happened. See chapter 12 below.
7. Except perhaps in agriculture.
8. Lefranc, **Histoire du mouvement ouvrier en France**.
9. See especially **Dossiers de l'action Populaire**, 10 July 1936; Jean Coutrot, **Les Leçons de Juin '36**; E Humeau, '*La Victoire du Syndicalisme*' in **Esprit**, July 1936; Simone Weil, '*La Vie et la Grève des ouvriers métallurgistes*' in **La Condition Ouvrière** (Gallimard 1951); and Prouteau, pages 142 and following.
10. Except in firms where women constituted the majority of the workforce.

11. Simone Weil is not to be confused with the rightist politician of the same name who was a cabinet minister under Giscard d'Estaing. This Simone Weil, the author of **La Condition Ouvrière**, was a Christian-inspired activist of the 1930s who, from being a highly-qualified schoolteacher, chose to take a manual job in the Paris engineering industy. Associated with Monatte's *Révolution Prolétarienne*, she visited Germany in the early 1930s, subsequently contributing an article which correctly predicted Hitler's rise to power. After spending some time with the International Brigades in Spain, she died young in hospital in London in 1943.

12. Delmas, page 92.

13. In the Chamber of Deputies, 6 June 1936.

14. **Léon Blum devant la Cour de Riom**, page 168.

15. See Chapter 3 above.

16. 'I am as thoroughly convinced today as I was at that time that the duty which came before all others in the order of priorities . . . was to maintain public order . . . I have reminded you, and I challenge anyone to contradict me on this, that no one ever asked me to do anything different, that at that moment, when we were faced with the reality, and not at six years' distance, no one proposed that I should have acted differently from the way I did.' **Léon Blum devant la Cour de Riom**, page 169.

*17. Tables 2 and 3 give totals for the whole of France, but detailed figures only for the most significant *départements*.

18. Williers, '*La nouvelle organisation du Travail*', lectures at the *Ecole d'administration et d'affaires*, November–December 1936.

19. Williers.

20. In the Chamber of Deputies, 26 June 1936. Salengro added: 'Would they have not brandished [the tools and weapons] if we had sent the police and the army against them?'

21. See Chapter 11 below.

22. Walter, page 318.

23. Delmas, page 93.

24. In the Chamber of Deputies, 26 June 1936.

*25. The original *soviets*, or workers' councils, of the Russian revolutions of 1905 and 1917 began as meetings of strike delegates from different factories, extending their control over the surrounding districts and growing into a national movement which, under Bolshevik leadership, was able to challenge for state power.

26. At the CGT national committee on 16 June 1936, Jouhaux revealed that Léon Blum had considered 'resorting to requisitioning the most essential consumer goods. The government has not had to make use of this weapon, but you should know that it exists.' In the end requisitions, which could only have been imposed by military means, were not even applied to the fuel depots, though seriously considered because of the risk of conflict with the workers. In any case the Radicals were opposed to any coercion against individual employers.

27. Humeau in **Esprit**, July 1936.

28. **Le Temps**, 12 June 1936.

Chapter Nine: THE WORKERS' ORGANISATIONS AND THE STRIKES

1. *'L'Union de la Nation Française'* in **Une politique de grandeur française** (Editions Sociales, Paris 1945) pages 13 and following.
2. Emphasis in the original.
3. Emphasis in the original, which reads *'jusqu'au bout'*.
4. Emphasis in the original.
5. Thorez, **Fils du Peuple**, page 30.
6. Joanny Berlioz, *'Une leçon de l'expérience du Front Populaire'*, in **Cahiers du Communisme**, January 1948. We should note that this article, written after the Communist Party's 'left turn' in 1948, is aimed at the Socialists, although in 1936 the Communist Party justified their own moderate attitude by referring to the Radicals' presence in the government coalition.
7. Raymond Millet, *'Le PCF dans le Front Populaire'*, in **Bilan du Communisme** (Librairie technique et économique, Paris 1937).
*8. See **Rapport au Congres d'Arles**, page 181. Louis Matin was as far to the right of the French political spectrum as it was possible to go without being a monarchist.
9. See Walter, pages 311 and following.
10. This became especially clear during the parliamentary debates on the events in Marseilles.
11. Report to Communists in the Paris region, 30 October 1936.
12. The words of Spinasse, the economics minister.
13. The Socialist Party, fearing an increase in the Communists' influence, opposed all the structural modifications in the organisation of the Popular Front which the latter put forward.
14. Antoine Roche, in **Esprit**, July 1936.
15. See Chapter 11 below.
16. **Le Populaire**, 5 May 1936.
17. **Le Populaire**, 12 May 1936.
18. **Le Populaire**, 27 May 1936.
19. Marceau Pivert, at the national committee on 10 May, told Blum: 'We have confidence in you. We know that you will always be at the service of the movement. We want you to listen to the voices from below, and their appeals. Heed their aspirations! And if the people want to go far, you must always remain at their head.'
20. A large number of opportunists were among the new recruits who flocked to the party in 1936. Strangers to the working class and to political action, they were drawn by the new aura of government. Naturally they reinforced the Socialist Party's reformist current.
21. Translated into English under the title **Leon Trotsky on France** (Monad Press, New York 1979).
*22. The *Parti Ouvrier Internationaliste* (POI).
23. Trotsky wrote: 'The Radicals are the democratic party of French imperialism.' 'It is an elementary principle of Marxist strategy that the alliance between the proletariat and the humble folk of town and country

can only be built in the course of a relentless struggle against the bourgeoisie's traditional parliamentary representatives. To get the peasant on to the workers' side we have to detach him from the Radical politicians who in turn subject him to finance capital. The Popular Front, on the other hand, being the result of a plot between the social-democrat and trade union bureaucracy and the worst political exploiters of the middle classes, serves only to kill the workers' faith in revolutionary methods and to throw them into the arms of the fascist counter-revolution. (**Leon Trotsky on France**.)

24. Trotsky, 'The decisive stage', an article written on 5 June 1936, reprinted in **Leon Trotsky on France**, page 155.

*25. Trotsky, page 163.

26. Trotsky, 'Before the second stage', article written on 9 June 1936, in **Leon Trotsky on France**, page 148.

27. This edition, seized by the police on Salengro's orders, does not figure in the collection of the *Bibliothèque Nationale*. Extracts are quoted in Lemarc, **Juin '36**, a Trotskyist pamphlet.

28. Under this heading the anarchists included the CGT unions.

29. **Le Peuple**, 19 May 1936.

30. Resolution of the CGT's *commission administrative*, 21 June 1936, page 144.

31. 'I remember a young girl who came from *Prix Unique* shop near Montmartre, trembling with agitation. She had just brought the place out on strike and didn't know what to do next, so she had come for help. Some comrades went off with her to make speeches, organise some discipline and draw up a list of demands.' Edmond Humeau in **Esprit**, July 1936.

32. The union growth was most spectacular of all among white-collar workers, where in most workplaces there had not been a single union section. For example during the month of June the number of union members in the *Bon Marché* department store rose from eleven to 1,800.

33. The archbishop of Paris communicated with the faithful through the medium of **le Temps** on 13 June 1936: 'Workers of all grades and both sexes are much solicited in these days to join trade union organisations. It should not be necessary to remind all, and especially Catholic, workers that the Church has many times recognised and encouraged the workers' right to group themselves into trade associations, and that we encourage all Christians to form professional associations. The CFTC, *5 rue Cadet*, which endeavours to bring to fruition the social teaching contained in the papal encyclicals, is the professional group to which Catholics should make it their duty and their joy to belong . . . Membership forms can be found . . .'

34. **Le Temps**, 19 June 1936.

35. See Maxence van der Meersch, **Pêcheurs d'hommes**, on the role of young Christians in the strikes in the north of France.

36. See the series of articles which Raymond Millet devoted to 'The CGT's rivals' in **le Temps**, March 1938.

37. Jacques Bardoux, '*Le Complot du 11 Juin*', in **Revue de Paris**, 15 August 1936.

38. **La Flèche,** 4 July 1936.
39. Léon Blum, speaking in parliamentary debates, 6 June 1936.
40. Notably Raymond Vidal, a Socialist Party deputy, in the Chamber, 26 June 1936.
*41. Henri de Kerillis, wealthy right fringe politician who, though never a deputy in parliament, set up and financed an information centre for right-wing ideas.
42. Simone Weil, **La Condition Ouvrière,** page 168.
43. Simone Weil, pages 177 and following.

Chapter Ten: THE GAINS OF JUNE '36

1. The first legislation in this field was on 19 March 1919.
2. **Rapport Laroque,** 20 November 1924.
3. The bill originally put forward by the government contained a clause giving the minister of labour power of arbitration in case of dispute. This clause was removed at committee stage after objections from Communist deputies.
4. **Léon Blum devant la Cour de Riom.**
5. Léon Jouhaux, **Les conventions collectives.**
6. J-P Maxence, **Histoire de dix ans** (Gallimard 1939).
7. Thery, **Un an d'audace et de contradiction** (Paris 1937).
8. Information from employers' statistics.
9. Simone Weil, page 172.
10. Thomas, **L'Echelle mobile des salaires** (Paris 1938).
11. The experience during the 1914–18 war, when a shop delegate system was introduced into firms working for national defence.
12. **Guide du délégué d'atelier** (*Centre confédéral de l'Education Ouvrière* 1937) page 12.
13. No statistics are available concerning the results of delegate elections which took place in 1936–7.
14. See, especially, Robert Mossé, **Un an de Front Populaire** (Editions du Sagittaire 1937).
15. Léon Blum to the Socialist Party national committee, 10 May 1936.
16. Law of 21 June 1936, raising the duration of compulsory schooling to the age of 14.
17. Calculated on the basis of average prices in the years 1911–13, multiplied by a coefficient which took account of the cost of living, of wages, and of the prices of products necessary for agriculture.
18. Which grew from 30,000 in 1935 to 130,000 in 1938.
19. Especially the weekly **Vendredi,** edited by André Chamson and Jean Guehenno. See also Jean Guehenno, **Journal d'une révolution** (Grasset 1938).

Chapter Eleven: THE BOURGEOIS COUNTER-OFFENSIVE

*1. The French word *patronat* is derived from *les patrons*, roughly to be translated as 'the bosses' or the employers.
2. Duchemin.

. The parliamentary caucus of the Communist Party, Socialist Party, Radical Party and other left parties.

4. Piettre, **La Politique du Pouvoir d'Achats devant les faits** (Librairie de Médicis 1938).

5. **Mouvement Economique en France de 1929 à 1939** (Imprimerie Nationale 1941).

*6. The *Cour des Comptes* and Council of State were constitutional bodies, independent of the changing political colour of the government, which were supposed to check the legality and regularity of government decisions. They were responsible for, respectively, public expenditure and the legality of state administration.

7. Marx Dormoy became minister for the interior in November 1936. Roger Salengro had committed suicide by gassing himself on 17 November, after a long series of slanderous articles published by the weekly **Gringoire** had impugned the honour of his record in the trenches during the First World War.

8. The gold reserve in the Bank of France had fallen from 82 billion francs to 66 billion.

9. Mossé.

10. For the remainder of 1936 alone, however, the actual deficit was four billion higher than envisaged.

*11. The danger in the Senate came as much, if not more, from the Radicals as from the parties of the right.

12. Mossé.

*13. 'One of the main purposes of devaluing the franc had been to attract capital back home. It failed. This was largely because the law-makers, in a quite commendable effort to prevent the speculators from making a 30 per cent profit, had provided that returning capital in gold or foreign exchange could only be exchanged for francs at the old rate. There was no profit incentive to return capital . . . It stayed abroad.' (William Shirer, **The collapse of the Third Republic**, page 290.) The return of the free market (Shirer gives the date as 7 March) left the holders now free to 'reap the 30 per cent profit denied them at the time of devaluation'.

14. Committee composed of Labeyrie, governor of the Bank of France, Charles Rist, director of the Suez Canal Company and of the *Banque de Paris et des Pays-Bas*, Jacques Rueff, former advisor to Laval, and Baudouin of the Bank of Indochina.

15. **Le Temps**, 8 March 1937.

16. See Dauphin-Meunier, **La City de Londres** (Gallimard 1939).

*17. When the Spanish republican government asked for arms to fight Franco's fascist rebellion, Blum succumbed to right-wing pressures and produced a 'Non-Intervention Pact'. He thus effectively tied the Popular Front's hands, while Hitler and Mussolini, who also signed the pact, continued to suply the Spanish fascists more or less openly with arms.

*18. The extent to which even quite moderate governments were vulnerable to the banks' machinations can be illustrated by the description which Malcolm Anderson, the historian of the French right, gives of the fall of the government headed by Edouard Herriot in April 1925. Successive governments had started to borrow more from the Bank of France than they were legally allowed to. They got round this by repaying the illegal excess shortly before the Bank of France accounts were due to be published, then borrowing again once the accounts were out. Private banks colluded in this by lending to the government for 24 hours to tide it over. To get rid of Herriot, 'they refused to carry out the normal manoeuvre'. The banks did not have to dream up anything special to deal with the Popular Front.

19. Georges Bonnet, well-connected and rightist Radical and apostle of monetary orthodoxy who became finance minister in the new government, speech at Périgueux, 7 August 1937.

*20. Members of the Finance Inspectorate, an elite branch of the French civil service noted for its links with business and financial circles.

21. Ferrat, **La République à refaire** (Gallimard 1945). Ferrat had by this time joined the Socialist Party.

*22. The *Anschluss* was the unification of Austria and Germany, a central plank in Nazi foreign policy.

23. The full text of this speech was published for the first time in the review **Les Temps Modernes**, September 1951.

*24. With Socialist and Radical participation, Communist support, and the right in opposition.

*25. All newly-formed governments had to present themselves for a formal vote of confidence. Blum meant that if the right would vote their confidence in him, he was willing to re-open negotiations to allow them into the cabinet. When they did not do so, he continued with the Popular Front coalition.

26. The Socialist Federation of the Seine, which was dominated by the *Gauche Révolutionnaire*, the party's 'revolutionary left' tendency, organised a demonstration outside the Senate and was disowned by **l'Humanité** as well as the leadership of their own party — who in due course dissolved the federation on 14 April 1938.

*27. Joseph Caillaux, chairman of the Senate finance committee.

*28. Ferrat, **La République a refaire**.

29. Meanwhile, under the same law, the leaders of the national-democratic Algerian People's Party were sentenced to several years in prison.

*30. The *Quai d'Orsay* is the French foreign office.

31. A Dauphin-Meunier, **La Banque de France** (Gallimard 1937).

32. One of them was nominated by the CGT.

33. '*La réorganisation de l'appareil bancaire*', in **Les Tâches actuelles du syndicalisme** (CGT 1939).

34. Maxence, **Histoire de dix ans**.

35. Maurice Ribet, **Les Proces de Riom** (Plon 1940).

36. Millet in **Le Temps**, 16 April 1938.

37. **Cahier du Militant**, quoted in Lefranc.

*38. '*Cagoulards*' means 'men wearing hoods'. The paper was mocking their conspiratorial behaviour.

39. Pozzo di Borgo, heir to a vast fortune, was formerly the chief financier of

the *Croix de Feu*, but had by now broken with Colonel de la Roque.

*40. Like so many socialist activists, Dormoy was held in custody by the Vichy authorities. Some of the Vichy prison warders placed a bomb under his bed.

Chapter Twelve: THE WORKERS' RESISTANCE AND DEFEAT

1. Sauvy and Depoid, **Salaires et Pouvoir d'achat des ouvriers et des fonctionnaires entre les deux guerres** (Presses Universitaires de France 1941).

2. **La CGT, ce qu'elle est, ce qu'elle veut** (Gallimard 1937).

3. **Syndicats**, 10 June 1937.

4. Preface to L Katz, **L'Arbitrage obligatoire** (Rivière 1938).

5. **Syndicalisme**, June 1938.

6. **L'Année Politique**, 1937.

7. **L'Année Politique**, 1937.

8. Lefranc.

9. Maxence.

10. The events at Clichy were preceded on 7 March 1937 by bloodshed at Metlaoui in Tunisia, where 19 miners were shot down by the *gendarmerie*.

11. **Ce Soir**, 18 March 1937.

12. Letter to the **Syndicat des Métaux** from the Paris West region of the Communist Party, reproduced in l'**Humanité**, 27 March 1938.

13. **Le Populaire**, 28 March 1938.

14. **Les Grèves de la métallurgie parisienne de mars–avril 1938**.

15. In reality this was a violent diatribe against the Socialist International from the pen of the secretary of the Communist International (Comintern), Dimitrov.

*16. '*Confédérés*' were former members of the CGT before its fusion with the CGT-U in March 1936.

17. Lefranc.

18. Belin was later to become minister of labour in the Vichy government from July 1940 until April 1942.

19. **L'Humanité**, 1 October 1938. Daladier signed the Munich agreement with Chamberlain and Hitler in September 1938.

20. The *Gauche Révolutionnaire*, expelled from the Socialist Party for, among other reasons, organising a demonstration against the Senate, transformed itself into the *Parti Socialiste Ouvrier et Paysan* (The Workers' and Peasants' Socialist Party), which the Trotskyist groups joined at the end of 1938.

*21. Roughly translatable as 'Syndicalist groups for class struggle'.

22. Sanctions included sackings, suspension of unemployment pay for six months, withdrawal of work permits for foreign workers.

23. Various intermediaries tried to renew contacts between the CGT and the government, but came up against government intransigence.

24. Thorez, **Fils du Peuple**.

Chapter Thirteen: SOME CONCLUSIONS

1. Jouhaux, **Les conventions collectives**.
2. Ferrat.

GLOSSARY

1. PEOPLE

Vincent Auriol (1884–1966): Lawyer and Socialist deputy since 1914. Minister of finance in the Popular Front government of 1936, then attorney-general.

François Blancho (1893–1972): Under-secretary for the navy in the Popular Front government of 1936. Socialist deputy, engineering worker and trade unionist from Saint-Nazaire.

Léon Blum (1872–1950): Prime minister in the Popular Front government of 1936. Son of a prosperous Jewish draper, he was well-known before 1914 as a literary critic and administrative lawyer whose only connection with the socialist movement was intimacy with the social circle around Jean Jaurès, founder of the Socialist Party (SFIO). Blum unreservedly supported the war effort after 1914, becoming assistant to one of the Socialist ministers. He became a deputy for the first time in 1919. From the mid-1920s he and Paul Faure were the undisputed masters of the Socialist Party, Blum in parliament and the press, Faure in the party organisation.

    After the German occupation of France in 1940, Blum was put on trial at Riom by the Vichy government. Because of his spirited defence, the trial had to be abandoned in 1942. Blum was sent to the Buchenwald and Auschwitz concentration camps, survived, and returned to France as the grand old man of French socialism, serving as prime minister again briefly before his death in 1950.

Georges Bonnet: Right-wing radical who opposed the Popular Front alliance with the Socialists and Communists. The apostle of strict monetary orthodoxy, he took over the finance ministry from Auriol in June 1937. Later foreign secretary, he accompanied Daladier to Munich in 1938.

Marcel Cachin (1869–1958): Founder-member of the French Communist Party. He was a member of the party's politbureau and central committee and edited the party paper **l'Humanité** from 1923 until his death in 1958.

Joseph Caillaux: Radical opponent of the Popular Front. Has been described as probably the most consistently influential politician of the 1930s. This influence he owed not to any formal position in the Radical Party, which he ignored, but to his semi-permanent chairmanship of the Senate finance committee. He used this position to veto plenary powers and bring down the Popular Front government in May 1937.

Camille Chautemps: Lawyer, Freemason and arch-wheeler-dealer among Radical Senators and deputies, his career aptly summrises the futility of the Socialists' parliamentary alliance with the Radicals. He was the Radical prime minister who was brought down by financial scandal in Janury 1934 (the Stavisky Affair); then Blum's deputy in the Popular government of 1936, taking over as prime minister in June 1937; then, after April 1938, he was a minister in Daladier's government which proceeded to dismantle many of the achievements of June '36!

Edouard Daladier: Leading Radical, son and grandson of bakers, who himself became a university teacher. Posed as the champion of the Popular Front inside the Radical Party, where he manoeuvred to the right in 1933 and 1934, to the left in 1935, and to the right again in 1938. Minister of defence in the Popular Front government, he clashed with the Socialists over his refusal to allow the Socialist and Communist papers into the army barracks. Prime minister in 1938, his government presided over the employers' counter-attack on the workes' gains of 1936. Daladier signed the Munich agreement with Hitler in September 1938, and was later put on trial at Riom by the Vichy government during the German occupation of France.

Jacques Doriot: Prominent Communist deputy and mayor in the Paris 'red belt', but expelled for questioning the sectarian line used against the Socialists. He set up the fascist *Parti Populaire Français* on 28 June 1936. Doriot helped to form and fought in the French anti-Bolshevik legion on the Eastern Front, went into exile in Germany as a member of the puppet French government in the last stages of the Second World War and is believed killed in an aircraft attack in 1945.

Marx Dormoy (1888–1941): Socialist deputy and mayor of Montluçon. Under-secretary for the interior, then minister after Roger Salengro committed suicide in November 1936. Himself assassinated while imprisoned near Lyons in 1941.

Duchemin: President of the main employers' organisation, the *Confédération Generale de la Production Française* (CGPF) and negotiator on behalf of the employers during the strikes of June 1936.

Jacques Duclos: Communist militant who joined Maurice Thorez in the party leadership in the early 1930s. Historian of the party Jacques Fauvet called them 'the Hammer and the Sickle'. Duclos, despite his stocky appearance, qualified as the sickle because of his sharp wits and sense of humour, which made him one of the most popular of all Communist leaders until his death in the 1970s. He is credited with never having left the suburbs of Paris during the Nazi occupation, while Thorez was in Moscow.

Paul Faure (1878–1960): General secretary of the Socialist Party and minister of state in the Popular Front government of June 1936. Later expelled from the party for his association with the Vichy regime.

Benoit Frachon (1893–1975): Assistant general secretary of the CGT union confederation in 1936. Son of a miner. Founder-member of French Communist Party in 1920, trade union activist and strike leader in 1920s in St Etienne engineering industry. Member of Communist Party polit-bureau from 1928 until he officially stood down on becoming one of two assistant general secretaries of the re-united CGT in 1935, though in fact he continued to attend politbureau meetings unofficially. Continued as party's number one functionary in the CGT after 1945. He is credited with appearing at a mass meeting at Renault in 1968, when he endorsed the strike call, overruling CGT general secretary Georges Séguy.

Ludovic-Oscar Frossard (1889–1946): Minister of labour in Sarraut's care-taker government in 1936. Primary-school teacher turned journalist. Former general secretary and founder-member of the Communist Party, he resigned in 1923, becoming successively a Socialist, a *néo-socialiste*, and finally a member of the Vichy 'National Council'.

Edouard Herriot (1872–1957): University teacher, life-long Radical and mayor of Lyons. Three times prime minister and most prominent Radical of his generation. Took a back seat during the Popular Front period.

Léon Jouhaux (1879–1954): General secretary of the CGT trade union confederation both before and after its re-unification with the CGT-U in March 1936, and main union negotiator during 1936 strikes. He was general secretary of the CGT from 1909 to 1947, with a break during the Second World War, then formed the class-collaborationist breakaway *Force Ouvrière*.

Jean-Baptiste Lebas (1878–1944): Minister of labour in the Popular Front government of 1936. Socialist deputy and member of the party's national executive from 1920 to 1939. Involved in resistance to Nazis and died after being deported to Germany.

Lebrun: President of France in 1936.

Marceau Pivert (1895–1958): Leader of the *Gauche Révolutionnaire*, the left current inside the Socialist Party, who declared after the Popular Front victory in May 1936: 'Everything is possible.' Son of a peasant who became a primary-school teacher and union activist. Formed *Gauche Révolutionnaire* in 1935, which was expelled from the party in June 1938. Rejoined the Socialist Party after 1945 but again expelled, for opposing party policy, which was in favour of war against Algerian independence.

Colonel de la Roque: Leader of the fascist *Croix de Feu* (see below).

Roger Salengro: Socialist mayor of Lille and Minister for the Interior in the Popular Front government of June 1936. He committed suicide in November 1936 after a series of slanderous articles impugning his record in the trenches during the First World War.

Albert Sarraut: Prominent Radical and head of the caretaker ministry that handed over to the Popular Front government of Léon Blum in 1936.

C Spinasse: Minister for economic affairs in the Popular Front government of 1936.

Maurice Thorez: General secretary of the Communist Party from 1930 to his death in 1964. The son of a miner, he was a founder-member of the party and first visited Moscow in 1925. It is possible that he played some role in persuading Stalin to adopt the 'Popular Front' line in 1934, though Thorez had himself been an enthusiastic supporter of the sectarian 'Third Period' policy. Spent years of Second World War in Moscow.

Raymond Vidal: Socialist deputy-mayor of Marseilles and parliamentary deputy for Marseilles.

Jean Zyromski (1890–1975): Left-wing activist and member of the Socialist Party national executive from 1924 until 1938. Founded and led the *Bataille Socialiste* tendency. Expelled from the party in 1945, when he joined the Communists.

2. POLITICAL ORGANISATIONS

The Socialist Party (SFIO): Leading party in the Popular Front coalition. Formed by Jean Jaurès in 1905, its proper title was *Section Française de l'Internationale Ouvrière* (SFIO), French section of the Workers' International. It was the amalgamation of several factions and successfully combined revolutionary rhetoric with reformism in practice. In 1920 the party split over affiliation to the Communist International, with the majority forming the French Communist Party. Until 1936 the Socialists, while making electoral agreements with the Radicals which helped the latter to achieve office, had consistently refused to participate in government apart from the war years. Its ruling body was the *Commission Administrative Permanente*, roughly equivalent to a national executive committee. There was also a larger and more consultative body, the *Conseil National* or National Council. Leading members in 1936: Léon Blum, Roger Salengro, Paul Faure, Marceau Pivert (see above).

The Communist Party (PCF): Formed in December 1920 from the majority in the Socialist Party who had voted to affiliate to the Communist International. The party also attracted many of the best of the pre-1914 revolutionary syndicalists. Many of the party leaders, however, were only skin-deep converts to communism, and between 1921 and 1923 the Communist International repeatedly intervened against reformist and opportunist tendencies in the party. After 1924, when the Comintern came under the control of Zinoviev and then Stalin, the party was slowly but surely transformed into a loyal agent of Moscow. Genuine revolutionaries such as Rosmer and Monatte were expelled. The party followed the twists and turns imposed by Moscow, including the disastrous 'Third Period' during which the French Socialist Party and trade unions were denounced as 'social-fascist' and the 'main enemy' of the working class. As Danos and Gibelin's narrative opens, party leader Maurice Thorez is seeking ways to break the French Communists' self-imposed isolation. The Popular Front alliance with the Socialists and Radicals was to be the result. Leading members in 1936: Maurice Thorez, Jacques Duclos, Marcel Cachin, Benoit Frachon (see above).

The Communist International: Otherwise known as the Comintern, this was the international body linking Communist Parties in different countries. Set up in 1919, after the 1917 revolution in Russia, it came under the control of the rising Russian bureaucracy led by Stalin and was, by 1936, merely a tool for Russian foreign policy.

The Radical Party: The *Parti Républicain Radical et Radical-Socialiste*. Official-ly committed to the defence of private property (preferably small), law and order, the nationalisation of private monopolies such as rail, electricity and insurance, and to profit-sharing — which was expected to abolish class distinctions. Party organisation was minimal: the executive committee in 1935 numbered 2,388 members! Most of the leading Radicals had only limited relation to the party structure. Leading members in 1936: Joseph Caillaux, Camille Chautemps, Edouard Daladier, Edouard Herriot (see above).

The Fascist Leagues: Most prominent in the 1920s was the *Action Française*, whose paramilitary wing, as well as breaking up university lectures and theatrical performances, engaged in street battles with the sellers of workers' papers. By the 1930s the leading fascist organsation was the paramilitary *Croix de Feu*, which claimed 50,000 members in 1934. Originally an ex-servicemen's association, its name referred to a 'military cross' *under fire*, and had nothing to do with the Ku Klux Klan. Its leader was Colonel de la Roque. The *Croix de Feu* was banned by the Popular Front govern-ment, and immediately reformed as the *Parti Social Français* (PSF). This grew enormously in the demoralisation following the end of the 1936 mass strike and the collapse of the Popular Front government.

3. TRADE UNION ORGANISATIONS

Trade union structure: The structure of the French trade union movement in 1936 reflected its complex history. The basic unit, or branch, was the *syndicat*. These were grouped into *fédérations*, usually covering a specific craft or industry at national level — the equivalent of the English 'trade union'. The basic units, however, were also grouped locally or geographi-cally into the *bourses*, *chambres*, *unions locales* or *unions des syndicats*, which, in their coverage of a particular town or district, resembled the British 'trades council'. The national *confédérations*, such as the CGT and CGT-U (see below), represented both these vertical and horizontal trade union groupings. The confederation's *Bureau Confédéral* was designed to represent these dimensions of the trade union movement equally, while the *Comité Confédéral National* was a larger body, consisting of one delegate from each affiliated organisation. The *Commission Administrative* was the small execu-tive committee which ran the day-to-day affairs of the confederation.

Confédération Générale du Travail (CGT): The main trade union con-federation in 1936, whose general secretary was Léon Jouhaux (see above). Its leaders attempted to damp down the wave of militancy that followed the First World War, themselves splitting away from the more militant unions in 1921. The latter formed the CGT-U (see below). The two re-united in March 1936 during the run up to the Popular Front election victory. The CGT claimed 70,000 members in 1935.

Confédération Générale du Travail Unitaire (CGT-U): Largely Communist-influenced trade union confederation formed from split with the CGT in 1921. Re-united in March 1936. The CGT-U claimed more than 200,000 members in 1935.

Confédération Française des Travailleurs Chrétiens (CFTC): The Catholic trade union confederation, small and lacking in influence compared with the CGT and CGT-U. Founded in 1919.

4. EMPLOYERS' ORGANISATIONS

Before 1936 centralised employers' organisations were weak in France. Most of the employers' bodies mentioned in this book represent the interests of employers in a particular industry, and these retained considerable autonomy *vis-à-vis* the **Confédération Générale de la Production Française**, the main umbrella body which first came to prominence as negotiator with the government and the unions in 1936.

The situation in engineering deserves special mention. The 'engineering employers' organisation' which appears frequently in the text is the **Union des Industries Métallurgiques et Minieres de la Construction Mécanique, Electrique et Métallique, et des Industries qui s'y rattachent**. As its name implies, this was a ramshackle organisation covering many branches of engineering. The vast majority of its members would be the heads of small family firms. The **Comité des Forges**, on the other hand, represented heavy steel and iron interests, though it also included firms that were steel-users. Between these two branches of the industry there was a latent conflict of interest, which had an influence on the negotiations of June 1936.

5. OTHERS

l'Humanité: Daily paper of the French Communist Party.
le Populaire: Daily paper of the French Socialist Party (SFIO).
le Temps: The leading Paris daily paper.

INDEX